River Bend Revisited:

The Problem Patron in the Library

River Bend Revisited:

The Problem Patron in the Library

by Bruce A. Shuman

ORYX PRESS
1984

The rare Arabian Oryx is believed to have inspired the myth of the unicorn. This desert antelope became virtually extinct in the early 1960s. At that time several groups of international conservationists arranged to have 9 animals sent the Phoenix Zoo to be the nucleus of a captive breeding herd. Today the Oryx population is over 400 and herds have been returned to reserves in Israel, Jordan, and Oman.

Copyright © 1984 by The Oryx Press
2214 North Central at Encanto
Phoenix, Arizona 85004

Published simultaneously in Canada

Printed and Bound in the United States of America

Library of Congress Cataloging in Publication Data

Shuman, Bruce A.
    River Bend revisited.

    Includes bibliographical references and index.
    1. Libraries and community—Case studies.   2. Public
relations—Libraries—Case studies.   3. Libraries—
Security measures—Case studies.   4. Public Libraries—
United States—Case studies.   5. Libraries and readers—
Case studies.   I. Title.   II. Title: Problem patron in
the library.
Z716.4.S5   1984   021.2   84-10451
ISBN 0-89774-125-0

To Bek, Benj, and Josh, tre bambini incredibili.
To Anne Thompson of Oryx, more interested in a better book
than a pampered author.
To Laureen, inspiration and comfort in my declining years.

Table of Contents

Foreword

People who do not use libraries tend to think of them as safe, quiet sanctuaries. People who use libraries know better. Chances are good that they have witnessed some incident involving drunk, disorderly, or disturbed persons in the library. And library staff know best of all just how unquiet and unsafe libraries can be.

Perhaps the River Bend Public Library is unique in the sheer number and variety of incidents that the harried staff must deal with, but every public library staff must deal with some of these cases. Librarians by nature tend to be unprepared to cope with the problem patron, but they are thrust into these situations almost daily. The number of security guards in libraries is a sign of the times and so is the number of libraries training their staffs in techniques of handling the problem patron.

In my thirty-five years of working in public libraries in Hawaii, Michigan, and California, I have faced many of the situations described by Professor Shuman, plus a few which could be the basis for his next book. The main thing I have learned is *be prepared*! The unexpected is sure to happen, and a panicky librarian will only make the situation worse. Every library should have a plan for dealing with emergency situations, and all staff members should know what they can handle themselves, when to call for staff backup, and when to call for outside help.

River Bend Revisited: The Problem Patron in the Library provides an excellent starting point for any library trying to develop an emergency plan. Follow the suggestions for using the cases, which are outlined in the Preface. And remember, *you are not alone*. Even the smallest community has resource people to draw on. Ask someone from the police or sheriff's department and someone from the city attorney's office to sit in on your discussions. The local college may be able to provide a psychologist and try the local hospital or mental health center for a psychiatrist.

Using appropriate cases from *River Bend Revisited*, staff and resource people can brainstorm solutions and procedures. The procedures should be written out, rehearsed with the staff, and posted by the telephone along with emergency phone numbers. This provides a consistent approach which will discourage inappropriate behavior by problem patrons and will instill confidence in the most timid librarian.

Good Luck!

Joyce Elliott, Regional Librarian
Los Angeles Public Library

Preface

We ought to get hazard pay and wear firearms. . . .

We try to forewarn new clerks about what to expect, but there's really no way to prepare them for what it's like.

People yell vulgarities and threats at them. Some jump up and wave their arms, concluding an invisible orchestra. Others talk to themselves. We get people who are infested with vermin, who smell so bad that it makes us sick to our stomach, and who chase our legitimate patrons out of the room. One night a man at one of the machines had a gun. . . . One man threatened to strangle me. I never did figure out why. . . .

One staff member was beaten up and off work for three weeks. The security guards come down here in pairs now; they're afraid to come alone.

. . . all public library employees have their favorite stories about how they encountered, in the line of duty, drunks, dopers, vandals, knife wielders, gun toters, purse snatchers, laser-eyed paranoics, raving schizophrenics, lice-infested derelicts, exhibitionists, peeping toms, child molesters, and sexual deviates of every stripe.[1]

Over a seven-year stint in public library and state library reference departments, I think I have seen it all. All of the types listed above by Easton (and more) had walked, raced, staggered, crept, crawled, slithered, lurched, passed out, committed offenses against themselves and others, presented massive affronts to public taste and decency, or stayed in one place lapsing into catatonia, somnambulism, slumber, or, in one case, even death in libraries where I've worked.

A range of problem people, from the innocuous sleeper to the homicidal maniac, enter public libraries every day and must be dealt with. The fact that each of these people is different precludes a simple answer to each question or problem s/he poses. Generally, for example, drunks who enter the library to sleep off the effects of alcohol are not dangerous, whatever else they may be. But can you count on it? As a rule, the flasher or exhibitionist, who gets his kicks from inspiring fear and revulsion in unsuspecting patrons (usually female and young), is not a rapist, but there is no guarantee of this, nor is there one prescribed procedure for handling such a disturbance.

Because we are as unalike as our fingerprints, no set of regulations or procedures can be written to cover all cases. Perhaps the safest way to handle the problems cited above is to summon the police forthwith. Yet, even that solution is not always the best one, because the police have their own variables to contend with. On a given day or evening, the response time of a police unit to the library may range from seconds to hours, and the nature of the reason for the call affects timing as well. One wouldn't call a police officer to deal with a sleeper, a constant talker, a foul-smelling patron, or an agitated retarded patron. A library staff member would typically attempt to deal personally with these problem situations. As a back-up plan, many libraries are able to employ security guards who are not armed but uniformed and often police trained. They are mainly intended to convey authority when patrons are told that they are violating rules and asked either to stop or leave the building.

How to Use This Book

This book was written to provide an array of 40 problem situations which might (and do) arise in a public library setting. The reader is asked to role play the various library staff members named, meaning that one becomes the person involved. No definitive answers are provided for these cases. That would defeat the purpose of the book and provide evidence of overweening pride into the bargain. Each case is expressly designed to suggest a variety of possible lines of action, usually a continuum, ranging from ''do nothing'' at one end to ''call the police'' or ''throw the bum out'' at the other. The reader is encouraged to consider all the facts, step into the character, take action, consider possible ramifications, and imagine consequences. For each case, a section is provided that provides questions for discussion, intended to focus attention on one or more anticipated or unanticipated consequences of each action. In the questions, one is asked to become each library staff member internal to the drama and state what s/he would do about the situation as it unfolds. Finally, for each case, a small number of resources is provided for further reading in the particular problem patron behavior described or for related investigation.

The cases themselves are taken from life or thought up by the author. Several arose from news items. Some are embroidered fantasies, and the rest are of the "what if . . ." variety.

This book may best be used by persons:

- In classes of graduate programs in library and information science.
- In inservice training sessions in a public library.
- In workshops for public employees, who must deal and cope with members of the public in a situation where all are free to enter.

It is most desirable to have experts on hand to supplement this book. Previous workshops on problem patrons have employed such outside-the-field consultants as police officers, first-aid instructors, psychiatrists or psychologists, social workers, assertiveness training instructors, self-defense instructors, *et al.*

These cases may be used:

1. For reading alone and attempting to map appropriate lines of subsequent action to the problem situation.
2. For reading and discussion by small groups, who meet to compare possible responses to the discussion questions and who may benefit from the interaction of group problem solving.
3. For assignment to library school students.
4. For use by panel discussion members, guest experts, or individual guest speakers, who discuss the cases and recommend how they would handle them.

The book has further application in providing a basis for a library to institute a policy and procedures manual. The Index might provide a list of potential situations that may arise, and the Table of Contents and cases themselves suggest categories or topics that should be included in a good, comprehensive policy. Several policies already in existence are recommended to the user in the various resource sections provided with the cases—any or all of which may serve as a model or template for one's own library's policy or manual.

So long as one keeps in mind the injunction that each situation is unique, one is within one's rights to seek common threads. Just remember that a drunk is not a drunk is not a drunk, nor do all sex offenders act predictably, and one will be somewhat forearmed in coping with problem behavior. In fact, the *definition* of problem behavior may be the toughest part of the problem. The introduction to the book attempts to define problem behavior and the problem patron, but personal definitions may vary, and situational circumstances will call for alternate methods.

With these points in mind, you are once again welcomed to the River Bend Public Library, more or less typical of its species, and told to watch yourself.

Reference

1. Carol Easton, "Sex and Violence in the Library: Scream a Little Louder Please." *American Libraries* 8 (9) (October 1977): 484–88.

Introduction

The City of River Bend

At the southern end of a midwestern state which encompasses some of the most arable land in the world lies the city of River Bend. Rolling hills, broad flatlands, and prairies are interspersed with forested areas, giving way, along the Pine River, to a wide belt of fertile farmland. The Pine splits into two streams at River Bend, each meandering across the state until both find their way into the Mississippi just north of Memphis. River Bend is a community of just over 180,000 residents and was founded in 1838 by settlers from further east, who were attracted by its rich soil and abundant water. Immigrants from many nations settled the area in the ensuing hundred years. The city is third in size in the state, supporting a variety of industrial and agricultural jobs.

During the four years since the *River Bend Casebook* was published in 1981, the city of River Bend has suffered significant erosion in its tax base. The more affluent segments of society have, whenever possible, moved from the city into the upscale suburbs north and west of the city and along the Pine River's eastern shore. This has left the central city, from which its public agencies derive their income, with significantly less money raised from property taxes. Some members of the River Bend community have prospered, but two of the area's dozen factories and foundries have closed since 1981, causing numerous families to relocate to the nation's Sun Belt (Texas, Florida, Alabama) in search of jobs (or better jobs), a less harsh climate, or new horizons. There has been major construction in the downtown area, including a gleaming new city building that houses a police station and municipal court facilities, but numerous shops and stores have gone under, leaving buildings vacant and properties unimproved. The once flourishing downtown area is now a shadow of its former self, as shoppers and those seeking amusement seem to prefer the various shopping centers and malls found on the periphery of the city, where crime is infrequent and trees are more numerous, and where automobiles may be parked at no cost, and in comparative safety.

The population of the city proper has decreased slightly since the 1980 decennial census, and all estimates point to a community more ethnically diverse yet less numerous. "White flight" seems to be the answer to urban problems, and River Bend is becoming, like so many cities of recent times, a "melting pot" for immigrants from Third World nations.

Governmentally, things haven't changed much in River Bend. Herbert Clemons, who was a newcomer to city hall in 1981, has just been reelected by a landslide to run the city for another four years. Clemons is seen as a get-tough, law-and-order politician, and the mood of the community seems right for his indolent (if affected) drawl, his western attire, and his notorious cronyism. A few years back, Clemons had to distance himself from a scheme confected by his brother and some of his associates in which southside properties were bought up and milked for what they could bring in, without improvement or remedy for the appalling conditions that residents reported. In that scandal, Clemons was depicted as being unconcerned with the plight of Black and Hispanic community members, who lived in the projects bought by the consortium of businesspeople, but whether such an allegation was right or wrong, he seemed to be able to wriggle out from charges of involvement in their malfeasance. It would appear that the citizens of River Bend rather take to the tall, rugged, and swaggering Clemons, and his vote margin of sixty-eight percent compared to thirty percent for his opponent, suggests that the people are either unconvinced that Clemons was involved in the landlord scheme or have forgiven him for it if he was.

There is still a city manager form of government in River Bend. Nineteen eighty-four's election saw a new, young city manager go to work on the city's budget and financial problems, but at this writing it is too soon to tell how it might affect the community's economic climate and the allocations of the various city agencies. One city government decision which has rocked people in the past year is the closing of the city's zoological gardens. Pleading the inability to maintain and feed a menagerie of zoo animals on the pittance provided by the current tax allocation, the directors of the River Bend Zoo have declared the doors closed on September 15, 1984 and begun work to turn the fenced-in park into a municipal recreation facility.

To those citizens who view the closing of a rather nice little zoo as an ominous portent of a city near death, the city's administration says "not so." The zoos of St. Louis, Chicago, Cincinnati, Indianapolis, Milwaukee, and Memphis are only a day's drive away, says City Manager Arthur Vaughn, and for River Bend to attempt to keep up such an expensive facility for the convenience of the Sunday driver and the local family is expensive, redundant, and unnecessary.

Attitudinally, it would seem that the community has taken a decidedly rightward shift in its politics. The pages of the local newspapers scream with crime headlines, and River Benders do not feel secure in their homes or businesses. Actually, and statistically, the crime rate is only slightly ahead of those of previous years, but the perception of the people is that crime is rampant and that the perpetrators are out there, awaiting their chance to commit illegal and sometimes life-threatening acts. The new police station, and the hiring of two dozen new uniformed officers in the past few years is meant to be reassuring, but those with their fingers on the pulses of the communities around town report a mood of fear and anxiety. What this means for city government is a felt mandate for more and more visible protection for citizens—more sophisticated electronic equipment, vehicles, and surveillance teams. What it means for other agencies of city government, especially those not concerned with protecting life and property of the citizenry, is murky, and heads of such agencies are holding their collective breath, afraid that to be conspicuous or obstreperous might cause them to go the way of the zoo director who is now relocated in Seattle, some 2000-plus miles distant from River Bend.

On the average, people aren't that much worse off economically from what they were in 1981. Of course, averages are concerned with great numbers of people, and individual families feel varying amounts of impact from the uncertain financial times. At one press conference, Mayor Clemons spoke approvingly of a scheme of which he had read where a southern city offered free bus fare out of town to any welfare families willing to go elsewhere and promise not to return. Clemons had wondered aloud if the idea might have some merit with regard to River Bend's mounting welfare and aid-to-dependent-children rolls. When severely challenged about that statement by antagonistic reporters, however, the mayor had smiled weakly and said he was "only kidding around," and the idea had not been raised since. Still, city council members and city hall are equally alarmed about the cost of supporting the nonworking segment of the populace in the city, and various schemes, radical and conservative, are being bruited about for alleviation of the numbers and cost of welfare families. Clemons knows that he has to tread softly here, however, because an already hostile press would love to portray him as the champion of big business and the oppressor of the downtrodden and homeless. Clemons already has a racial problem, as he receives little significant support in the Black community and is not perceived to be welcoming of newcomers from foreign countries. His conservative politics are seen as a thin disguise for institutionalized bigotry, and most minority groups would like to see him out of office.

Religious fervor is, at present, alive in River Bend. With uncertain social, political, and economic conditions, people seem to be turning to religion for solace and comfort. Revival meetings taking place in tents each spring and fall, and attendance at churches is up over similar figures for previous years. Mayor Clemons publicly fosters a back-to-religion mood in the city, and he likes to be photographed entering and leaving the Congregational Church over on Union Street every Sunday.

In the area of education, River Bend is at a crossroads. More and more families are pulling their children out of public schools and entering them in private ones, some for the increased educational opportunity, and others because of the parochial curriculum of instruction. School prayer is not presently Constitutional, according to the law of the land, but teachers in River Bend, in public and private schools alike, have been leading their students in silent prayer as a regular part of each morning's activities for years. This is not so much a law as it is a "custom," and no one has complained as yet. The student is merely asked to bow his/her head and reflect for a minute or two, and no doctrinaire religious beliefs are given in the public schools. River Bend is, at bottom, a religious community, and most of the city's residents feel that, so long as no one's freedom is abridged, prayer in the schools is a useful and pleasant part of the day.

In higher education, the city has been unsuccessful in getting the State University to open a branch campus within corporate limits. The continuing presence of a community college and private (Catholic) college provide higher education for the people. Increasing numbers of young people in search of college degrees are going elsewhere, and a feasibility study for a state university campus is under way, with a site selected on the southwest side, and architectural drawings for fourteen campus buildings having been approved. The state is balking, however, at extending its university into the southern region of the state, as River Bend is the only city of any appreciable size there, and conservative legislators do not see the necessity for another downstate campus to further dilute the higher education funding they vote each year. Consequently, the status of "River Bend State" is in limbo and will probably not be decided until several critical decisions at both state and federal levels are made.

Summing up, the city of River Bend is better off today in some respects and worse off in others. There is always tradeoff in every decision or event (for example, the closing of the two industrial plants has sidelined over 300 workers—some of whom now reside in Texas and other southern states—but has resulted in noticeably cleaner air in and over the metropolitan area). Change comes slowly to such a city, for most of the people don't want, or even fear, change, but gradual transition is inevitable. Some ask why River Bend thinks that it can survive by standing still, while others hold the philosophy that, unless it is proven to be necessary that the city change, it is therefore necessary that it not change.

In such an environment, consisting of so many factors, obvious, subtle, and concealed, the River Bend Public Library continues to exist. Progress is hard to achieve, and is not always forward, but Patricia Broughton and her generally capable crew of staff members is doing its level best to survive and grow under such straitened and uncertain circumstances.

The River Bend Public Library Revisited—Transition and Change

The economic changes that have affected the city have, of necessity, filtered down to the library. As a tax-supported creature of city government, the library flourishes and declines along with the fortunes of the rest of the city. The tax rate is fixed by the state, which has authorized a ceiling on the millage per $100.00 of assessed valuation in which a city may tax its residents for governmental purposes. Beyond this current rate of 4 mills per $100.00, a city must place a referendum on the ballot at election time.

River Bend's library is luckier than most, for it has a durable, relatively modern structure to house its downtown main operations. The central library, while somewhat small, is not dangerously overfilled with materials. The structure is still adequate to the needs of the community, and three branches in outlying parts of the community are designed to permit residents of those neighborhoods to visit a more conveniently placed building than the one downtown, which is lacking in all but the most rudimentary free parking.

When two large factories closed down last year, the library felt the shock waves of the event as laid-off and fired workers came looking for information on employment or benefits for the unemployed. As a result, subscriptions to the *Houston Chronicle, Tampa Tribune,* and the *Miami Herald* have been purchased, and, at times, fought over by those willing and able to relocate. A more ominous effect of the closings has been the sudden erosion of a large chunk of the tax base from which the library draws its financial lifeblood. When Midwest Steel and Continental Rubber went belly-up and their gates were padlocked, taxes formerly paid by those companies were no longer available to city agencies, which responded in different ways. The police and fire departments were affected very little, due to their claim on the support of the community as bulwarks against threats to life or property. The library doesn't think of itself as a frill, of course, and a dedicated readership keeps circulation figures respectable. Unfortunately, but typically for an American city library, only about 20 percent of the adult populace really considers itself numbered among "library users." This means that about 80 percent of the citizens don't use the library (at least for its intended purposes) and some of them doubtless would probably just as soon have the money for its upkeep and operation either refunded or rechanneled.

For Library Director Pat Broughton and her staff, this presents a thorny public relations problem. How does one convince four-fifths of an economy-minded city that it should subsidize the leisure and educational pursuits of the other one-fifth? Pat doesn't know, but she is trying. Somehow, it works. The library has survived attempts to cut into its acquisitions, curtail its hours, reduce its staff, and abandon it branches. Bloody but relatively uninjured, the library continues to serve the community, with its only significant loss being the discontinuance and subsequent sale of the bookmobile, back in 1982, which proved to be too expensive to staff, fuel, drive, and stock. So while much could be improved, in a financial manner of speaking, Pat is grateful for what remains.

Administratively, Pat governs the library with the help of Mike Ross, her capable and generally supportive assistant director, and a mixed bag of support and interference from her five-person board of directors. Just now, she would really like to add a secretarial person to her tiny office staff of two, but she sees the realities of her situation only too clearly and is not about to jeopardize the triumph of having been authorized to fill a line in her Performing Arts department last year by appearing insatiable.

The staff has shown little turnover since 1981, which is just as well, because the city is apt from time to time to slap a hiring freeze on all departments, perhaps causing an important vacant payroll line to go unfilled should anyone quit. Since 1981, her staff is up one line, although there has been a small amount of rearrangement. Two staff members previously charged with outreach and programs have been reassigned from downtown to various outlying locations, and one staff member has been added to the complement working downtown at the central library. It may not be all Pat might have wished for, but it's better than it might have been. Pat remembers only too well the January day in 1983 when she opened her correspondence to find the simple typed request that she make contingency budgets showing how the library would cope with 5 percent, 10 percent, and 20 percent reduction in funds. That was a chilling experience, as she and her department heads labored far into the night to try to propose cuts that could be made without excessive bleeding. By luck, state aid held up by a legislative logjam was suddenly released, and Pat and her brave co-workers have not had to deal with any of the grim alternatives to the lean budget in force at that time.

In the public relations arena, Pat has managed to deflect or evade excessive criticism. Once in a while, someone from city government (occasionally it's Mayor Clemons himself) gets a notion to "do something about the library," but Pat has learned how to jawbone such economy moves down to manageable proportions. She has also learned the joys of delegating responsibility for public relations and has discovered to her pleasure that some of the best ideas come from the rank and file—the librarians, clerks, and even the pages—who work in the building.

The library board of directors, after a disastrous attempt to create and implement policy for Pat and her staff a few years ago, has subsided into a body of people who really want to help, even if they aren't always in accord with Pat or with one another as to how this should be done. The retirement from the board of Mr. Alfred Meninger, an archconservative retired industrialist, and his subsequent replacement with the fairminded and politically independent Samantha Hurst, an economist at the local junior college, has helped Pat in keeping the board on her side on most points of controversy.

Physically, the library still occupies a lovely site on a small mounded hill surrounded by ancient trees and amid a parkland setting across from the carefully maintained Riverfront Park, which runs along the city's eastern boundary from north to south. The city has determined, however, that upkeep and maintenance of the square block occupied by the library and its surroundings are the responsibility of the library, and the onerous job of mowing, trimming, planting, watering, etc., has fallen on the already beleaguered shoulders of the library's small (two-person) maintenance and custodial staff, Irwin Rossiter and Peter Bourdelle. Worse yet, the city's police department cannot spare any uniformed police for security and will not authorize the hiring of a special security patrol, so Irwin and Peter must also take on themselves the job of guarding the library against disruptive forces. Peter doesn't mind this extra job too much, because he likes all the overtime he is piling up by being a security guard when his custodial day ends. Irwin, however, is no longer a young man, nor single as is Peter, and, despite his proprietary attitude toward the building and grounds, he is having some difficulty in wearing all the hats he must wear as custodian, walking guard, lawn care specialist, occasional referee, traffic cop, floor-walker, father-confessor (to staff members), and night watchman. He has on many occasions threatened, only half joking, to bring a cot to the library and give up his little home on the north side. Then, he says, he could always be at work in the morning just by rolling out of bed and wouldn't have a weary drive home when he was ready for sleep at night.

A serious problem has recently centered around the lovely flowering bushes which line the walkways leading to the library from all directions. Young muggers and thieves are using the bushes as places of concealment from which to ambush their prey, and attempts to catch them and stop them have failed so far. The reaction of the police, when told of the minor-league crime wave, has been drastic. Threatening to cut down and remove the bushes if the muggings don't stop, the chief of police has thrown a serious scare into Pat and all those who love the color and texture of the forsythia, crepe myrtle, lilac and sumac bushes which festoon the walks in three seasons of the year with colorful borders. So far, Pat has managed to keep the city from bulldozing the library's parkland setting into something resembling Berlin just after the war, but every time some poor child is set upon and mugged outside the building, the cries go up that the bushes must go.

One feather in her cap, Pat thinks, is the way in which the library has begun experimenting with the many applications of electronic machines in her library. So far, she has overseen the purchase and installation of a small number of microcomputers, which can handle acquisitions and circulation routines together with accessing online search services an enhancement to her library's reference capabilities. In the future, she envisions "closing the catalog" and replacing the customary and traditional card catalog drawers with online access terminals, which could be used by the public and would greatly facilitate use of the collection. Such upgrading of the library would take much money ("Megabucks," as Mike Ross calls it) and would call for terminals located at various and numerous spots around the building and in all of the branches.

Worse than the cost, perhaps, is the opposition Pat has encountered to her desire to bring the library "kicking and screaming into the twentieth century" by the addition of computers and terminals with their ancillary equipment. Religious groups within the community have taken strong stands in opposition to the presence and use of computers in the library, and even though Pat has privately tended to brush off such complaints and diatribes as "the crank ravings of the last of the dinosaurs," increasing numbers of River Bend's people appear to be alarmed or even angry about the fact that Pat wants to spend her library's allocation, at least in part, on *machines* as well as on books and magazines. Murmurings are heard that computers have no souls, that they are programed by godless Communists and Atheists, and that they will turn the children of River Bend into a legion of button-pressing, game-playing automatons.

Still to date and into the foreseeable future, the question is academic. There is little money available to cover anything but the bare necessities of keeping a library staffed and equipped. Pat wonders, however, just how much entrenched resistance she is likely to encounter should she elect to automate the catalog and require that patrons use terminals. She sees so many benefits to such a plan that she is puzzled (and at times enraged) that others don't see them too.

The strengths and weaknesses of the library are perhaps equally balanced, although Pat, always the optimist, prefers to concentrate on the strengths. The library is still blessed by and large with a strong, creative, enthusiastic, and dedicated staff. The building is pleasant and attractive, and the collection, while not what it should be (after years of systematic strangulation by budgetary constraints), is at least responsive to the changing needs and demands of the citizens of the community. On the other side of the ledger, hours of operation are down from where they were five years ago, and the staff hasn't grown in numbers or diversity as much as Pat would like to have seen. Outside interference with the library's selection policies, usually manifested through censorship attempts, still continues to plague the staff, and the usual run of problem patrons require more security personnel to keep them from wreaking their customary disruption on staff and other patrons alike.

The Problem Patron in the Library

There seem to be more problem patrons than there once were at the River Bend Public Library and at other libraries across the nation, although it may be that library staff members are just getting more sensitive to their presence and talking about the difficulties more. At any rate, whether because of improved (or at least different) treatment of mental patients, more stress attached to day-to-day living, or something to do with the overall ambiance of the library itself, incidents involving problem patrons are on the upswing. Now, more than ever, the problem patron poses a tough dilemma for librarians.

Increasing numbers of homeless and mentally ill citizens use the library as a place to pass their time. Shortages in library service staff have made immediate service delivery more difficult, resulting in more complaints and aggressive actions from inconvenienced patrons. With growing frequency, librarians find themselves forced to respond to a "special breed" of patrons who are misusing library facilities, creating disturbances, and even threatening the safety of library users and staff. Most librarians have never learned how to respond to these problem patrons. With the orientation of "service at all costs," many well-intentioned librarians are caught unprepared to take on the responsibility of enforcing rules and setting limits with problem patrons. When the staff lacks consistent approach, dealing with problem patrons becomes something that is avoided or handled with such tension that an even larger crisis is precipitated before the situation can be brought under control.

Essentially, problem patrons can be categorized into five classes. There is, first, eccentric behavior, differentiated from true problem behavior because of the basically harmless nature of the activity in which the patron is engaged. Examples include patrons who talk to themselves, gesture nonthreateningly at other patrons or staff, hum, wear bizarre clothing, speak in tongues, etc.

Then there is mental illness, often difficult to diagnose. Persons so afflicted may appear or even be normal for most of their time spent in the library and then may be "triggered off" by some outside stimulus or something occurring within themselves. A third type of problem behavior has to do with noncompliance with library rules and may overlap any of the other categories. Noncompliance, of course, ranges from library to library, as the rules themselves vary. Sleeping, for example, may be expressly forbidden by one library's policy or procedure manual, forbidden but overlooked in another library, and tolerated or not discussed in a third. A fourth type of objectionable behavior is harassment of library staff or other patrons. Harassment is variously defined but entails more than just occasional (or perhaps even justifiable) anger or irritation at alleged rude treatment or inordinate delays. Persistent badgering, verbal abuse, following, or even staring intently at library staff or patrons can fall under this category. Finally, there is intentional misbehavior, in which the perpetrator knows that s/he is doing something forbidden or dangerous yet intends and proceeds to do so. Examples include physical violence, destruction or multilation of materials, assaults on the physical structure of the building, or the carrying or use of controlled or prohibited objects or substances.

Somewhere, there is a fine line between that behavior which is only annoying (such as the patron who won't go away and persists in engaging a library staff member in protracted discussion) and that which is disruptive or harmful to other persons. In the gray area between the clearly defined extremes of the continuum may be found patrons who smell so bad that no one wants to go near them, complaining patrons whose voices grow louder and shriller as their levels of frustration increase, and persons who emit unexpected sounds at random, startling those around them and causing them fear or loss of concentration.

> The problem patron has been a difficult fact of library life . . . there's a
> new vigilance about just who should be allowed in libraries. Arson,
> still a big problem for libraries, has most often been blamed on today's
> youth. Libraries are all too vulnerable to lawsuits . . . some are
> protecting themselves with liability insurance.[1]

Strange people hang around in libraries. *Newsweek* (April 14, 1975) describes James Ruppert, who shot and killed eleven members of his family on Easter Sunday offering no statement of motive for his bloody act, as "a quiet, unemployed draftsman, (who) spent a lot of time reading in the public library.'' The fact is that anyone is free to enter, needs have no reason to be there, nor need state such a reason, and may, if interested, avoid talking to anyone, buying anything, showing identification, or explaining his/her presence. Then, too, the hours are long, the location is usually central to a city, the furniture is often inviting, and libraries are warm (or cool), dry, and as inviting as the staff can make them. What more ideal location for the drifter, the idler, the psychopath with no place to go on a long, boring day? What better spot to plan one's next move, stalk a victim, choose a quarry, or commit a crime than in one of the darker, less-traveled parts of a cavernous building with inadequate security?

Concern about the people who frequent libraries is nothing new. Charles A. Cutter, one of the all-time movers and shakers in the history of American libraries, wrote an article entitled ''Library Discipline: Rules Affecting the Public'' in which he attempted to list and deal with various forms of problem behavior in reading rooms and stack areas.[2] Nor is the problem uniquely American in nature, or even especially western. It was reported in *American Libraries* some years ago that the *Bangkok World* for March 9, 1971 reported that:

> The National Library (of Thailand) was the scene of student 'hooliganism.' Kaimuk Milithorn, deputy director of the National Library, told the press that 'students from government and private schools used the library as a place for making love, smoking heroin, and misbehaving in other ways.' According to Miss Milithorn: 'At present, the library officials dare not even warn or check the students, for when they do, they are molested every time.' One possible solution to some of the library's problems seems to be postponed for the present: 'We are thinking of closing up the way that leads to the back entrance,' said Miss Milithorn, 'but we do not know how far we can proceed with that. Very often the students have made appointments to fight in the compound of the library. There have been cases of hand grenades being thrown and guns being fired.[3]

Then there are authors who have speculated in print that the library tends to be a natural and powerful magnet for persons who are, in one way or another, not quite right in the head. One writer put it this way:

> G.K. Chesterton thought it was mainly mad people who hung around reading rooms. He called the British Museum a temple of hobbies, and by hobbies he meant any pursuit which began as one part of a life and then consumed all of the life (misers, drunks, the man who spends 20 years building a model of the Brooklyn Bridge from toothpicks, and George Eliot's Mr. Casaubon, who was looking for a key to all mythologies). There was a rumor, Chesterton said, that any family with a madman in it dropped him off for the day at the British Museum.

"When I first discovered that some of the other people (who come to libraries) there were drunk, crazy, or had come in to get out of the rain, I was surprised but I took it in stride. We readers are tough-minded. Once at the Tompkins Square Branch (of the NYPL), a man tried to attack me in the 800s, but after the janitor threw him out, I went right back because I had to have something to read. Non-readers may be surprised at my perseverance, but readers won't."

"I have seen many strange people (in the NYPL) . . . the people who work there look nervous, guarded, or weary. Besides helping the customers find books, they have to patrol the bathrooms, phone booths, entrances and exits, and all of these extra rooms like the picture collection, magazine room, etc."[4]

Strange places, libraries. People walk through the doors every day who exhibit the most bizarre or anti-social behavior imaginable. Others are only annoying or pitiable. Staff members will, at varying times, want to slap, shake, talk to, talk about, run to, run from, avoid, counsel, protect, comfort, help, dispense with, dispose of, take home, refer, arrest, vaporize, or ignore such "problem patrons." But it isn't supposed to be that way. Lincoln in his *Crime in the Library* points out that "the public image of the library is generally that of a quiet, comfortable, inviting place, a place where people read and study, and certainly a place where people and their belongings should be safe."[5]

And yet, somewhere at any given moment, someone in a public library is the victim of some manner of crime. Even though the term "crime" is susceptible to all types of definitions, Lincoln maintains that it must be *intentional* behavior and may include theft, vandalism, mutilation, drug use and/or sale, harassment, obscenity, verbal abuse, complaints, assaults, vagrancy, psychologically abnormal behavior, arson, indecent exposure, voyeurism, and a host of other types of incidents that annoy, threaten, or victimize staff or patrons. A recent incident in one Virginia public library brought to light a series of events that might justify a description of the public library as a Combat Zone. Griffith reports that, "during a single year, 41 physical assaults against staff members were recorded (in the United States), but the problem is considered 'negligible.' "[6] O'Neill lists in his findings the eight most common problems reported by libraries: (1) perverts, (2) youths threatening malicious mischief, (3) loitering and vagrancy, (4) dangerous neighborhood between library and parking lot, (5) patrons sneaking into restricted areas, (6) mentally unbalanced patrons, (7) threat of personal injury by smart aleck youths, and (8) muggings.[7]

Since the reality seems to be that libraries can be dangerous and sometimes even menacing places rather than the conventional stereotype which presents them as quiet havens enshrining the dead thoughts of dead men from a dead past, measures must be taken to deal with the criminal, the scofflaw, the weirdo, and the loiterer, with or without intent.

A recent incident saw a library director demoted by a city administration after a library clerk was killed while attempting to close a branch library building. The assailant claimed no motive for his attack on the woman and another staff member who was stabbed. The son of the slain woman has filed a five million dollar lawsuit against the city (Norfolk, Virginia), charging that officials "negligently and recklessly" failed to provide adequate security for library employees, even though they realized that "dangerous, hazardous, and unsafe conditions had existed for some time."[8] The branch librarian had written several memos to the director warning of dangerous conditions at the library and appealing for better security measures. Among incidents reported in such memos were "the theft of a bicycle, fire in a mailbox, deflated tires on cars of library patrons, damage to the interior of the library, and . . . incidents of beer drinking, masturbation, and indecent exposure inside the building."[9]

To secure themselves and their premises against the numerous and demonstrable hazards of working in library buildings, library staff members have suggested a number of measures that would go a long way toward remedying the situation. Lincoln lists the following:[10]

1. Closed circuit television
2. Plainclothes guards or police
3. Portable signalling devices
4. Uniformed guards or police
5. Security screens on all windows
6. Unbreakable windows
7. Intrusion alarms on all doors
8. Book theft detection systems
9. Automatic communication links with police
10. Electronic intrusion system inside
11. Security locks on all outside doors
12. Police patrol coverage
13. Smoke detectors
14. Locked storage room

One might add to the list. Dogs, for example, may be excellent deterrents to break-ins, and metal-detectors, such as those used at airports, might deter the weapon-carrying crazy from doing his/her thing in the library. Some libraries have found a relatively simple method to help them deal with problem patrons. Such libraries as Tucson Public and Schenectady County Public Libraries have written and posted rules for behavior in the library. Library employees including security guards at the main branch of the Tucson Public Library have found that it is easier to ask problem patrons to leave or desist from a particular type of misbehavior when the staff is able to point to a printed list of rules when confronting the offending patron. Below is such a list of rules that the Schenectady County Public Library finds useful.

Schenectady County Public Library
RULES
governing the use
of the library

WHILE IN THE BUILDING, PLEASE DO NOT

- Smoke

- Consume Food or Beverages

- Loiter or Solicit

- Sleep

- Bring Pets into the Building

- Harass Patrons or Library Personnel

- Be Drunk or Disorderly

- Leave Pre-School Children Unattended

- Enter with Bare Feet

- Place Feet on Tables or Chairs

The violation of any one of these rules may subject the individual(s) involved to exclusion from the library premises.[11]

All of these remedies, however, cost money—some of them requiring a great deal of money. Even with them, the library cannot be assured of rendering its staff or its patrons safe from the unprovoked actions of the people who pass through the doors of the building every day. It is because the unexpected so often arrives, and at the least expected time, that this book came to be written. River Bend is your town, and its library is your library. Read on.

References

1. Mary Rouse, "Cover to Cover: Libraries, Letters, Messages," *Village Voice* (April 18, 1974): 28.
2. Charles A. Cutter, "Library Discipline: Rules Affecting the Public," *Library Journal* 28 (1903): 65–67.
3. *American Libraries* 2 (September 1971): 544.
4. Rouse, p. 28.
5. Alan Jay Lincoln, *Crime in the Library* (New York: Bowker, 1984), p.1.
6. Jack W. Griffith, "Of Vagrants and Vandals and Library Things," *Wilson Library Bulletin* 52 (June 1978): 769+.
7. James W. O'Neill, "From the Editor's Desk: Staff and Patron Safety . . . Eight Most Common Problems, " *Library Security Newsletter* 1 (September–October 1975): 3–5.
8. "Virginia Library Director Loses Position," *Wilson Library Bulletin* 58 (September 1983): 495.
9. "Virginia Library Director Loses Position," p. 495.
10. Lincoln, p. 161.
11. Used by permission of the Schenectady County Public Library. © 1983. Schenectady County Public Library. *Problem Patron Manual*, December 1981.

River Bend Public Library
Administrative and Staff Roster, 1984/85
Central Library Building

Administration

Patricia Broughton, director
Michael Ross, assistant director
Catherine LaFleur, budget officer
Marjorie Strazinsky, executive secretary
Christine Darnell, clerk-typist

Circulation Department

Frederica Bondanella, head
Carolyn Harada, clerk
Althea Jackson, clerk
Donna Campbell, clerk
Herbert White, page (part-time)
Hilary Brewer, page (part-time)

History and Travel Department

John Collins, head
Emilia Parsons, librarian
Burton Stone, librarian
Joshua Williams, clerk-typist
Susan Camaraoes, page (part-time)
Daniel Ortega, page (part-time)

Science and Technology Department

Robert Castlebury, head
Suzanne Arakawa, librarian
Martin Ellis, librarian
Cynthia Brookings, clerk-typist
Ginny Christopher, page (part-time)
Lenny Newman, page (part-time)

Technical Services Department

Allan Costerman, head
Vera Hemphill, acquisitions librarian
Marie O'Shea, cataloger
Karen Talbert, cataloger
Joyce McDonald, clerk-typist
John Levinson, page (part-time)
Artemis Matsoukis, page (part-time)

Custodial Services Department

Irwin Rossiter, custodian
Peter Bourdelle, janitor

Reference Department

Martha Forsch, head
Randall Gardner, librarian
Nancy Groves, librarian
Robert diMarzo, librarian
Cindy Abelson, clerk-typist
Barrett Johns, page (part-time)
Julie Carroll, page (part-time)
Stanley Lewis, page (part-time)

Performing Arts Department

Joann Larabee, head
Lawrence Green, librarian
Lauren Soltani, librarian
Virginia Watanabe, librarian
Kay Brown, clerk-typist
Patricia Pergolesi, page (part-time)
Kevin McConnell, page (part-time)

Children's Services Department

Eve Shelton, head
Barbara Prell, librarian
Gretchen Schroeder, librarian
Bonnie McKibben, librarian
Pauline Snyder, clerk-typist
Billy Jo Macklin, page (part-time)
Rebecca Benjamin, page (part-time)

River Bend and Environs

Scale: 1 inch = 1 mile

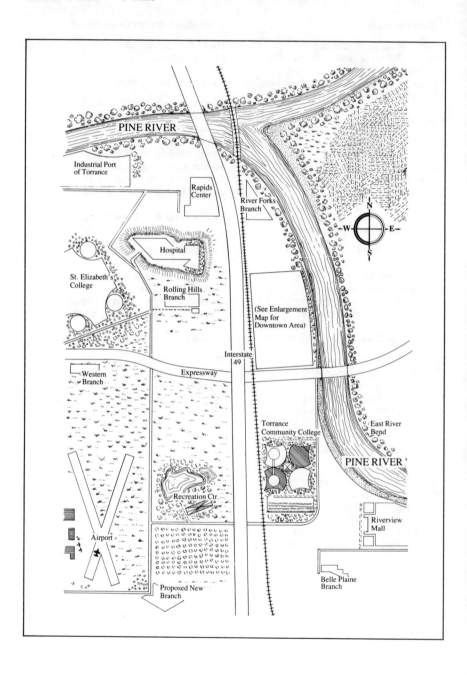

Downtown River Bend (Inset Map)

Scale: 1 inch = ¼ mile

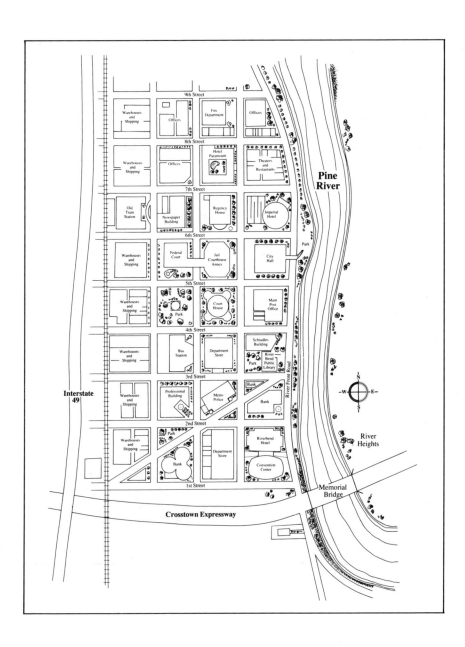

River Bend Public Library, Main Building Floor Plan, 1984

Scale: 1 inch = 40 feet

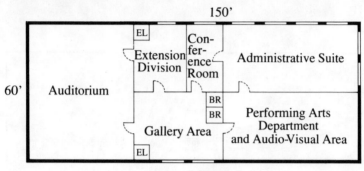

150'

EL	
Extension Division	Con-fer-ence Room	Administrative Suite
	BR
	BR
Gallery Area	Performing Arts Department and Audio-Visual Area
EL	

60' | Auditorium

LEVEL 2

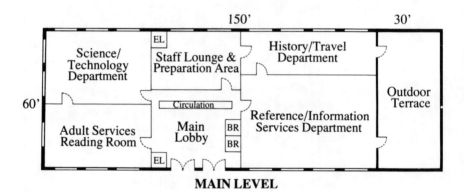

150' 30'

Science/ Technology Department | EL | Staff Lounge & Preparation Area | History/Travel Department | Outdoor Terrace

60'

Circulation

Adult Services Reading Room | Main Lobby | BR BR | Reference/Information Services Department

EL

MAIN LEVEL

150' 30'

EL			Drive-Through
Reserve Stack Area	Custodial Area	
Children's			Book-mobile Area & Loading Dock
Lower Lobby	BR BR	Technical Services Department	
EL			

60'

LOWER LEVEL

Total-27,000 square ft. + terrace + bookmobile area.

River Bend Revisited:

The Problem Patron in the Library

Section 1

Emergencies and Hazards Cases 1–20

Case 1
I'm Not Going to Hurt You!

The little girl came around the corner of the children's room and propelled herself into the arms of a startled Bonnie McKibben. Bonnie, a children's librarian at the River Bend Public Library, had only enough time to notice that the child was in a highly agitated state but didn't seem to be injured or bleeding, so she quickly decided that holding her and talking soothingly seemed to be the best course of action.

After a short while, the girl's convulsive sobbing abated, and she lifted her small face out of Bonnie's bosom and looked nervously around the room. "What is it, child? What happened?" asked Bonnie, but the girl, appearing to be about eight years old and wearing a nicely coordinated sweater-and-slacks outfit, refused (or was unable) to speak. Bonnie finally had the girl climb down from her lap, and she led the way into the small office, adjacent to the large children's room, she shared with Eve Shelton. "Eve, would you take the desk for a few minutes?" asked Bonnie. "This little girl and I have something to discuss in private." Smiling, Eve arose and left the office, closing the door behind her. Now that they were alone, Bonnie regarded the girl seriously. Except for the tear streaks on her face, she didn't seem to be any worse for her experience, but Bonnie, who had raised four children herself, knew that nothing could be decided until she could get the girl to tell her about it.

"So, what's the story?" she asked, seating the girl once more on her lap. "What happened out there?"

"There was this man. . . ." began the small girl, starting, as she spoke, to show signs of renewed crying.

"Go on," said Bonnie, and then she found herself waiting patiently while the whimpering girl tried to decide what to say next.

Bonnie finally picked up the office telephone and called the circulation desk. "Freddie? Yeah, this is Bonnie in Children's. Will you ask Irwin to come down here right away? No, not really an emergency, but we need him as soon as possible. Thanks, Freddie. See you later. Bye."

Turning back to the girl, she decided to begin with simple questions. "Tell me your name," she said.

"Jennifer."

"Jennifer what?"

"Randall. Jennifer Randall."

"Jennifer, did a man bother you today? In the library?"

An affirmative shake of the head.

"When was this?"

"Little while ago. Ten minutes."

"Where?"

"Elevator. In the elevator."

Just then Irwin Rossiter, the security guard on duty, came puffing up to the office door and entered without knocking. "Sent for me, Bonnie?" Bonnie was suddenly aware that the girl on her lap was cringing and peeping at Irwin in terror, her arms wound tightly around Bonnie's neck.

"It's all right, Jennifer," said Bonnie. "This man works here, and he wants to help." Slowly, hesitantly, the girl's grip loosened.

"Now please start over again, and tell us both what happened—can you do that?"

Jennifer, a bit more composed now, told, in a clear, high voice, that she had come to the library that morning on the bus, her first time downtown alone. She arrived at the library about 20 minutes past nine, to be plenty early for the 10 o'clock children's program and to give her time to look at some of the new books in the department.

She had gone out to the bathroom but had discovered that, for some reason, the basement-floor restrooms were locked. Ringing for the elevator to take her up to the main floor, she had found the car occupied. A tall man ("How tall?" asked Irwin in his booming voice, but the girl's fear reaction caused Bonnie to signal with her hand for Irwin to hold his questions for later) had said something about wanting to go up but being taken down by the elevator. When the door had closed on them, the man had reached out a hand and pressed the STOP button, causing the elevator to stop between floors. At that point, he had approached Jennifer and attempted to fondle her, saying, "I'm not going to hurt you; I only want to touch you." When Jennifer had started screaming, the man had said "Okay, okay!" and had released the STOP button, allowing the elevator to rise to the main floor landing, where he had hurried out without a word.

When pressed for description, Jennifer hadn't been able to be very helpful. The man was "tall" and wearing "dark clothes" with no distinguishing features that the girl could remember and nothing unusual about his voice. Irwin, with little to go on, walked out of the office, wearily promising to look around for someone answering the description but obviously not optimistic about bringing the man to justice.

4

Bonnie, doing what she could, elicited from Jennifer the name and telephone number of the girl's parents. The mother, reached by telephone and told of the circumstances, said that she would leave immediately and be at the library in half an hour. Before she hung up, she shouted at Bonnie, "What's the matter with you people at the library? Can't you even protect a little kid from the perverts and weirdos who come in there?" Bonnie thought it best to make no response to this, which was, after all, a good question and instead promised Mrs. Randall that she would personally look after Jennifer until she arrived.

After a call to the police, telling what she knew, Bonnie broke out a box of lemon drops and, taking one herself, offered several to Jennifer. "But he didn't hurt you, then?" she asked, just to make sure.

"No. But he was scary. There was no way to get out of that elevator and he wanted to do things to me." Jennifer shuddered at the vivid memory.

"I know. Well, your mother's on her way; the police have been told; Irwin, the guard, is prowling around looking for the man who did this to you; and I'll stay with you as long as you need me. Is that all right?"

"Yes. Thank you."

Spontaneously, Bonnie put her arms around the girl's thin frame and gave her an affectionate squeeze. "One more thing," she decided to ask, "Had you ever seen that man before?"

"No," said Jennifer, "I don't think so. I don't know. Maybe." Later conversations with her co-workers persuaded Bonnie that the man in question had been seen (unless it was someone very much like him) walking in and out of the children's department for several weeks. Because of his nondescript appearance, and the presumption that he might be somebody's father, no one had said or done anything about him.

At about 10:30, a worried looking mother swept into the children's department staff office and swept Jennifer off the floor in a hug. In a few moments, mother and daughter were on their way home. Bonnie watched them depart, feeling several emotions, first among which was relief. "Well, no real harm done and a happy ending," she remarked to Eve Shelton, who was standing beside her.

"Yeah, this time," said Eve laconically. "But what about *next* time?"

Questions for Discussion

1. Should a library (especially one with a children's department) monitor the behavior and movement of "suspicious persons" who seem to be hanging around or looking at children?

2. What, if anything, can a library do to discourage such people from loitering around children?
3. How can library staff be alerted and prepared when such persons are spotted?
4. Should children be notified of the presence of such suspicious-looking patrons, and, if so, how?
5. As the library director, subsequent to this incident, what steps would you take or commission to reduce the future possibility of repeated assaults against children?

Resources

1. "Kids Warned about Strangers by Hit North York Library Play." *Library Journal* 108 (November 15, 1983): 2122.
   A stage play with music made the rounds of the branches in this Ontario library system. It is shown to children and depicts some of the hazards they may face in encounters with strangers and is designed to be followed by discussion.
2. *Problem Patron Manual.* Schenectady County Public Library, Schenectady, NY. December 1981.
   See section on "sexual deviants" on p. 37. This booklet covers many of the problem situations likely to happen in public places, sooner or later.

Case 2
The Winter of '84

Even the old-timers couldn't remember a winter like the one River Bend experienced in 1984. George Orwell, the author who had written a book entitled *1984*, had predicted many dire things for the world in that year, but he couldn't have envisioned that the weather during that season was to be the equivalent of all-out warfare, for that's just the way it seemed.

Snow had fallen on River Bend on the average of twice a week from early November through early March, without benefit of a January thaw or any other reprieve from the unremitting cold. By the middle of March, the weather bureau claimed that afternoon temperatures should have been in the low 50s (Fahrenheit) at that time of year, with nights rarely falling to the freezing mark. Snow, therefore, should have been a rarity. Yet the blizzard which blew up on March 14, and extended for a full two days, dumped a record-breaking 26 inches of new snow on the city and its surrounding countryside and brought virtually all transportation and travel to a complete halt.

With all local radio stations advising residents to remain at home, if possible, and to emerge only if and when they must, people made the best of an unscheduled two-day midweek holiday. The St. Patrick's Day parade up Central was cancelled, and all private and public business was suspended until road crews, working feverishly, could open or reopen the streets and render them safe for travel. Finally, on the 19th of the month, things began to regain a semblance of normalcy. Stores and government offices opened, bus lines were again in operation, and children returned to school.

The public library also reopened on the 19th, with Peter Bourdelle, the janitor, arriving a full hour and a half before the 9:00 a.m. opening time to shovel walks and scatter salt and sand on pedestrian approaches to the building, while Irwin Rossiter, who doubled as custodian and security guard, operated the library's elderly snowplow to attempt to uncover as many spaces as possible in the parking lot.

By the middle of the day, thanks to a warm sun and rising temperatures, Peter and Irwin had made all approaches to the library passable and could resume their customary indoor duties. That night, however, foul weather returned to the city as a Canadian air mass descended from the North, bringing with it cold temperatures and light precipitation. The result was that, by morning, all of the carefully exposed walkways were glassy sheets of ice, and the backbreaking work of making them safe had to begin again.

About 11:00 a.m., Althea Jackson, a clerk at the library's circulation desk, looked up to see Peter Bourdelle leading a middle-aged woman slowly over to her, a look of concern on his craggy face. "This lady fell down on that ice out there, Althea," he told her, "and she cut herself some on something. Can you do anything for her?"

Althea took a brief look at the head of the woman, who seemed to be more frightened than injured. "Well, doesn't seem too bad to me," she said, smiling. "Why don't you come on in the back, honey, and let me clean up that cut."

The woman touched her bleeding scalp a few times with her gloved hand, then permitted herself to be led into the staff lounge, where Althea took her over to the sink.

"I'll just give that a good washing and some peroxide and you can be on your way," she said, cheerfully. Peter, who had followed the women into the lounge, cleared his throat and asked, quietly, "Want me to get an ambulance or contact the police or anything?"

The women looked at each other and grinned. "For this?" Althea found confirmation of her thought in the other woman's eyes. "I get worse than this when I fight with my children. No, Peter, you don't have to do anything about this," she looked inquiringly into the face of the older woman, "unless you think that you require medical attention, of course," she added as an afterthought.

"No, thanks. I just took a lick upside the head from an icicle or something. Just wash the slush off it, if you don't mind, and I'll be on my way to the stacks in search of a good novel."

"Thanks for bringing her in, Peter, and mind your own step when you go back outside, hear?" said Althea, smiling at the tall, shy janitor. Peter acknowledged her thanks and clomped out of the room, his rubber boots making squishing noises on the linoleum.

Althea examined the cut. "Just as I thought, it's just a scratch. Let me clean it up for you." With soap and water and paper towels, she washed the small wound. Then she applied a few drops of hydrogen peroxide and a Band-aid from the first aid kit which was kept in a drawer next to the sink. "There," she said, professionally admiring her work. "Now keep that clean and, for heaven's sake, watch your footing on the sidewalks."

The woman thanked Althea profusely, which Althea swept aside with a cheery "all part of the service" and walked her to the door, giving further instructions on how to navigate the library's slippery footpaths and stairs. After she had gone, Althea wondered whether she should have taken her name and address and filed some kind of accident report. Well, it was too late now, she thought, dismissing the incident from her mind as the day warmed up and more and more people ventured into the library. As she left to go home that evening at 6:00, she noticed that Peter had done his usual good job of shoveling and salting, for the sidewalks leading from the building to the parking lot were dry.

The next day Althea was rocked to find out that the woman she had helped, a Mrs. Vera Contini, had collapsed later in the day at home and had been rushed to Parkside Hospital with a concussion. She was now unconscious, and doctors gave her condition as "guarded," a term which Althea hated for its ambiguity. Worse yet, Pat Broughton, the library's director, called her into her office later in the day to inform her that the family of the unfortunate woman were considering a major lawsuit against the library for negligence.

Althea, shocked, slumped in a chair and, after Pat brought her a cup of coffee, she told the director what had happened the previous day, and how she had assumed that the woman's injury was minor, deserving of no more than routine first aid. "What do we do now, Pat?" she asked, in a small, contrite voice. "What can anybody do?" said Pat. "Wait."

"But the lawsuit. What if the woman dies? What if she's in a coma for years? How much trouble are we in? How much trouble am *I* in?"

"Althea," said Pat, "I know what you're thinking and I can imagine what you're going through, but at this time, all we can do is wait and hope, and maybe pray."

Althea thought a bit and asked Pat if there was any way she might take the rest of the day off. Pat, compassionate as always, said "certainly," and Althea departed, deciding to head for Parkside Hospital. She felt terribly guilty and fearful, and she wanted to be there if there were any developments in the condition of the poor woman she had helped, yet not helped at all.

Questions for Discussion

1. What procedures should be in place and understood by all staff members in the event of accident or injury to a member of the public?
2. How would you judge Althea's actions subsequent to having the woman led to her desk?
3. Now that a lawsuit is in the offing, what would you, as Pat Broughton, say or do to exercise "damage control" and to see to it that the library avoids charges of negligence?

4. As Pat, what would you say to Althea concerning her role in this accidental tragedy?

Resources

Sections on procedure in cases of accident, injury, sudden illness, and the like are available in several library policy manuals. In addition to the Schenectady manual mentioned in Case 1, one may consult:

1. Haley, Anne, and Gail Johnston. *Manual of Library Policies*. Baker, OR: Pacific Northwest Library Association, 1979. 143 p.
2. Hawaii State Department of Education, Honolulu. Office of Planning and Budget. *A Plan to Improve School and Library Environments*. March, 1976. 309p.
   This document is available from ERIC on microform (only). Price $1. Among its chapters is one entitled "Campus Safety—Preventing Injuries on the School Campus." Obviously, this document does not deal with snow-related injuries, but it does cover all sorts of accidents and prescribes procedures for staff to follow.

Case 3
Every Friday Afternoon, Like Clockwork

Frustration didn't come near to describing what Irwin Rossiter was feeling this afternoon. Rage was more like it. Again, today, the library had received a telephoned bomb threat, forcing him to activate the alarm and begin evacuation of the building. Again, today, Irwin and Peter had explained to patrons reluctant to leave the warmth of the building and stand around in the snow why they must do so, and again, today, the bomb threat had turned out to be bogus, obviously a malicious prank played on the library by someone unknown.

As he stood with dozens of people of all ages, milling about in the slush on the sidewalk across from the main entrance to the library building, Irwin cast suspicious eyes on everyone who had left in answer to the strident alarm bell. Most of the people looked as cold and miserable as he was, huddled against the fierce north wind in the lowering dusk of a February day, stamping their feet to keep them from freezing in the wet, crystalline mush that lay all about them.

A small knot of teenage boys stood apart from the rest, sharing cigarettes and private jokes. Irwin decided that they were collectively to be considered suspect #1. Searching his memory, he tried to recall whether they had been among those in the library the previous Friday, and the one before that. Clearly, there was a pattern to these annoying bomb threats, even if no obvious motive could be discerned. Irwin sighed, reflecting that the weather had been better on the previous two Fridays than it was today, but philosophically remembering that one day soon it would be springtime.

From previous experience, Irwin knew that the bomb squad and the fire truck were on their way. Even though he was privately sure that there was no bomb, and that everyone could safely go back inside right away, he knew that it was a matter of both prudence and procedure for the police bomb squad and the fire truck to race to the scene of the threat and for all emergency evacuation procedures to be implemented every time someone telephoned in a threat.

"Rotten punks!" Irwin mumbled as he surveyed the young boys laughing and jittering around in the snow near him. "Bet they're behind this, even if they have to stand out here and turn into popsicles like the rest of us." For a while, he contemplated the five or six young boys standing in a circle and having a fine time, as their collective exhalations gathered and rose in the frosty air. Some of them looked familiar, but as to whether they came in every Friday, and what it would prove if they did, Irwin couldn't say. All he knew was that he'd get them somehow. Nobody could just drop a coin into a public phone and tell the switchboard operator that there was a bomb set to go off in the building and get away with it week after week after week. Such people didn't belong in a library. They belonged either behind bars or in a zoo. Reform school, anyway. But first, just to get his hands on them for a few moments for a private and enduring lesson on citizenship!

Irwin's private thoughts were broken into by the scream of sirens, and he turned to watch a police van glide to a halt in front of him, accompanied by a long, red hook-and-ladder fire truck, and the fire chief's red Chevrolet. As the police bomb squad, accompanied by trained dogs and some sort of robot were deployed, the fire chief sauntered over to Irwin, shaking his head beneath his helmet. "Hey, Irwin," he called, grinning ruefully at his old poker buddy, shifting from foot to foot in the snow. "Lookin' mighty cold."

"Lo, Chief," responded Irwin.

"Y'know, this is getting monotonous. How many Fridays now, Irwin? Four? Five? Every Friday afternoon like clockwork, another damned phony bomb threat."

"Awwww!" rumbled Irwin, his expression showing exaggerated compassion. "Interrupt your poker game down at the station? I hope you had aces full when the alarm went off."

The chief turned serious. "Anything suspicious this time? Anything to suggest that there might be a bomb?"

"Naw," said Irwin. "I'm positive it's the usual. Kid's voice, bomb threat. You know how it goes by now."

"Yeah, I do. But we have to act on each one as though it's three sticks of dynamite and five pounds of plastique, dammit! So . . . everybody out of there?" His gesture took in the library building which glowed invitingly and warmly across the street.

"I think so, chief. If not, I figure it's the ones who're doing this and I hope they go up with the building."

"Irwin, you know and I know that there's no bomb in there, but we gotta go through this, so stand back and let us work. Any suspects?"

"You might try that bunch over there," said Irwin, indicating the small knot of boys who had fallen silent at the arrival of the police and firemen. "I can't prove it, but I'll bet you ten to one that they know something about these things."

Irwin and the chief were joined by Mike Ross, the library's assistant director. "Chief," he said, "this can't go on. Aside from the danger in the unlikely event that one time there *will* be a bomb in the library, our staff is losing a lot of time standing around out here for an hour each week. Any ideas on what we can do?"

"Yeah, some ideas. Few solutions, though. And most of 'em are going to cost you some money. Wanna hear 'em?"

"Yes, sure. Anything to get my mind off my frozen feet," said Mike as he turned his back to the biting wind.

"All right. First, we want to stop these calls. Figure that the calls are being made from inside the library, right? So on Friday afternoons, we try discreet surveillance on all the pay phones in the place. How many you got, four? Okay, have somebody watch them. Then, try to tape all incoming messages, or set up some kind of system so that the switchboard people can activate the recorder when it's that sort of call. Then there are television cameras, fingerprints, and, let's see. . . ."

"What good are fingerprints?" asked Mike. "Lots of people use the pay phones every day, and anyone we nail can say he was just calling his mother or somebody. Then there are gloves."

"Yeah. I know. Chances of catching this guy are not too great. And besides, the call could come in from outside, couldn't it?"

"I suppose," said Irwin, "but whoever's doing this is going to want to be there to watch the fun."

"Anyway, you should work on your evacuation and emergency procedures. Some of these folks are gonna take some persuading to leave your nice warm library on a day like this."

"You got that right," said Irwin. "I practically had to heave two sweet old ladies out into the snow this time. I felt like a villain, and I knew all along that there was no bomb. Just some kids who're bored and mean, tryin' to put some excitement into a Friday afternoon."

"I agree with you," said the chief, as he watched the policemen and firemen begin to return to their vehicles and put away their equipment. One of the firemen came over to the chief and gave an eloquent shrug of his shoulders, saying "Nada!" "But we have to act on every call, and so, boyo, do you. See you tomorrow night for our game, Irwin. Hang in there, Mr. Rossiter. And try to find whoever the hell is doing these nasty pranks and put 'em out of business best way you can, willya? I like slow, lazy days at the station house, especially when it's snowing."

He got back into his car and slowly drove away, followed by the lumbering trucks, and Irwin bellowed in his famous deep voice that everyone could once again go back into the library. As he passed Irwin, one of the young men, a pimply youth of perhaps 16 years of age, said, just loud enough for him to hear, "Don't you just love Fridays?" Irwin had to exercise all of his self-control to keep from grabbing the boy by his woolen scarf and flinging him into the street.

Questions for Discussion

1. How can a library best counteract phony bomb threats, fire alarms, and other malicious pranks played against the library?
2. Is there any justification for refusing to evacuate a public building because of a belief that a threat to public safety is bogus?
3. Which of the chief's alternatives seems most viable for the library, given the budget situation and the fact that, to date, no bombs have been discovered?
4. How would you go about catching the perpetrators in the act, and what would you do with them, if you did?

Resources

1. O'Neill, James W. "From the Editor's Desk: Staff and Patron Safety—8 Most Common Problems." *Library Security Newsletter* 1 (September–October 1975): 3–5.
   O'Neill offers practical solutions to problems similar to bomb threats, such as silent alarms, surveillance cameras, closed-circuit recorders, etc.
2. Remsberg, Charles. "Crackdown on Bomb-scare Pranksters." *Popular Mechanics* 116 (October 1961): 146.
   An oldie but a goodie, this article details ways in which those who phone in phony bomb threats have been caught.
3. Timko, Lola C. "Teaching Communication with Problem Patrons in Emergency Situations." *Journal of Education for Librarianship* 18 (Winter 1978): 244–46.
   Explores alternatives for conducting an orderly evacuation of a library, with emphasis on methods for treating those who do not understand or will not comply.

Case 4
The Torch

It all started over fines. A routine check of the circulation records of the River Bend Public Library revealed that a man named Jerome Carnes was overdue on nine books to the tune of forty-five days apiece. The library was authorized to assess borrowers who kept books out past their allotted time period the sum of five cents a day (including Sundays) up to the total cost of the book. The purpose of such fines was dual: it was designed to provide an incentive to procrastinating borrowers or slow readers to bring things back on time, and it provided a small sum of money each year which could be used for the purchase of replacement titles. Therefore, while delinquency was never encouraged, it did serve a useful function.

Normally, a courteous reminder in the form of a post card was sufficient to stir the overdue borrower into bringing back the books in question and paying the extremely nominal fine. When the postal reminder didn't do the trick, the policy and procedure manual for the circulation department provided a sequence of increasingly severe measures for dealing with the problem. First, the fines continued to accrue at the nickel-a-day rate. Second, the library was empowered to suspend the delinquent borrower's borrowing privileges until the record was cleared. Finally, the library had researched the problem and found that there were no legal impediments to suing a borrower in court, although that solution had never been implemented for reasons ranging from cost to the possible public relations problem it might cause. If all else failed, of course, there was always the ultimate weapon in the library's arsenal of resources: Irwin Rossiter.

Irwin Rossiter was a huge man who wore two hats in the library. He was legally the custodian, entrusted with maintenance of the building and grounds, ably abetted by the janitor, Peter Bourdelle. He also, and unofficially, had awarded himself the title of "chief of security," due to his duties as the library's on-site guard. A beefy ex-marine in his early sixties, Irwin was devoted to the library and to the enforcement of order therein, and had on many occasions staved off crisis situations by the sheer forcefulness of his personality. During the library's operating hours, he was normally to be seen patrolling the reading rooms, hallways and stack areas, smiling generously at staff members and familiar faces and scowling discouragement at anyone young or old who threatened the sanctity, safety, or order of those who had come to the library to use its resources or enjoy its restful atmosphere.

Jerome Carnes had received the post card informing him that nine titles were forty-five days overdue each, resulting in a fine totalling $20.25 (and counting), payable when the books were returned. He appeared at the circulation desk one afternoon, demanding to know who was in charge, and harangued Frederica Bondanella, the head of the department, for twenty minutes on the subject of his having returned all the books in question. Claiming that he owed nothing whatsoever, and stating flatly that he didn't want to hear any more about the overdue books from the library, he strode out of the building furiously, disappearing into the gloomy afternoon rain.

Two weeks later, when the circulation control computer program reported, as part of its statistical printout, the fact that Mr. Carnes was now sixty days overdue on nine titles (now the sum involved was $27.00), Freddie reported the matter to Mike Ross, the assistant director, for further action. Mike, after thinking about the problem for a while and hearing Freddie's report of her interview with the irate Carnes, decided that this might be a good time to experiment with Irwin as a retrieval system for the library.

So it was that on a bright autumn Saturday morning, Irwin Rossiter, dressed in his civilian clothes, walked up the steps of a small apartment building on the south side of town, found the bell marked J. Carnes, and pressed it forcefully and at length. When a metallic voice issued from a speaker recessed in the faceplate of the building's directory asking, "Who's there?," Irwin rasped out his name and mission in a voice calculated to suggest to the other party that he would brook no nonsense.

The next minute and a half were filled with oppressive silence, as the man seemed to be debating whether or not to let his caller enter past the downstairs door. Finally, a buzzing noise told Irwin that he was cleared for entry, and he walked slowly up the three flights of stairs to apartment 3-G where Carnes, a small, nervous looking man of perhaps forty, with thinning hair and a disreputable bathrobe on his back, awaited him.

Irwin, fighting to catch his breath from the difficult climb, assumed his best no-nonsense expression and quickly told the man that he owed the library just over $27.00, and that he was there to see if he couldn't expedite the return of the books and the payment of the fine at the same time. The man seemed indisposed to let Irwin enter his apartment, preferring to talk in the hallway, and Irwin, knowing there were limits on just how far he could go in seeking to retrieve the library's property, wisely elected to remain on the landing and chat.

"You're seriously overdue on nine books, fella!" he growled, looming menacingly over the much shorter man.

"Hell I am! Always return 'em when I'm done. Ask anybody. Don't have any of the library's books. Told the blond lady that. Anything I borrow, I bring back. No need to send some big goon round to wring 'em outta me when I don't have 'em."

Irwin ignored the slur and proceeded with his agenda for trying to bring the man to compliance with the library's rules. "Well, see, the computer says that these nine titles," he waved a double sheet of greenbar fanfold computer paper in the man's face, "are over sixty days late apiece, and I was sent here to help you look for them and, of course, to collect the fine. Computers don't lie, buddy, so why don't you just go and look for the books and write out a check? I'll wait right here."

"Just get out of here, man. This conversation is over, see? I don't have no library books in my place, and I am not about to write you no check for twenty-seven dollars for books I don't have, so get out of here, or I'm gonna call the cops!"

By now, Irwin had recovered his normal breathing, but the smaller man seemed to be hyperventilating; his breathing was labored, his eyes rolled comically, and he had broken out in a sweat. For a moment, he looked as though he might try to push Irwin down the stairs, but perhaps he quickly thought better of it when he saw the combative glint in the older man's eyes. "Computers make mistakes! This is one of them. I don't have the books! I ain't payin' the money! Just go!!" Jerome Carnes' voice had risen to such a loud timbre that two neighbors opened their doors and peeped fearfully out, while Irwin could hear the click of a security lock on a third.

Turning to descend the stairs, Irwin fired one parting shot. "It just gets worse and worse, my man!" he shouted, angrily. "A nickel a day times nine is forty-five cents a day, and that's day after day after day. Then there's your borrower's card. Suspended as of today, how d'ya like that? And wait until you get that subpoena commanding you to appear in court, with conviction meaning three, maybe even four months in the slammer. Then we'll see who's made mistakes!" Irwin was bluffing, and he knew it, but he figured that the other man couldn't be sure.

The man's anger had turned to hysteria. "Just leave me alone! Alone, you hear? Go away and don't bother me no more or you and that big, beautiful building you work in are gonna pay!"

Irwin, halfway down from the top stair, suddenly froze in midstep. "What's that, a threat? What do you mean, 'me and the building?' "

The man looked startled. "Just never mind," he said, in a softer tone, swallowing several times. "But I mean what I said. Keep off me or you'll all be sorry, I swear it!"

As he walked away from the building a few moments later, fuming in impotent rage, Irwin could still hear the shouts and threats Carnes, clearly a man beside himself with anger, was shouting.

The next Monday afternoon at the library, as Irwin was walking his customary rounds of the building, he noticed that a small man with thick glasses and dramatically styled blond hair was regarding him thoughtfully from one of the reading tables in the Reference department. When Irwin looked intently back, however, the man looked studiously down at the book he had before him. Several times in the following week, Irwin, who had developed a sixth sense for things that didn't seem quite right in the building, felt hostile eyes on him as he strolled along in one department or another, but he didn't see the blond man, or anyone else who looked out of the ordinary, again.

It was almost a week later that Irwin, slowly walking the second floor corridor heard muffled shouts and screams coming from the Reference department. Quickening his step, he was about to enter the department when he collided unexpectedly with someone running out the door. Before he could speak, or even think about it, the person had bounced off him and had run headlong down the stairs to the main floor. Irwin looked after the fleeing figure, but all he could see was a flash of yellow hair and a green windbreaker jacket. Then the person who had run into him was gone.

Turning back to the Reference department, Irwin entered to see that a small pile of books on the floor had been set ablaze, and Randy Gardner, one of the reference librarians, was wrestling with a wall-mounted fire extinguisher, trying to get it free of its mounting, while several staff members and perhaps twenty patrons stood around ineffectually watching. Soon the fire had been extinguished, and Irwin gained the chance to ask questions.

Questions for Discussion

1. In what ways can a public library maximize its chances of recovering books and other materials which have been charged out by patrons?
2. What is your opinion of Mike Ross's decision to send Irwin around to collect overdue books and fines? When overdue notices are ignored or disputed, is the employment of bullying "collectors" justified in the interest of preserving the collection?
3. How would you evaluate Irwin's behavior with regard to Carnes?
4. What procedures would you write into your library's policy and procedure manual for dealing with the surveillance of suspicious persons in the building?

5. In the absence of police, what can library security officers do to deter members of the public bent on vandalism, arson, drug dealing, or other criminal activities?

Resources

1. Brashear, J. Kirk; James J. Maloney; and Thorton-Jaringe, Judellen. "Problem Patrons: The Other Kind of Library Security." *Illinois Libraries* 63 (April 1981): 343–51.
   Among the categories listed of disturbed persons who frequent libraries are arsonists.
2. "Is Your Library Safe from Fire?" *American School and University* 28 (April 1980): 60–63.
   Some preventive steps that a library might take to reduce fire risk are included.
3. Kennedy, John. "Library Arson." *Library Security Newsletter* (September 1976): 1–2.
   Arson is a very real possibility in libraries, and this article deals with ways to prevent, if possible, and combat, if necessary, suspicious fires.
4. Myers, Dorothy. "A Survivor's Tale of Service Under Siege." *American Libraries* 9 (October 1978): 525–28.
   This branch librarian's tale of woe includes the fact that "in 1972, arsonists burned down one-third of the building."

Case 5
How're You Fixed for a
Quarter?

Sergeant Frank Bronsky of the River Bend Police Force looked exactly like Pat Broughton had expected him to look after hearing his voice on the telephone. He sat in one of the guest chairs in her office at the library, slush dripping off of his enormous rubber boots, idly turning a glass paperweight over and over in his huge hands. "And how many people have reported being robbed in such a manner?" he asked Pat, his flat, gray eyes starting intently at her.

"Six that I know of," responded the library director, wondering what Bronsky might do to any pint-sized criminals he caught. "There might be others, I don't know. Six children have reported such assaults to me."

The police detective put down the paperweight and drew from his jacket pocket a small red notebook and a pen. "Is there any kind of pattern to the attacks?" he asked, frowning in concentration. "Any common thread which might help us to find and apprehend the perpetrators?" Pat smiled at the word, wondering why policemen always sounded like bad television shows, or was it the other way round?

"Well, yes. One common thread would be that all of those who were assaulted report that their assailants were their size or smaller, something around or under five feet tall."

"That narrows our search," muttered Bronsky dryly. "Kids. We're looking for a band of kids who prey on other kids, is that what you're telling me, ma'am?"

"I guess so. It would appear that that's the case. Another thing these assaults have in common is that they always occur just outside the library building between 6:00 and 6:15 p.m. on Fridays and Saturdays. It seems that whoever is doing this stands out there, behind the bushes maybe, and waits for unescorted children to come by just after we close. Probably wouldn't happen if it weren't wintertime and dark, but it is, so it does."

"Anybody been hurt in this little crime wave of yours?" asked the sergeant.

"Two boys received some minor bruises. A girl got her coat torn at the sleeve when she resisted and wouldn't surrender her purse. That's about it, but who knows what could happen next time?"

"That's right. That's why we got to stop them now. Before anyone gets really hurt. Now tell me, about how much money did they get in these robberies?"

"That's the sad part. Pathetic, really. One boy claims he was carrying six dollars in his wallet. The others had anywhere from about fifteen cents to a couple of bus tokens. You'd think that these kids would hit on adults, who might have significant amounts of cash, credit cards, and the like."

"Yeah, but adults might be armed, or fight back. When they go after kids their ages or younger, they have a reasonable chance of getting away with it, even if 'it' isn't all that much."

Pat looked thoughtfully out of the window for a moment, then said, "Why do their parents let them go alone like that? Don't they take any notice of the fact that it's dark and cold these days when the library closes?"

"Some do and some don't," said the sergeant. "But any kid walking alone around here after dark is a sitting target."

The sergeant stood up and stretched languorously. He reached reflexively for a cigarette, spied the "Thank you for not smoking" sign placed prominently on Pat's desk, frowned, appeared to reconsider, and sighing, put it back in its pack. Pat smiled and nodded, and he shrugged.

"So, from what you know, Mrs. Broughton, can you give me an idea of how these attacks occur?"

"We close at 6 on Fridays and Saturdays, and when small, unaccompanied children are making their way homeward or to the bus stop across the park, somebody, or several somebodies, jumps out of the bushes alongside the walkways. They wear red or gray ski masks, they appear to be between 10 and 12 years old, with child's voices, and they either demand money or just take it. Anyone who resists or hesitates too long is likely to get pummeled or knocked down to the ground, but the . . . perpetrators . . . don't seem to use violence for the fun of it."

"Any weapons used, that you know about?"

"No. They strike suddenly, they say very little, and they run away. No fingerprints. No weapons. No traces, except maybe footprints in the snow, but there are so many."

"Any way to tell the racial or ethnic grouping of the muggers?"

"How? They wear ski masks and their victims are so frightened that they really don't remember much about what happened afterwards."

"Yeah. I got it," said Bronsky, beginning to lean out of the door of Pat's office, obviously anxious to get on his way. Then, as an afterthought, he mused in a reminiscent tone, "Funny thing. The wife and I came down here from Chicago almost thirty years ago when I was a young street cop. Figured River Bend would be a much safer place to live and work and raise a family. Now, I don't know. I just don't know.''

A smile of commiseration and sympathy creased Pat's face. ''So please keep in touch. My secretary will give you the names and addresses of the six children we've talked to about these incidents. Do you think you can do anything with their descriptions?''

''Hope so, ma'am. In the meantime, try to get kids leaving the building to walk in groups or have their parents come with them or pick them up. Just for my own information: what would you think if the city came and took down those tall bushes that run along the walks leading up to the library?''

''It might come to that, but I'd rather it didn't happen. They are so pretty for three seasons of the year, and the whole block would look naked without them,'' Pat lamented.

''It comes down to whether you want safe walks or pretty ones, sometimes,'' said Bronsky, pragmatically.

''I suppose,'' said Pat with a weary nod of agreement. ''Sergeant,'' she called after him just as he was leaving her office, ''what will happen to any young people you catch committing these robberies?''

''You're not one of those bleeding heart liberals, are you?'' asked Bronsky with a sardonic grin. ''The bottom line is that we put them out of business. People, especially children, have the right to walk around town without getting hit or robbed or raped or even murdered. The job of the police is to stop them. Which reminds me: the library might be called upon to press charges, if we arrest some of these kids. Without your testimony, they could be out on the streets doing it again the same day. Remember that.''

''I will,'' said Pat Broughton, unhappily.

''Meantime, why don't you pressure your city council friends for more lights in the park, and maybe more police, while you're at it?''

''Will do.'' Pat watched the officer as he stopped at her secretary's desk to consult a typed list of names and addresses. ''I don't want anybody hurt. I just want the library *and* the park to be safe for everybody.''

''Mrs. Broughton,'' said Bronsky, finally lighting a cigarette, ''that's all any of us wants. The trick is how to get it.''

Questions for Discussion

1. To what extent is a public library legally or morally responsible for the welfare and safety of its users after they have left the building?

2. How can a library maximize user safety, especially with regard to young patrons, without hiring additional security personnel or resorting to the installation of new lighting, surveillance cameras, and the like?
3. For the present, what measures would you, as Pat, take to protect unescorted children until the police can put a stop to the assaults on them?
4. Should those responsible be apprehended? How far would you go, as library director, to assist in their prosecution? What are some of the pros and cons of the library administrator's decision to press charges?

Resources

1. Griffith, Jack W. "Of Vagrants and Vandals and Library Things." *Wilson Library Bulletin* 52 (June 1978): 769+.
   Warns that libraries often make themselves too attractive to the wrong people, and tells what can be done about it.
2. O'Neill, James W. "From the Editor's Desk: Staff and Patron Safety—8 Most Common Problems." *Library Security Newsletter* 1 (September/October 1975): 3–5.
   Among the eight most frequently cited problems for public libraries are: (#2) "youths threatening malicious mischief," (#4) "dangerous neighborhood between library and parking lot," (#7) "threat of personal injury by smart aleck youths," and (#8) "muggings."
3. Starr, Carol. "Youthomania: The Care and Treatment in the Public Library." *Wisconsin Library Bulletin* 68 (January–February 1972): 37–38.
   Explains how to make the library attractive to young people without sacrificing fun or discipline.

Case 6
A Harmless Crush

For a moment, she wasn't certain that she felt anything at all, but when she turned her head to look, Cynthia Brookings was all too aware that the man was stroking her hair. He was just standing there by her desk in the Science and Technology department, caressing the tips of her long, brown hair, not even smiling, but peering intently down at his well-manicured fingers as he ran them gently through her hair.

A scream began to form in Cynthia's throat. Quickly, she suppressed the urge, whipping her head away from the man's grasp and moving across the room. From the comparative safety of the other side of the circulation counter, she watched as the man shrugged and returned to the pile of magazines he had been pretending to read.

It was the same man who had been staring at her for weeks. She had been continually aware of him, but since he had done nothing of a threatening or suggestive nature, she had chosen to ignore his staring, pretending that he wasn't there. She had pondered the problem, of course, thinking up and then rejecting the several potential remedies that came to her. She could confront him, telling him to get the hell away from her, but that might create a scene and, if he were truly a disturbed man, it might also set him off somehow—with unwelcome consequences. She also thought of turning the matter over to Irwin Rossiter, the large and gruff custodian, who also served the library as security guard some evenings and who took an avuncular and protective attitude towards the young women who worked in the library. But Cynthia was afraid that Irwin might go overboard with the man, possibly threatening him or ordering him out of the library for good. Nobody wanted that. Irwin was kind, benevolent, and fierce in defense of his friends, but he would never win any prizes for tact or diplomacy, and Cynthia hadn't considered the matter serious enough for Irwin, prior to today. Today, however, the man had quietly approached Cynthia, while she was bent over, absorbed in her work on the vertical file reorganization and had reached out and begun stroking her hair.

Cynthia was always modest in dress and demeanor, partly by nature and partly as a means of trying to discourage unwanted attention from men.

Blessed with sunny good looks, she was anything but ostentatious, wearing muted colors and more tailored than flamboyant fashions. She strove to appear cool and professional always and had, heretofore, never been the victim of any of the strange types who frequent library reading rooms. Yet this man had been staring at her for weeks. It seemed as though every time she looked up he was watching. The man was nondescript in appearance, with, Cynthia thought to herself, no-color hair and eyes. Neither tall nor short, he was seemingly devoid of remarkable features other than his unwillingness to smile. He just stared and had been more or less easy to ignore, but this time he had gone too far.

Cynthia remembered having confronted him before. Several weeks ago, she recalled, she had had a particularly bad day. First, it had rained incessantly, and she had become drenched on the way to work, despite the folding umbrella she had held for protection. Then, she had had a headache from the sinus congestion rainy days always gave her. Finally, at lunch, she had spilled boiling hot coffee on herself. She, therefore, when she returned to work, was in no mood to be stared at by this creepy-looking man, and when he began his usual game of stare and return to reading when she caught him at it, she just could not take it any more. She had stridden directly to the science books stacks just behind the man's chair. He had pretended to be oblivious to her movement, of course. Then, without warning, she had darted forward to him and hissed loudly in his ear, "Stop it, you sickie!"

Unfortunately, as Cynthia remembered with chagrin, the man had managed to ignore her remarks after an initial flinch, but her voice had been louder than she had intended it to be, and she had caused everyone else in the room to resemble the actors in one of those investment broker commercials where everyone stops whatever he or she is doing and cocks an ear. Blushing at her remembered embarrassment, Cynthia told herself that no such incident would serve any practical purpose today.

Calming herself by the force of her will, she looked casually around the room. The man was studiously reading a magazine, to all outward appearances, and the twenty or so patrons also in the room were occupied as usual with whatever they were doing. She made the following observations: First, staring was one thing, but touching was quite another. Cynthia remembered meeting an old friend at a party a month before. The man was a psychologist, and Cynthia discovered that he didn't mind talking shop during a recreational evening. When Cynthia had described the man's staring and general behavior to her friend, the psychologist offered the opinion that it was probably only "a harmless crush" and should be ignored, as much as possible. She wondered now what he would say if he knew that the man had graduated from looking to touching and pondered calling the psychologist that evening to talk about it. Second, it seemed no longer safe to assume that the man was harmless, in any event, and it was high time that someone deal with him immediately before he hurt Cynthia or some other unfortunate to whom his mind formed an attraction. Third, this entire matter ought to be reported to someone, whether it be Irwin or Pat Broughton, the director, or the police, or somebody else. The man needed help, and so did the library. Checking to see what the man was up to now, she was somewhat surprised to note that he had arisen and left the room while she was reviewing her array of action steps. Picking up her telephone, she dialed the custodian's line to summon Irwin to Science and Technology. He may be a bit crude and rough, she decided, but he's just the man who'd know what to do about this problem.

Questions for Discussion

1. Some libraries have procedure manuals that cover courses of action in cases of threatening or violent behavior. Does this case fall into a category that would be covered in a typical manual?
2. As Cynthia, how would you handle this problem patron, given that you cannot be sure of his motivations or future behavior?
3. What is the role of "security" in such situations? When does a library problem become a police matter?
4. Where is the dividing line between a "harmless crush" and a case of sexual or psychopathic behavior?
5. As director of the library, how would you instruct your staff to behave when confronted with unwanted (and possibly dangerous) attentions from members of the public?

Resources

1. Easton, Carol. "Sex and Violence in the Library: Scream a Little Louder Please." *American Libraries* 8 (9) (October 1977): 484–89.
   Examines especially the problems that women library employees and female patrons have faced.
2. "New Security Problem: Staff Safety." *Library Journal* 100 (March 1, 1975): 434.
   This article explains the need for library staff to worry about themselves as well as their patrons. In addition to the violent confrontations of assault (see resources for Case 7), there is the possibility of sexual advances, ranging from staring to attempted rape.

3. Samet, Norman T. "Why Does That Man Stare at Me?" *Library Journal* 94 (January 15, 1969): 156–57.
A former librarian turned psychologist offers a sympathetic view of schizophrenia, urging tolerance in staff dealings with them. Gentle but bizarre behavior, he says, needs understanding more than outright rejection. This would probably extend to staring, but not to physical contact.

Case 7
If You See Me Comin',
Better Step Aside!

The man stood well over six feet tall, and looked even taller, due to the pair of black leather books he wore on his immense feet. He was totally bald, and his glistening head was adorned only with a red-and-blue bandanna which he wore just above his eyebrows. His work clothes seemed dusty, as though he worked outside, and perhaps the most intimidating feature of his appearance was the perpetual scowl on his face.

Two or three times a week, he would stride through the glass doors of the Performing Arts department of the River Bend Public Library, his boot heels clicking across the linoleum of the foyer and falling silent as he entered the room's carpeted interior. Surveying his surroundings, the man would usually select a victim and walk over to him slowly. The victim would normally be a man, but several times, it had been a teenage boy. In any case, the victim would be either brushed or bumped by the passing man, sometimes softly and sometimes hard, and then the man would bellow out something like: "Watch it, buddy!"

The startled patron, normally one just standing by the periodicals shelves, would glance up at the towering bully and mutter a brief apology.

"Just watch it, I said!" he would snarl, watching the other man carefully for signs of combative response. If the victim offered the slightest argument, the tall man would begin shoving him, pushing him backwards with massive hands, hoping for a fight. If, however, the combination of physical assault and taunting words could not provoke anger or violence, the man would saunter out in search of braver prey. After a few weeks, Virginia Watanabe, a librarian in the department, had become well-aware of the man and his methods. She had been unsuccessful in trying to find out who he was, because none of the circulation desk personnel had ever seen him check out any materials, and asking him any direct or personal questions seemed unwise.

Virginia had, of course, notified security of the man and his behavior, and Irwin Rossiter, the custodian and guard, had followed him around for a while, but the man never seemed to pick on anybody while Irwin was in the room and was clever enough to wait and seize his moments when no one in authority was around. After comparing notes with Kevin McConnell, a page who worked afternoons and Saturdays in the department during the season when football was not played, Virginia had found that the man had accosted at least eight other men, had threatened most of them, and had engaged in a brief shoving match with one of them, but that no injuries or actual violence had resulted. For his own private reasons, the man was bent on getting into fights and looked as though he wanted action at any cost.

At Virginia's urging, Irwin had approached the man, telling him that the library was a place for study and relaxation and that no fighting or even yelling was permitted. The man had chosen not to respond except for a contemptuous roll of his massive shoulders and had brushed past Irwin slowly. When Irwin reported the exchange to Virginia in Pat Broughton's office, he described the man as ''an accident looking for a place to happen'' and ''250 pounds of trouble on the hoof,'' which seemed to be an entirely accurate description of the man's bearing and behavior. Still, according to the library's policies, the man, like everybody else, was welcome to use the library as long as he was not doing anything inappropriate or dangerous. The word ''dangerous'' of course, might have applied to him, but so far no one had risen to his challenges, and therefore no one had been placed in actual danger.

Then one evening in January, when few people were in the department and Virginia was looking forward to getting home to her dinner and a warm night under several quilts, the glass doors opened and the big man walked in. His customary sneer seemed even more pronounced that evening, possibly because his face was bright red from the cold wind, and his shaven head was snugly surmounted by a navy knit watch cap which came down almost to his dark and angry eyes. He carried his pea jacket in one hand as he paused to survey the occupants of the Performing Arts department on this particular Wednesday evening. Few people were seated at the work tables. Since it was between semesters, few high school students had ventured out into the intense cold of winter to do any library research. Over by the record turntables, an old woman, a regular on most evenings, was listening intently through a set of earphones to ''French, Self-Taught,'' as she closed her eyes and softly repeated the words and phrases she heard on the recordings. A middle-aged man was standing alone, flipping through the library's collection of framed art prints which could be borrowed for four-week periods, and three girls of perhaps twelve years of age were quietly discussing the career of a noted ballerina whom they hoped to emulate.

The man stood for a short time indecisively by the door, then nodded his head quickly, heading over to the man in the trenchcoat who continued to search through the art prints, oblivious to the danger. By prearranged signal, Virginia alerted Kevin to the presence of the man, and both staff members watched, in horror and fascination, as the man in the blue knit cap made his approach. Finally, he was in place, and he abruptly walked past the patron who stood with a large print of a Renoir painting in his hands. As he passed, he furiously whipped his pea jacket into the man's face, startling him to the extent that he cried out loudly.

With practiced ease, the huge man glared down at the much smaller person and snarled, "Why don't you watch where you're going?"

For a few seconds, the man didn't respond, seemingly shocked at the suddenness with which he had been hit in the face. Then, recovering, he said sharply, "Where *I'm* going? What about you?"

This was exactly what the large man had been waiting for, and he licked his lips in anticipation of a fight. "Friend," he said, loudly enough to be heard throughout the room, "You're going to be real, real sorry you said that!" Throwing his coat and hat on a nearby chair, he assumed the crouch of a professional wrestler, hands extended and feet well apart.

"Now, wait a minute," began the smaller man, "All I said was. . . ."

It was at this point that Kevin McConnell finally sprang into action. "Excuse me, gentlemen," he said, smiling winningly as he walked toward the two men, "Let's just cool off here and forget this whole thing."

"Back off, sonny boy," roared the big man, "or I'll get to you next, after I clean this turkey's clock for him!"

Positioning himself between the two patrons, Kevin stalled for time, talking steadily and warily watching the hands of the menacing giant with the practiced eye of a linebacker. Out of the corner of his eye, he could see Virginia on the telephone, and he hoped that the police would be there quickly.

"Sir, if you will just put on your hat and coat and leave the department, everybody will be better off," he said quietly.

"What the hell for? This little creep stuck his foot out and tried to trip me as I was just walking by. He needs to be taught some better manners, that's all," said the big man, smiling for the first time that Kevin or Virginia could remember.

"I was just standing there. Minding my own business. Then this big bozo swung his coat into my face for no reason at all!"

"I believe you, sir," Kevin said softly to the outraged older man, his eyes never leaving the assailant in case he reacted violently to being called a name.

"Kid," the belligerent man growled, "You have ten seconds to get out of the way, and then I'm going through you to get to him!"

Suddenly, Kevin was convinced that the man meant what he said. Desperately, he tried quoting the rules. "Fighting in the library is against our policy. Couldn't you take it outside to settle it?"

"Suits me," said the angry giant, grabbing the smaller man roughly by the shoulder of his coat and propelling him rapidly toward the doors of the department.

Imploringly, the small man turned in the grasp of his assailant to shout to Kevin, "Don't just stand there! Help me! This guy's going to kill me."

"Damn right!" Kevin heard the large man say as he succeeded in getting his victim out of the department and into the 2nd floor foyer.

As he watched them stumble toward the stairway, Kevin stood helplessly watching for a moment, then whipped around and ran back to the desk. "Virginia!" he screamed, "where the hell are those cops?"

"They said right away, Kevin!"

"Well, if somebody doesn't do something fast, there's going to be somebody hurt." Bolting for the doorway, he prepared to do something about the malicious and dangerous man, but without any time to reflect on it, he didn't have the first idea as to what he would do when he reached him.

Questions for Discussion

1. What can a library do to deter chronic troublemakers from finding their victims in the building?
2. If you become aware that a man like the one in this case is using the library to choose those he hopes to goad into combat, how would you handle him?
3. As Kevin, what would you now do to prevent harm to the innocent patron until the police arrive at the scene?
4. What factors would influence your decision as to when the library staff can handle a problem and when law enforcement officers are needed?

Resources

The following representative sample of news notes from the library literature constitutes proof, if proof is needed, that there is plenty of reason to believe that library work can be extremely hazardous to the health of staff members, not to mention the public.

1. "Knife-Wielding Youth Slays Public Library Staff Member." *American Libraries* 14 (April 1983): 174.
2. "Librarian Grapples with Killer as 7 Are Slain in Library." *American Libraries* (July 1976): 428.
3. "Librarian Stabbed at Desk." *American Libraries* 6 (April 1975): 213–14.
4. "U of Fla. Library Director Shot by Former Employee." *American Libraries* 14 (June 1983): 334.

Case 8
Can't You Take a Joke?

Summers get long, hot, and sticky in River Bend, and temperatures sometimes rise to 90 degrees and beyond for several days in a row. The wind seems to die down, and the relentless sun beats down on the midwestern city with a vengeance. The park, which runs along the riverbank for several miles, turns from a pleasant haven of shaded trees and fresh breezes into a hot, still, and stifling place where the humidity is worse than anywhere else.

The park's usual denizens, seeking relief from the persistent, sticky dampness, are driven away to seek relief elsewhere. Those with the money may take in a daytime movie downtown. Shopping malls are comfortable on hot days, but none of them are located within convenient walking distance from the park. A few go in for culture and frequent nearby museums and galleries. Many of the park's regulars, however, find themselves short of funds and disinclined to walk great distances. For them, the closest place to keep cool without being expected to state one's business or to buy something is the public library. The River Bend Public Library staff understands this and is reasonably receptive to the basic premise that all are free to enter, and all, if they observe certain rules of conduct, may stay as long as the building is open, doing whatever they choose, if they do it quietly.

The History and Travel department of the library seems to attract a coterie of vagrants on hot summer days. The travel books and periodicals, with lovely photography and evocative descriptions, are inviting. Some come only to sleep in the five or six padded armchairs scattered around the department. Sleeping is, of course, forbidden by the library's policy manual, but most of the staff, and even members of the small security force, are willing to look the other way when someone is spied slumped over , gently snoring, in one of the chairs. Noisy snoring is another matter, but an afternoon nap, while not exactly condoned, is at least tolerated in the spirit of humanitarian *laissez-faire*.

On such a sultry afternoon in River Bend, the usual crowd of park residents was taking its ease in the sedate precincts of the History and Travel department. Their true names were seldom known to the staff members, but after some time, Burt Stone and Emilia Parsons, librarians in the department, came to know quite a few of them by their "handles" or nicknames. Big Bob was there, as were Louisville, Blackie, Spike, and Little George. It was the latter individual who captured most of whatever sympathy Burt and Emilia might have for the homeless men from the park. Little George couldn't have been much over five feet tall, had weak, watery eyes behind chipped and taped-together eyeglasses, and seemed to be the butt of a variety of practical jokes which the others played on him.

From time to time over the long, hot summer, poor George had been victimized by the placement of unexpected treats on his chair: thumbtacks, puddles of Coca Cola, dead cockroaches, and an assortment of overripe fruits and vegetables. Burt and Emilia had also borne witness to episodes in which George, about to sit down, had found his seat suddenly whisked out from under him, resulting in a surprising, usually painful, descent to the linoleum floor. His possessions had been hidden when he had been in the restroom and mysterious little wads of paper, propelled with considerable force from stretched rubber bands, snapped noisily and alarmingly off his backside when he rose to leave the room. Most of these coarse jests were accompanied by hoarse laughter, which left fiftyish George torn between outraged protest and shy smiles. He was after all the most inoffensive of people, which must have been why they all picked on him.

Once Burt Stone had been so bold as to ask Big Bob, who seemed to be the ringleader of the jokers from the park, why he and the others did such mean things to innocuous George. Bob had shown his array of yellowed snaggle teeth in what Burt had been forced to consider a warm smile. "Hell, man," he had bellowed, clapping Burt on the back heartily, "we spend long hours in here most days, you know? Gets boring, right? You gotta do something to, like, relieve the monotony. And George? He don't care. Really, he don't. I think he likes the attention, myself."

To Burt's insistence that some of the jokes were edged with cruelty and left George in obvious physical pain, Bob seemed unconcerned. "Like I told you, man, he don't care. Look at him. Does he seem any the worse for all the stuff we been doin' to him? Naww! Truth is, we all love old George. He's a good old boy, and we don't mean him no harm. It just gets boring up here all day, is all. So I 'preciate your asking, but you don't gotta worry about us. Nothin' mean in it. No way."

Burt had returned to Emilia at the desk, shaking his head. "They must both like it that way or it wouldn't happen," he explained, after he told Emilia what Big Bob had said to him.

As the summer progressed, the nature and intensity of the jokes played on George seemed to worsen, especially during the two weeks that security guard Irwin Rossiter was on vacation. Someone had stolen his eyeglasses once when he had put them down for a moment, and George had gone careening about the room in pursuit of his dimly seen antagonists, shouting, "Give them back! Give them back to me, right now, you hear?" Emilia, who had been on duty at the time, had become concerned and had approached John Collins, the department head, with her belief that George's companions ought to be banned from the department unless they would agree to stop playing tricks on him all the time. Besides that, Emilia pointed out, the other patrons in the area were being disrupted by the park gang, and it was beginning to be "like working in a real zoo." John had merely chuckled and dismissed her concern, saying that "boys will be boys," and that, unless someone were *seriously* hurt or inconvenienced, he was not anxious to intrude on the men's activities. Dismayed, Emilia reported her conversation with John to Burt, asking if they should have a word with library director Pat Broughton about the state of affairs in their workplace, but Burt counseled discretion and patience, saying that he didn't want to hassle John unless it seemed necessary and that the summer wouldn't last forever.

A few days later, however, John was summoned from his office about 4:30 on a steamy afternoon by Dan Ortega, a part-time page in the department. To his questions about what was going on in the reading room, Dan said that he thought that John had best come and see for himself. When John arrived on the scene, he beheld the little man known as George being helped through the door of the department, seemingly unable to walk on one of his feet. In the middle of the room stood Big Bob, wearing his habitual smirk of derision, calling after the hobbling George, "Whatsamatter? Can't you take a joke?"

Bob turned with a smile when John Collins approached him. "Hey, Mr. Collins, you missed it. I really got Little George good this time."

"Mind telling me what happened here, Bob?" said John.

"Aahhh, nothin'. Just a harmless little joke to kinda liven up the day."

"Tell me about it, anyway."

"Nothin' to tell. Me and some of the boys was just doin' a number on George and he tripped or stumbled, and I guess he hurt himself. But I didn't cause him no harm."

"Did you see this?" John asked, turning to Dan, who stood quietly behind him.

"Yes, sir, I did."

"What happened?"

"This guy here gave that little man a hot foot. When the guy, who I guess was asleep, felt it, he jumped up and must've tripped, 'cause he fell over and came up with some kind of ankle problem. That's all I know. Man, that's mean!''

"You keep out of this, boy!'' Big Bob warned 18-year-old Dan, who shrugged unconcernedly.

"A hot foot? I don't understand. What is a hot foot?'' asked John Collins.

"Easiest trick in the book. You wait until the guy's asleep. Then you put a match in his shoe, with the head facing out, see? Then light the match and wait until it burns down to the shoeleather. It gets the guy's attention right away, I assure you. Hey, did you see that sucker jump when the match began cookin' his foot inside the shoe?'' Bob asked his confederates, who had been lurking in the background. A few smiled; most didn't.

"But the man seems to have really hurt himself,'' said John, uncertainly.

"Oh, that. Well, yeah,'' conceded Bob. "But it wasn't from the hot foot. He musta twisted his ankle bone when he got up so suddenly. I dunno. Anyway, Louisville and the boys are takin' him to the hospital, and he'll get fixed up just fine, so what's the problem?''

John stood first on one foot and then on the other. There didn't seem to be anything constructive left to say, so he went back to his office, instructing Dan Ortega to tell him if anything else happened between or among the bunch from the park. As he stepped into his office, he turned and saw Emilia Parsons, who was just reporting back for duty from her dinner hour, staring at him.

The next afternoon, even though he had been expecting it, John felt his palms grow sweaty when he was summoned by telephone to report to Pat Broughton's office. When he walked in he saw Pat, unsmilingly sitting next to Burt Stone and Emilia Parsons, and he knew that he would have to do some fast talking to get out of this one.

Questions for Discussion

1. What is your opinion of the library's practice (if not policy) of letting people sleep in the reading rooms during the hot summer days?
2. Under what circumstances does patron behavior become inappropriate? Do you feel that practical jokes perpetrated on members of a group by other members fall outside the definition of acceptable library behavior?
3. As John, how would you have reacted to Burt and Emilia's request for action? What can a department head do to control such problem behavior?

4. Should Burt and Emilia have gone to Pat or some other person in administration before the incident depicted?
5. As Pat Broughton, now that this has happened, what would you say to John Collins, to Burt and Emilia, and, if desirable, to Big Bob and the others, to reduce the likelihood of future "practical jokes" in the library?

Resources

1. Caputo, Janette. *The Assertive Librarian*. Phoenix, AZ: Oryx Press, 1984.
   In this book, Caputo makes the point that, by the nature of their helping profession, librarians often feel compelled to put up with behavior that they shouldn't tolerate. The book contains complete guidelines and techniques for dealing assertively with patrons, colleagues, and superiors.
2. "The Library: Fortress of Dreams." *American Libraries* 13 (February 1982): 12.
   Presents results of an informal survey of public libraries concerning policy and practice with regard to sleepers.
3. Vocino, Michael, Jr. "The Library and the Problem Patron." *Wilson Library Bulletin* 50 (January 1976): 372–73.
4. Vogel, Betty. "The Illegitimate Patron." *Wilson Library Bulletin* 51 (September 1977): 65–66.
   The Vocino and Vogel articles argue the library's problem of differentiating appropriate behavior from inappropriate behavior, and what to do about each.

Case 9
Drug Awareness Week

According to a report to the mayor of the *ad hoc* Citizens' Commission on Drug Use and Abuse, River Bend was a city awash in illegal narcotics and their users. Once thought to be a problem that only affected the inner-city poor in big cities and the Beverly Hills type of wealthy, drugs were now clearly a serious and growing problem, especially among the young, who sought and found diversion from what they considered their ordinary midwestern lives.

The report, after documenting the existence and menace of River Bend's drug problem, went on to make several recommendations. Among these, and perhaps the most easily achieved, was the hiring of a popular television star to come to the city and speak to young people on the perils and risks of drug use. Colossus, as he was called, was a former bodyguard, pimp, and self-confessed drug user and retailer who had cleaned up his act and begun a new life as a movie star.

The huge Black actor affected an outlandish fashion style but was widely respected for his willingness to preach to young people in their own language against experimentation with drugs. He was spending the summer barnstorming around the country talking to youth groups about the problem, asking only his expenses. Pursuant to the recommendation of the mayor's commission, a call was made to Colossus, who agreed to speak in River Bend on August 22 and to be interviewed on two television programs while he was in town. The River Bend Public Library, possessor of a 200-seat auditorium, was selected as the site for Colossus's talk, and director Pat Broughton and her staff set about the preparations for it with attendant publicity and refreshments.

Colossus and his small retinue arrived in River Bend on the 21st, and the musclebound, not-too-articulate actor made himself available to the news media to answer questions about the next day's program at the library. As a result of the publicity, and the recognition factor of the actor's face and appearance, the auditorium of the library was packed with people, mostly teenagers, an hour before the announced 7:30 p.m. program on the 22nd.

Library custodian Irwin Rossiter had volunteered to coordinate security that evening, partly out of his desire to get a little overtime money, and partly out of curiosity about what the crusading actor might have to say to deter some of the more delinquent members of the community from their interest in narcotics. A police officer was also assigned to the evening program, but his function was limited: he was under strick orders not to interfere in the library's management of crowd control, which Irwin prided himself on handling well, unless there were outbreaks of violence.

Promptly at 7:30, Mike Stewart from the mayor's office introduced the speaker, who needed no introduction, resplendent as he was in dreadlocks, a dazzling red silk vest, and costume jewelry. After Colossus strode to the podium of the auditorium to friendly applause, practically everybody fell silent to listen to his words.

Glaring around the room, his eyes flashing with conviction, Colossus began his remarks in a low voice and spoke in the argot of the streets. His rapt audience uttered no sound as he stabbed at the air with bejeweled forefingers and told them why he had come that night.

"Some of y'all gone be dead this time next year!" he began, solemnly. "Thass right, chump, I'm talking to you, and you, and you." Thick fingers pointed at random faces in the audiences. No one else made a sound. "Whichever man or woman think he bad. Figure he too smart or too strong to get put down by drugs. Wants to impress somebody, maybe. Or just fit in. Show the damn world he tough. Do a little dope, yeah, and fly all night."

The impact of these words hit most of the audience like a shock wave. A few stirred restlessly in their seats, but most almost forgot to breathe, so impassioned was the huge man's delivery. Somebody in the back of the room said something, making a few others laugh, but Colossus chose to ignore it and went on with his speech, his voice rising in a crescendo as he warmed to his topic.

Whatever his acting skills, the man had charisma beyond imagining. Everybody in the house, with the exception of three or four teenage boys in the last row, was hanging on his every word. He sounded street-smart, invulnerable, experienced, and completely confident as he detailed his one-time life of petty crime, strongarm work for a loanshark, procurement of women and drugs, and eventual drug dependency. When he described conditions in prison, where he had spent eleven months for armed robbery, many in his audience gasped, and even Irwin, who had never tried drugs in his sixty-four years, and who had sneered at the appearance and demeanor of Colossus, found himself drawn into the emotional grip of the actor. As Irwin looked around the room, he noticed that everybody, or almost everybody, seemed to be intent on the actor's words.

As the speech continued, the whole room gradually became aware that the small group of boys in matching green leather vests in the last row were beginning to create a disturbance. Irwin, hoping to catch their eyes, put his most menacing scowl into his glance. Colossus chose to ignore them, loftily convinced that he could deal with a little laughter and some derisive catcalls; he had done that before, and if all else failed he knew what to do next.

The three young men had filed quietly to their seats in the back early in the evening and had been escalating the volume and spitefulness of their comments ever since. Now they were giggling at their own remarks and competing with Colossus for the attention of the crowd. Finally, one of them, a small boy with long, blond hair and a thin face, said in a loud stage whisper that speeches like the one he was hearing would turn more people onto drugs than it would get them off them.

With this, Colossus executed his prepared routine for dealing with obstreperous listeners. Feigning fury, his face contorted and he leapt from behind the podium and ran up the aisle to confront the startled young man who had uttered the sarcastic remark. "Listen, sucker," he bellowed. "This is serious stuff I'm talkin,'" and if you can't deal with it, take a walk now!"

Quietly, but with defiance on his young face, the boy murmured, "Make me!"

Colossus was ready for this, too. Gently, but with an appearance of great menace, he grabbed the boy's shirt lapels and said, "You're tempting me, man!"

Irwin had been as surprised as the boy had been when the huge man had rushed down the aisle of the auditorium. Now, he hesitated to act, figuring that the kid wouldn't say or do anything else after this display of wild anger on the part of the speaker.

Irwin was right about that, because the boy fell completely silent for the rest of the evening, along with his friends who were now also in a subdued mood. Colossus jauntily walked back to the front of the room and finished his speech in a rousing manner, urging his audience to avoid drugs lest they "wake up dead" some morning. When he was done, there was enthusiastic applause and a circle of autograph seekers and well-wishers surrounded the sweating actor as he left the podium. Irwin scanned the room for any sign of the troublemakers, but they had evidently gone sneaking off in disgrace or fear of further humiliation. As he supervised the closing of the library building that evening, Irwin reflected on the obvious ability of Colossus to get his point across and to quell disturbances without serious incident, and he revised his previous estimation of the hulking actor's value to the world.

The next morning, when Irwin reported for work, he was astonished when Pat Broughton told him that an attorney had phoned her promptly at 9:00 a.m., informing her that the Harris family, which included the young man who had been reprimanded by Colossus the previous evening, were suing the actor for aggravated assault and were pressing charges against the library for permitting it to happen. Pat and Irwin stared intently together at her desk pad where she had scribbled the dollar amount which the lawyer had told her he was seeking from the library for young Tom Harris: it began with a five and had five zeroes behind it.

Questions for Discussion

1. When police officers are not available for crowd control, how can a library staff best keep order and discipline, while maintaining the rights of all concerned at public programs?
2. As Irwin, entrusted with coordination of security, what might you have done *before* the incident described in an effort to defuse or minimize the situation?
3. As Irwin, what action might you have taken *at the time* that Colossus left the podium and charged up the aisle toward the heckling boys?
4. As Pat Broughton, assuming that the library's attorney feels that there is a possible case for the lawsuit, how would you go about trying to assemble a viable defense for the library?
5. In general, to what extent do you feel that libraries are responsible or financially liable for the actions of persons who are employed or appear under their sponsorship?

Resources

1. Grotophorst, Clyde W. "The Problem Patron: Toward a Comprehensive Response." *Public Library Quarterly* 1 (Winter 1979): 345–53. Guidelines for managing the disruptive user in libraries, together with the information that "50 percent of all police problems involve unruly youths under the age of sixteen."
2. Starr, Carol. "Youthomania: The Care and Treatment in the Public Library." *Wisconsin Library Bulletin* 68 (January–February 1972): 37–38. Recommendations for dealing firmly with teenagers, such that they feel welcome but are not given license to annoy others.

Case 10
Take the "A" Train

It all seemed too good to be true. Jonas Meacham, once a boy growing up poor in River Bend and now a millionaire industrialist in a suburb of Chicago, had just called Library Director Pat Broughton and offered, free of all costs, a fully equipped library branch on wheels. Meacham explained that he had received a shipment of a dozen superannuated subway cars, that were intended to be melted down and recycled for their steel content, from the city of Chicago. Instead, Meacham told Pat, he had inspected the cars and had seen in them a potential for libraries.

Meacham's proposal was that he convert one of the old cars to a fully equipped, state-of-the-art library branch and send it to his former hometown, where it could be used as a stationary branch or as a floating one, limited only by the availability of railroad tracks in the community. Pat, whose fondest wish through the past several years had been to have a branch serving the west side of town, but who again and again had run up against the financial realities of a city undergoing recession, felt that this opportunity was exactly the chance she had prayed for.

River Bend, as a city, was growing rapidly. Originally, the downtown (main) library building had sufficed to serve the community; then two branches were added to serve residents of the south side and north side who couldn't (or wouldn't) come downtown to get books or avail themselves of other services of a city library. That left only the west side unserved, but the west side had, since about 1970, become the fastest growing area of the city. It was also, by any measure, the poorest and was home to a large portion of the city's Blacks and Hispanics. Through the years, pressure had been building on the city, and on Pat, in particular, to build a branch in the west side area, so that minority members of the population would not feel that the city was neglecting them. Besides, it had been pointed out again and again, minority children needed good, free library services more than the more affluent ones. Until the call came from Meacham, however, Pat had felt both frustration and embarrassment at her inability to be more optimistic when confronted by west side residents who sought to pin her down to a commitment to a branch in their midst.

Until the mid-1970s, that area had been served, in a manner of speaking, by a bookmobile, which made regular weekly stops at several shopping areas in the neighborhood. Unfortunately, however, the "oil crisis" had stopped the bookmobile, as a manifold increase in the cost of fuel had rendered the big vehicle to be less and less cost-effective. Since 1976, Pat reflected, there had been no service west of Central Avenue, with the understanding that when funds became available a branch for the west side would be a high-priority item.

Not only would such a branch provide a needed service to a large segment of River Bend's growing population, but it would diminish or end the unfair charges of racism, which occasionally were heard at city council meetings when it was announced that the money just wasn't there to make such a branch possible. Those who testified at budget hearings pointed out that it was not that easy for west siders to just hop on a bus and get downtown. Pat and her board registered sympathy, and made vague promises, but until now it had not been possible to be specific about facilities or timing.

When Meacham announced that, if Pat would simply authorize the delivery, he would send a gleaming new car all fitted out with library shelves and tables and chairs within a month's time, she personally telephoned each member of her board and got their unanimous approval. The following Monday, she drove to Chicago to meet Meacham in person and to see the plans for the new branch facility. True, Pat conceded to herself, the car didn't look like much yet, as she toured the weatherbeaten and rusty car, sitting on a rail spur next to Meacham's Steel Works, but the plans indicated a paint job to restore the car to its former appearance when it had been part of the north-south "A" train route in Chicago. There would be shelving between the windows inside, and four wooden work tables, with matching chairs, bolted to the floor. Additionally, one end of the car was to be fitted out with a staff area, a charge desk, workspace, and a tiny bathroom. There was one small condition for Pat to agree to: a plaque bearing the name of Jonas Meacham and the bequest was to be displayed prominently just beside the door. Pat considered this fair, given the generosity of the giver and the need for the gift.

Arriving back in River Bend, Pat thought it best to assemble a few of the west side leaders in her office and to consult them about the ideal placement of the branch, which had the additional benefit of being capable of relocation, anywhere the rails, which crisscrossed the city, might go. Five community members attended her meeting: a minister, a priest, two businessmen, and the woman who ran the settlement house over on Hill Street. They all expressed pleasure in the plan, and Pat, encouraged by their response and enthusiasm, went forward with plans for a grand opening with speeches, refreshments, and dignitaries in attendance.

Three weeks later, Pat received word that the car had left Chicago behind a freight locomotive and would be available for positioning on the following Wednesday just after noon. With much news media coverage, Pat scheduled the grand opening for the following day and told reporters that the entire city owed a debt of gratitude to Mr. Meacham and his firm for this useful and beautiful tribute to the city of his birth.

Even the weather cooperated on the day of the grand opening. Pat counted well over 200 people in attendance, as the mayor, the city manager, a representative of Meacham Steel, and Pat herself spoke briefly about the opportunity that the new branch presented to the west side. Balloons were given to the children, cookies were consumed, and the branch opened for business at 1:00. By 3:00 p.m., when the branch closed until the following morning when regular hours of operation would begin, over 500 books had been checked out, and everyone in attendance pronounced the day a success. Pat drove home in a mood of elation, feeling very "up" about everything that had happened and all that would follow. In her mind, she composed a letter of appreciation to Mr. Meacham, to be dictated and sent the following day.

Pat was therefore both stunned and saddened that night when the desk sergeant of the west side police precinct called her with the news that vandals ("person or persons unknown," he said) had broken into the new branch, completely trashed it, inside and out, and had spray painted it with graffiti. Every window was broken, all the books had been strewn about or dismembered, and the furniture had been mutilated with knives and other pointed weapons. Most of the spray painted words and messages were obscene, the sergeant said, but one, obviously written by someone with more than senseless destruction on his or her mind, read: "Take your second-class services and put them where the sun don't shine!"

Pat got little sleep that night, and in the morning, she phoned the same people who had consulted with her on the planning and deployment of the new branch library. They expressed sadness, surprise, and a sort of resignation that things had turned out so badly. One of them, the owner of a west side hardware store, said, "You know, Pat, we seem to be guilty of one of two things: either we didn't ask enough people what they thought of the project, or we didn't ask the *right* people." Sadly, Pat acknowledged that this seemed to be true. Evidently, some members of the community did not agree that a subway car, even a retrofitted and brightly painted one, could take the place of a new, permanent branch in their community. To them, the location of such a facility in their midst might seem a polite way of telling them to stay in their ghetto and not to come downtown and mix with the upscale White members of the city's populace. The angry reaction might be another example of senseless violence against property, or it might be a clear message to the city and its library from a hostile group of insulted and frustrated residents. Sighing, Pat dictated a memo to her department heads for a meeting the following Monday to try to decide what should happen next.

Questions for Discussion

1. How can a public library's planners involve the community in its decision making in a meaningful way to avoid misunderstandings that can result in destruction and waste?
2. As Pat, what would you have done to maximize communication and understanding before the new branch facility was delivered and set in place?
3. What would you do to attempt to salvage the branch idea, now that this incident has happened?
4. Should the perpetrators of the vandalism be caught and arrested, what would the library stand to gain or lose by seeking to press criminal charges against them?

Resources

Unlike most of the cases in this book, this one is based loosely upon an actual incident. For background reading on it, see:

1. Howard, Edward N. "Terre Haute: No One Has Asked." *Wilson Library Bulletin* 43 (May 1969): 888–92.
2. "Terre Haute's Railroad Car Spurned by Militants." *Library Journal* 94 (June 15, 1969): 2381.
3. "Train Wreck in Terre Haute." *ALA Bulletin* (July–August 1969): 981–84.

And, just to demonstrate that abandoned railroad cars can become valued library facilities in a community, you might read Robl, Ernest H. " 'Reading' Railroad Revival." *American Libraries* 9 (April 1978): 195.

Case 11
You'll Never Take Me Alive!

A heavy snowfall and a stiff wind kept the usual Saturday crowd home that day. The public library opened as usual punctually at the stroke of 9:00 a.m., with janitor Peter Bourdelle twisting the key in the lock of the outside door and turning on the pressure treadle that caused the door to swing open, but no one was waiting to enter. By noon, there were no more than two dozen people in the building, exclusive of staff members, and virtually everyone kept a sharp eye on the out-of-doors to warn them of the possibility of blizzard conditions.

Larry Green, a librarian in the Performing Arts division, rather enjoyed the day for two reasons. First, he was not too displeased to be working on a day when the weather would have prohibited all but the most necessary outside activity, and second, there were so few people around that he had almost uninterrupted time at his desk to get a few bothersome but backlogged things done. He looked around the room. Patricia Pergolesi, the teenager who was his regular page on weekday afternoons and Saturdays, had long ago finished her task of shelving books that had come back and was now seated at one of the tables reading a movie magazine. This didn't bother Larry in the least, for he really couldn't think of anything for her to do. Saturdays were often hectic, and this slow, snowy one was a break for him and for Pat.

Because it was such a dull day, Larry welcomed the distraction when he saw the door to the department open and watched a man wearing a Viet Nam era camouflage battle jacket walk in, lugging the department's circulating 16mm film projector and a large shopping bag. Despite the heaviness of the self-threading projector (Larry had carried it to and from his car many times and he knew its weight well), the man seemed to have no trouble carrying it or raising it to deposit it on the desk. He was slim, perhaps thirty years old, wiry, and had an attenuated moustache of a sandy rust color. He didn't look directly at Larry but dropped the projector in its protective cover in front of him and mumbled, "Returning this, okay?"

"Certainly, sir," said Larry, politely. "Your name?"

"Garrity. Borrowed this last week about this time."

Larry checked his file of film and equipment rentals and found a card showing that a Mr. L. Garrity had indeed charged out the projector on the previous Saturday. He made a notation of the date under the column marked "return" and gently tugged upward on the green cover of the projector for the required superficial inspection. What he saw next almost caused him to gasp. The projector had been dented, its film track was twisted, the projector lamp seemed to be missing, but most disturbing of all, the arm that held the take-up reel was missing, its winding mechanism dangling loosely out of the body of the machine.

"What happened?" Larry muttered to Garrity, searching the man's face for explanations.

Garrity, smiling broadly, leaned over the desk between them and gave Larry the benefit of a conspiratorial wink. "Figured somebody'd ask that," he said, looking around the room, still almost empty of other people. "See, I borrowed this projector to watch some special films that a friend of mine got from Argentina or somewhere. I mean, you wouldn't believe what those girls do, you follow? Six films, all different, in color, and every fantasy you ever had is right there, man. Six of them!"

Larry, striving to keep his voice free of moral nuances, said, "Oh, I get it. Hard core stuff. X-rated?"

"X don't come near what we got a hold of. Triple X is too tame for these little movies, friend."

Concealing his distaste, Larry, who was by no means a prude, shrugged. It wasn't the library's business, or his, to worry about what uses were made of the equipment. Safe and sound return, however, was quite another matter.

"Seem to be a few problems here. Parts missing, some damage," he said evenly, relishing the understatement.

"Well, yeah," said Garrity, reaching into his shopping bag. "All the parts are here, see? I just didn't know where everything went and figured that I'd better not try to stick it back in any whichaway."

"How did this machine get wrecked like that?" Larry asked.

"Well, I really can't tell you. Some of the guys I served with and I made a night of it this week. It was snowing again. It's always snowing. And we had these films and the projector and some dynamite stuff to smoke, so. . . ." His voice trailed off as he remembered the events of the evening in question. "Somebody started throwing things, I guess. And a full can of beer knocked this projector right off the table and onto the floor. That's what I remember, anyway. Next thing I know, I wake up and everybody's asleep or gone home, and this projector is lyin' there on the floor just runnin' and runnin'. Ruined the film, too. Carlos ain't going to like that, I tell you."

Larry didn't know or care who Carlos was, but he wanted to understand what had happened to the projector. "So what you're telling me is that you and your friends got ripped out of your minds and you broke this projector."

"You got it," agreed Garrity with a rueful grin.

Larry took the projector, such as it was, over to a nearby electrical socket and plugged it in. Nothing happened when he tried various buttons for forward, reverse, or lamp. To his appraising eye, the machine looked like a total write-off. "How do you intend to pay for this?" he asked quietly.

"Pay?" Garrity seemed not to have considered the idea before. "Well, I dunno. I'm on welfare and a government pension. I can't pay for this. How much d'you figure, anyway?"

"I'd have to guess a minimum of five hundred dollars. Maybe closer to six."

"Forget it, man!" Garrity was beginning to look angry.

"Somebody's got to compensate the library for its broken equipment. If not you, then who?"

"Look, I'm sorry the thing's broke, but I can't deal with it, you know? I've been out of a job a long time. Ever since 'Nam, I've had problems keeping work. My nerves, the doctors say."

"Sir, you signed an agreement. Did you read it before you signed it?"

"Well, no. I mean, who thought that the damn thing was gonna topple off a table and smash to pieces?"

"Nevertheless," said Larry. "You're on the hook for its replacement or repair costs. I'll have to report this to the director's office and our board of trustees, and they'll send you a statement of damages and costs."

"Man, I got no money. That's why I come to the library so much. And no job. I just can't deal with this now, you hear what I'm sayin' to you? I don't need this. Now look, I brought it back to you. So you fix it, and don't be tellin' me that I'm going to have to pay for it. I can't deal with it, man."

The man's voice was growing louder by the second, and Larry decided that he had best say nothing further. Out of the corner of his eye, he saw Pat Pergolesi and three or four startled patrons beginning to edge to the door.

Suddenly the man screamed. It was a sound of agony, ripped from his chest, and very clearly and unmistakably a signal that he was feeling violent. "All right!" he shouted, and in one smooth motion, he had reached into his field jacket and withdrawn a hand grenade, whose safety pin he pulled out, seemingly preparatory to detonation.

"Now, hold on," said Larry, horrified. "You don't have to. . . ."

"Shut up, fool! Just shut up! Not another word!" The man was waving his arm in a large circle with the fragmentation grenade firmly (for the moment) clenched in his fist. Larry tried making placating gestures, but he could see that the man was beyond talking to.

Also, out of his peripheral vision, Larry gratefully noticed that Pat had quietly slipped out of the Performing Arts department and had run down the stairs, presumably to summon help. Three women and a man, who just happened to be in the reading room at the time, were attempting to follow in Pat's footsteps, when Garrity spied them trying to get away.

"Don't!" he commanded, and beckoned to them to return to the room, while his right arm made a pantomime of throwing the grenade baseball style.

Larry had, to some extent, recovered his wits by this time. "Nobody has to get hurt now, Mr. Garrity. Do you really want to hurt me or those ladies over there? And why kill yourself? What good would that do?"

"Right," sneered the man. "About now you're going to tell me that life is really beautiful and that a job and a girl and an '84 Mercedes sports coupe are just around the corner waiting for me. You watch too much television, man! Life stinks!"

"But this is all over a lousy damaged film projector," said Larry, hoping that it was the right psychological ploy. "Why does anybody have to be hurt or anything be blown up over a projector?"

"Just keep back and let me think!" bellowed Garrity, slumping into a chair, his knuckles visibly whitening as he squeezed the grenade in his shaking hand. Larry thought that that was a hopeful sign, so he too sat down and signalled the confusted and frightened other occupants of the room to follow his lead.

Several minutes passed, with the only sounds in the room coming from one of the women at the far table, who seemed to be moaning involuntarily in her fear. Larry, desperate to get the man talking again, was nervously sorting out his next words, when a sound in the hallway caused Garrity to jump out of his chair, as he held the grenade aloft.

"Mr. Green," came a stern voice through an electronically amplified loudspeaker. "Can you hear me? Are you all right?"

Larry peered through the department door but could see nothing except the water fountain across the hall. He looked at Garrity for a moment and called out, "Yeah. I'm not hurt. We're all okay in here."

"This is the police," came the voice, blaring into the department. "You in there. Put down that explosive and come out with your hands above your head and you will not be harmed."

Garrity's response was immediate, loud, profane, and to the point.

"I say again: deactivate that weapon and come out slowly and you will not be harmed."

"Or else what, huh? I got four other people in here, you know? You'll never take me alive . . . or anybody else! If you get me, you get all of us. I'm squeezin' a general purpose frag here, buddy, and my hand's gettin' tired even as we speak."

Larry, following the conversation between the disturbed man and the unseen police officers, noticed that he was momentarily forgotten. Never one to be a hero, he was at this moment wondering if there was any way to do something to save the day before anyone, including himself, got maimed or killed. Feverishly trying to remember what he had learned about grenades during his peacetime two years in the army, he tried frantically to figure out a plan.

Questions for Discussion

1. What procedures should be in place in a library before a potentially violent or destructive incident happens?
2. As Larry, what might you have done or said after the disturbed man pulled the grenade to try to reduce the tension in the situation?
3. What is the most effective way to evacuate a large public building in the event of a hazardous situation?
4. Now that the police officers are just outside the door, and the man seems even more agitated, what would you, as Larry, do to try to bring the incident to a harmless conclusion? Must you necessarily proceed on the assumption that the grenade is "live" and that Garrity will throw it?

Resources

1. "Crime Risk Revealed." *American Libraries* 11 (September 1980): 479.
   Relates the potential perils arising from dealing with the general public in today's libraries.
2. Fichtelberg, Leo. "More on the Troublesome Patron." *New Jersey Libraries* 12 (February 1979): 10+.
   Deals with ways to anticipate emergency situations as well as ways to deal with them when they occur.
3. "New Security Problem: Staff Safety." *Library Journal* 100 (March 1975): 434+.
   Tells how various urban libraries deal with emergencies.

Case 12
Graffiti Wars

Custodian Irwin Rossiter had spent his lunch hour eating his sandwich in the air-conditioned comfort of the staff lounge at the River Bend Public Library. He was pleased that he had thought ahead to bring his sandwich and a thermos of iced tea, because there was no way he was going to venture out into the searing heat of this July day until 6:00, when his workday was over and the sun was beginning to drop down over the city's western skyline.

He had just finished eating and was settling back on the couch for a twenty-minute read through *Time* and *Newsweek* when the door burst open and Marie and Karen walked in. Marie O'Shea had been in charge of cataloging for the library since Irwin could remember, and Karen Talbert had joined her little crew in the last two years. A warm friendship had grown up between the widow nearing seventy years of age and the vivacious young library school graduate, and Irwin knew that they enjoyed working together and felt that they made the place more fun to work in, with their good cheer and amusing stories.

"Irwin," said Karen, "have you seen what's been painted on the western wall of the building?"

Groaning aloud, Irwin sat up straighter on the couch and muttered, "what is it this time? Phantom spraypainter strikes again?"

"Oh, yes, he struck again. Or *they* struck again, anyway. Somebody sure did!" said Karen, with Marie nodding in agreement.

"And what's the message for the world today?"

"If I told you, you'd wash my mouth out with soap," giggled Karen, receiving a playful nudge in the ribs from her companion.

"Just tell me this," said Irwin. "Is it something that can wait to be taken off until the temperatures moderate a bit?" He scratched unobtrusively at a spot that had begun madly itching beneath his gray uniform shirt. "It's just too damn hot to do it now."

"Depends on how many see it, I suppose," said Marie, "but I wouldn't wait too long. This one's really . . . what's the word the kids are using again, Karen?"

"Gross," her young colleague supplied.

"Exactly. Gross. Somebody has an unlimited budget or spray cans of red paint and a vile sense of what's proper for depiction on the sides of public buildings."

"Yeah, yeah. I'll go right out," Irwin said, reluctantly, already imagining the heat and humidity of a July day in River Bend, which was a flatlands community along a riverbed in the middle of a prairie state.

"Sorry to make it necessary, Irwin, but . . . you'll see why your immediate attention is needed when you get out there."

Muttering to himself about the intelligence and parentage of people who paint things on concrete walls at night, Irwin went to his locker, found his sunglasses, slipped them on, and walked sedately through the library's staff entrance into the dazzlingly bright parking lot area. The library was situated in a landscaped two-acre lot just across Riverside Drive from the park, and beyond that the river. Its front entrance faced a busy office building, and its backside overlooked the parking lot. Its western face, however, looked out on a wooded slope, which led down to a busy street. It was this face of the building, with few windows and few passersby after dark, which someone, usually teenagers, always chose for a display of artistic talent. Over the years, Irwin and Peter, his helper, had wiped and scoured plenty of legends, logos, and pictograms off the wall.

Sometimes the wall contained messages of what Irwin in his military days would have called "unit pride." Examples were: "The Regents are #1," "Horsemen Forever!," and simply "Blazers." Another category of painted slogans were presumably insulting to one gang and reflected another gang's opinion of their collective manhood or abilities. Such disparagement might be accompanied by ethnic or racial slurs, depending on the identities of both painter and subject. Once in a while, Irwin found a message having to do with religion or politics ("Jesus is Lord" or "Down with the Shah!"), and a few were cryptic to the point of bafflement (Irwin had once found the wall covered with huge black spraypainted letters saying, without explanation, "Arbitrary Donuts!")

As he puffed around the corner of the building to the west face of the concrete structure, he became aware of two things: the summer sun was bouncing off the porous wall of the building, giving off heat that could fry eggs quite easily, and there, centered on the west wall of the structure, covering parts of numerous earlier graffiti, was a stunning work of art.

To Irwin's anger and amazement, someone had taken the time and trouble to paint an anatomically accurate representation in black on the wall and had covered the area behind the depiction with a red background that must have required four or five cans of paint. The background made the featured objects themselves stand out in startling relief, and Irwin, as he wiped his perspiring brow with his handkerchief, imagined that the entire representation, perhaps five feet square, could be seen from several blocks away, even though trees in full leaf covered the library's western grounds.

Furiously, Irwin slapped his palm stingingly against the desecrated wall, shouting "Damn punks!" as loudly as he could, despite the fact that he could see no one who was listening. Scratching against the paint with a fingernail, he found that it was standard wood paint, the kind one might use to cover a chair or table, and that, in time, it would wash off in the rain. But Irwin realized that he didn't have time. Very soon, the huge picture would be seen by someone in authority, who would probably object and demand that it be instantly removed, since it was a public affront to taste and decency.

He squinted, despite his sunglasses, critically appraising the wall and wondering about the best method for removing the offending picture. If only the artist hadn't filled in the rest of the square with that red background, he thought, it would be easier to take care of it. But the kid had taken his time and exercised uncharacteristic thoroughness, making Irwin's job all the more time-consuming and difficult. Looking behind him to the west, Irwin scanned the horizon that he could see behind the tall buildings, hoping that an afternoon thundershower was on its way to assist him in getting rid of the blot on the wall. The pitiless sun beat down, however, in a blue sky and not a cloud was to be seen.

Mentally, Irwin made a list of the preparations he would have to make before tackling this sweaty and thankless task. Let's see, a bucket, a couple of those stiff wire brushes, some industrial strength detergent, a hose, maybe a bottle of turpentine, and, of course, Peter, to help him. Then he'd see about trying to find the little rat who had painted this . . . this thing . . . on the wall, and make him pay for his pleasure.

Lost in thought, Irwin at first didn't hear the sound of running feet and he was startled to discover that four small children, perhaps seven years old apiece, were standing behind him, surveying the huge *object d'art* on the pitted wall.

"Did you do that, Mister?" asked one little boy, a dark-haired kid in a striped T-shirt, dark jeans, and sneakers.

Irwin was so upset by the idea that these children were viewing the wall's new adornment and the horrifying suggestion that he might have painted it that he couldn't speak for a moment. His already perspiring face assumed the general color of an overdone lobster shell and he waved his arms flappingly, first at the painting and then in the general direction of the children, who stood in a fascinated semi-circle, poised for flight.

"Get the hell out of here!" he finally managed to scream and took two menacing steps toward the children. They took off at a dead run, and Irwin stood there perspiring and listening until they had disappeared from sight. Sighing, he trudged around the building and into the staff entrance. "Yo, Peter!" he called.

"Over here," called Peter from the loading dock.

"Better take off your shirt and come outside with me, kid," growled Irwin as he stood in the blissfully cool air of the library's interior.

"Oh? What's up?"

"If I told you, you wouldn't believe me," muttered Irwin, mopping furiously at his brow where sweat was not cooling in the frosty air near the compressor.

"Gotta be done now?" complained Peter.

"Now," said Irwin tersely. "We don't get rid of this one, we'll be busted for public obscenity."

With resignation, Peter took off his uniform shirt and, stripped to his "muscle shirt," he grabbed a bucket and some brushes and followed the older man out into the sunlight, blinking and squinting in the moist heat.

"This crap's got to stop, Irwin," he growled, as he walked around the side of the building, laden with cleaning tools.

"Yeah, but how?" asked Irwin, rolling up his sleeves.

Questions for Discussion

1. What is the best way to discourage nocturnal artists from decorating the library's exterior with words or pictures?
2. As Irwin and Peter, what ideas can you come up with that might catch and stop those who are doing this to the building?
3. If the perpetrators of this act are caught, what should the library do about them? Consider the costs associated with the constant cleaning up after such incidents.

Resources

1. Ingwerson, Marshall. "Scrubbing the Graffiti off America: A New Legal Approach." *Christian Science Monitor* 75 (June 7, 1983): 1.

Points out the magnitude of the graffiti problem and a few cases in which perpetrators are being made to atone for their crimes when they are caught.

2. Myers, Dorothy. "Babysitting, Band-Aids, and Blood: A Survivor's Tale of Service Under Siege." *American Libraries* 9 (October 1978): 525–28.
Myers' urban library branch is described as "the unwitting, unintentional, center of activities in the complex, (with) . . . nonstop vandalism and graffiti."

3. Starr, Carol. "Youthomania: Their Care and Treatment in the Public Library." *Wisconsin Library Bulletin* 68 (January-February 1972): 37–38.
Suggests ways that teenagers may be "mainstreamed" into the library community through involvement and participation in cooperative library projects.

Case 13
Outpatient Therapy

Odd patrons came with the territory for librarians working at the River Bend Public Library. It seemed that the library building served as a magnet for the confused, the deluded, the oddly dressed, and the "not quite right" people in and around the city, and the staff tried to learn to deal effectively with the difficult ones and laugh off the rest. Lauren Soltani, a new, young, and energetic professional librarian working in the Performing Arts department, quickly learned the ropes under the careful guidance of her older, more experienced colleagues, but one can't be prepared for everything.

On her first day of work, Lauren had been taken on a guided tour of the building by Joann Larabee, her department supervisor. She was shown, among other things, some of the chronic "weirdos" who frequent the library. That was her first exposure to such interesting but more-or-less harmless people as "Crazy Harry," who conducted imaginary conversations with unseen partners, and the woman known only as Bessie, who had the habit of walking up to unsuspecting browsers in the stacks and telling them that their days were numbered and that she had foreseen the time and circumstances of their deaths. Most of these people, Joann had said, were not dangerous and should be, as much as possible, ignored. A few never washed or were apt to emit shrill noises at random and unexpected times; many, it seemed, had little or no contact with reality, but it was all part of the job and not to be worried about overmuch.

Lauren was counseled to take such irritations in stride, and to be ready and willing to call a guard, or even the police, if circumstances seemed to warrant it. Whenever people seemed disruptive, or getting to that point, she was not to hesitate to summon assistance and, at her own discretion, to get out of the way.

The lesson of that first day stayed with Lauren, and behind her ready smile and her friendly greeting, she had acquired, in her first three months of employment at the library, a pretty good knack for sizing up patrons and classifying them into those who could pretty much be left alone and those who bore close watching.

Recently, she had been informed, Riverview State Hospital, located about three miles north of the library, had instituted new procedures for the treatment and possible cure of its mentally ill patients. Outpatient therapy, thanks to advances in drug therapy and a revision of previously held attitudes, permitted Riverview to discharge some of its patients, who were then permitted to live in town, work, and attempt to reintegrate themselves into society, returning to the hospital only for medication and therapy sessions. The implications of this for the library, Pat Broughton had told the staff at a recent meeting, was that former inmates of Riverview were going to be coming to the library as part of their recommended courses of treatment.

Shudders of foreboding and a few coarse jests had greeted that news, but Pat had gone on to explain that the library wanted to participate fully in the hospital's experiment as a cooperating public facility, dedicated to improving the life of the community.

"Why the library?" someone had asked.

"Why not?" Pat had responded.

"First of all, it's free. It has long hours of operation, has few routines for the public to follow, and does not press people who come in to identify themselves or to state their business. Finally, our books and other materials provide opportunities for bibliotherapy, and doctors from the hospital will be available for consultation with you, if you have questions or problems."

Lauren had liked the idea, personally. A young woman who cared about people and wanted to help, she welcomed the opportunity to do some good and to know that her work made a difference. Her idealism was admired by some of her colleagues and mocked by a few others, but Lauren put herself on notice to expect the unexpected when people came into her department, and she tried to think of more and better ways that the arts and music she dealt with could assist people to find themselves again.

On an overcast February morning, while Lauren was alone on duty sorting through several *Schwann* catalogs in search of new titles for the phonorecord collection, an earsplitting shriek of triumph roused her from her work. Startled, Lauren looked quickly up to see that a middle-aged man was standing over one of the turntables used for listening to records and capering around in what appeared to be joy. Several other patrons, who had been using turntables or tape playing equipment, looked up and quickly away to avoid the appearance of staring. Lauren, not sure whether to grin or frown, walked slowly and cautiously over to the man, saying, "Anything wrong?" to him in a neutral tone.

The man was about to respond when something he heard in the earphones he had on his head caused him to pause and assume a stiff, awkward pose. Quickly, he sat down and began scribbling furiously on a notepad. "There it is, again!" he bellowed, drawing a few "Shhhhhh" sounds from others in the room. Obviously excited, he held out his arm, offering the earphones to Lauren.

"Just listen to this and you'll see. They'll all see. Called me crazy, but I have proof, now! Listen!!"

Lauren hesitated, noting that the rubberized earphones were slicked with the man's perspiration. Absently, he wiped them against his trouser front and extended them again. "Will you just do me a favor and bear witness to my discovery?"

"What is it that you want me to hear?" asked Lauren, noting that the cover of the album the man was listening to read "Fusion: The Peanut Butter Conspiracy," which meant nothing to her, as her musical interests lay primarily in the Baroque and Rococo periods.

"This! This proves conclusively that these guys aren't just singing gibberish. I figured something was up when I first heard this song, but it wasn't until I found out how to play it *backwards* that I knew how to unlock the secret. Please, miss! Indulge me. Listen to this one song and tell me what you hear."

Curious, but a trifle reluctant to get involved in this man's obsession, Lauren slipped the headset over her ears and watched as the man picked up the phonograph's needle and replaced it at the beginning of the title cut of the album. In seconds, Lauren's ears were bombarded by something resembling music, only much less melodious. A peculiar and twangy instrument was being plucked or strummed to an insistent and syncopated backbeat, while a voice, vaguely recognizable as human, caterwauled meaningless syllables at a volume considerably beyond the threshold of pain. Lauren, unobtrusively turning the volume control knob downward, listened patiently and with growing bewilderment until the singing and playing stopped.

"Well?" demanded the man, sitting uncomfortably close to her. "Well?"

"Well, what? I'm sorry, whatever it is, I don't seem to be getting it."

"Don't you hear them singing about Satan? Don't you catch the name 'Reagan' three times in the song? How can you miss it?"

Lauren, hoping to placate the man and uncertain as to whether she might have missed something that was really there, said, "Maybe if I could hear it over again? This time, I'll concentrate harder."

"Forget it," the man snapped, pulling the earphones off of her head with one hand and giving her a little nudge with his shoulder. "You're just like all the rest of them, aren't you? So smug and serene in your little shell. Don't you see that this song, when you play it backwards, foretells the end of the world and the advent of the devil as the new power? Doesn't it matter that this song tells us that President Reagan is the only one who can save us? Sure, what do you care? Get out of here. Just leave me alone.''

The man subsided into gloomy meditation as he slipped the head-phones over his ears and replayed the first song on the record. Lauren noticed that the turntable was turning in a counterclockwise direction, and that the man, once again lost in his own thoughts, was writing something on his notepad. Blinking at the man's bizarre mood swings, and unsure as to what to do about him, she went back to the desk. For several minutes, the man made not a sound, except for the audible but nonthreatening scratch of his pencil as it dug deeply into paper. Then he was shouting again and waving his arms in all directions, reacting to something he had heard through the earphones.

This time, at least four people in the room made shushing noises, and one man, large and powerful looking and dressed in a navy pea jacket, called over to Lauren that if she didn't ''do something about this nut case,'' he definitely would. Lauren still felt that the intently listening man was nonviolent and could be tolerated, but she had the comfort and possible safety of all the room's occupants to think about, and so, reluctantly, she dialed the library's custodial office and spoke briefly to Irwin Rossiter, the man in charge of security that morning.

When Irwin had heard the nature of the problem, he said that he was on his way up and to try to keep things cool at her end until he could get there. Lauren was just about to tell Irwin that there was no emergency and that he could take his time, when she heard angry voices off to her right.

Irwin, evidently, had heard them, too. ''What the hell is that?'' he demanded.

The man who had heard the voices warning of Armageddon was now backed against a filing cabinet, shouting in fury at everyone else in the room and holding the library's copy of *Fusion* aloft. Advancing toward him was the burly man in the pea jacket, saying nothing, but his intentions were rather clear. ''Irwin,'' shouted Lauren into the telephone, ''get up here quick, will you?''

Questions for Discussion

1. At what point must a librarian who seeks to be warm and supportive disengage and become impersonal when dealing with a disturbed and potentially unstable patron?
2. How would you evaluate Lauren's conduct with respect to the patron in question thus far?

3. Is there any way to differentiate those patrons who are potentially or actually dangerous from those whose behavior is merely bizarre or unusual?
4. As Lauren, following this incident, how would you seek to modify your future behavior with respect to out-of-the-ordinary conduct on the part of patrons in your department?

Resources

1. Elliott, Joyce. "Working with Disturbed Clients in Libraries." *The Communicator* (Librarians' Guild AFSCME Local 2626, Los Angeles, CA 90071) (January–February 1982): 15–18.
   This article paraphrases advice to librarians from psychologists at a workshop given at the Los Angeles Public Library and is full of good advice on dealing with schizophrenics, paranoids, alcoholics, and other types of problem patrons.
2. Leijonhufud, Marta. "Are California's Librarians Responding to the Needs of the Mentally Disturbed? Well, Some Are Trying." *California Libraries* 35 (July 1974): 27–35.
   Details ways in which librarians are working with hospital personnel to create a therapeutic environment for patients in the public library.
3. "Mental Patients: A Forgotten Minority in the U.S." *U.S. News and World Report* (November 19, 1979): 49–52.
   Deals with the problem of release of outpatients by mental hospitals from society's perspective.
4. "Pratt Holds Seminar on the Problem Patron." *Library Journal* 105 (December 1980): 2461–62.
   Full of good advice on effective countermeasures to problem behavior in library buildings.

Case 14
Let Me Do That!

Newspapers are an essential ingredient for any library reference service. The River Bend Public Library is proud of its reference service and seeks to provide, despite severely limited resources, adequate coverage of local newspapers for factual information and historical perspective on events and issues. For example, not only does the library have cover-to-cover indexing of the *River Bend Herald* since 1916, when the library was founded, but it performs that indexing through a cooperative arrangement with the newspaper. The library staff goes through the newspaper each day, clipping out obituaries, wedding announcements, and the like and mounts them on cards that are placed in the River Bend file, maintained as a public service for the community. In comparison to online indexes such as the *National Newspaper Index*, this may seem a primitive service, but the library staff is proud of its felicitous knack of coming up with the clipping it is asked for, and few complaints have ever been voiced.

Another important newspaper service is contained in drawer after drawer of little black and yellow boxes bearing the distinctive label of *The New York Times* on microfilm. Over seventy years of world events are stored on reel-to-reel microform in the *Times,* and the library has every reel and the necessary indexes to make them accessible. The reels take up five large steel storage cabinets, and a sixth one is on order, because a year's accumulation of the *Times* represents dozens of reels in identical-looking but differently marked square boxes. The cases sit in the reference room and are very frequently used for a variety of information.

One Thursday evening in November, Nancy Groves was seated at her desk in the Reference department, going over some figures for the periodicals budget, when she noticed that a familiar scene was about to be played out in front of her. Two patrons were advancing toward her desk from two different angles, and they seemed to be about to reach her at the same time. One was a tall man who walked with a lurching, rolling motion, and the other was an extremely pretty young girl, probably a high school student.

As she had foreseen, they arrived before her at the same moment. Observing this, both the man and the girl laughed, and Nancy joined in. Looking from one to the other, she smiled and said, "Well? Who's going to be first?"

"Ladies first," said the man. He seemed to have a thickening of his speech, somewhere between a lisp and a cleft palate. Looking closely into his eyes, Nancy realized that he might be retarded, although probably not too seriously.

Turning to the girl, she took a breath and asked, "What can I do for you?"

"I need for you to get me some reels of the *New York Times*," said the girl, consulting a legal pad. "I'll be needing the reels that cover, aahhh, October 25, 1982, October 29, same year, and January 21, 1983."

"Certainly," said Nancy, reaching into a drawer to retrieve the little key that unlocked the microform cases. Before she left the desk to get the girl's microfilm boxes, she looked up at the man and asked, "Can you tell me how I can help you? Maybe it's something I can do on the way to those cases over there."

The man smiled and said, "Yeah. I think it is. I want those newspapers, too."

Nancy was delighted to hear that. Now she could serve both patrons at once and set them up at the viewers in the little carrels off to the side, and no one would be kept waiting while she wrestled with the cantankerous reel-to-reel machines that were necessary to view the *Times*. "Good," she said. "If you'll both follow me, I can fix you up with the things you need at the same time."

She led the way to the steel cabinets, key in hand, thinking how sometimes things just seemed to work out and that her job was not only rewarding, it was fun. When she got to the cabinets, she said to the girl, "Now let's see, you wanted some dates from late '82 and early '83, you said?"

"Right," said the girl, and repeated her requests, while Nancy opened and closed drawers, selecting the appropriate reels. When all three reels were in her hands, Nancy said, "Now just let me get the reels the gentleman wants, and I'll set you up and you'll be on your way."

"Oh, that's not necessary," said the girl. "I've done this so many times that I know the procedure backwards and forwards. It's simple. Really. Just give them to me and I can set them up myself, okay?"

"Well, okay," said Nancy, relieved that she could then give her full attention to the man, who might need some help with the tricky threading of the film. Handing the three boxes to the girl, she smiled gratefully and said, "Well, you're on your own, then."

The girl smiled back and disappeared into one of the three microfilm carrels recessed into the wall of the Reference department, closing the glass door behind her.

"And what was it you wanted to see?" said Nancy, smiling now at the man before her.

"Well," the man spoke haltingly. "I got to wondering what was happening on the day I was born, you know? So I heard that you had newspapers here in these little boxes, and I want to look at the headlines when I was born."

"I think that can be arranged. What's the date?"

"The 9th of March in 1958," said the man slowly.

"Fine." Nancy went to the appropriate drawer and extracted a box of film. "Now I'll set it up so you can see it."

"Let me do that!" said the man, vehemently.

"Wouldn't you like me to do it for you? It's really no trouble, and I can do it quickly and easily." Nancy was thinking about his difficulty with speech and motor coordination but knew that it would be tackless and possibly cruel to point out such obvious things to the young man.

"I'll do it, I said," said the man, holding out one huge hand for the box of film. "You let *her* do it," he said, gesturing over his shoulder toward the girl in the viewing carrel. "I can do it, too."

"Well, all right," said Nancy, a bit uncertainly, and handed the small carton to the man, after which she watched him make his way clumsily into another carrel and close the glass door behind him. Returning to the reference desk, she got distracted and thought no more about the man until she heard him calling to her from the open carrel door.

"Hey, lady," shouted the man. "I got a problem here!"

Hurrying over, Nancy entered the boothlike room and saw that the microfilm had been completely pulled from the reel and lay collapsed in a mound of spaghetti-like plastic on the floor.

"What happened?" she asked, fighting for control. "What have you done?"

The man, despite his towering height, visibly flinched. "Ahh, the reel was no good. It kind of cracked, see? And then I tried to get it back to the beginning but it started to unwind. . . ." His voice trailed off as he contemplated the mess on the floor. "I'm sorry, lady, but it could happen to anybody."

Nancy won the struggle with her temper and swallowed twice before speaking. "It's all right. I think I can get it all back the way it was," she said slowly. "So why don't you just go somewhere else, and I'll clean up here, okay?"

"I'm not finished," said the man, evenly. "I told my sister I'd look up her birthdate, too. Now I need May the 5th, 1963."

Nancy paused in the act of trying to gather the loose coils of film into her arms. "Er . . . . okay. But only if you'll let me set it up for you, this time."

"Well, see. That was an accident. That wasn't my fault just now. The reel is cheap plastic and it just cracked and the film fell out, that's all. I didn't do it. Let me do the next one by myself, please? I don't want help. I can do it. Really!"

"No way. You have two choices, Either I set up the film for you and come take it off when you're done or you don't use any more films. Now, you decide."

"It's not fair," mumbled the man.

"Maybe not, but I'm protecting the materials. These little reels are very important and difficult to replace, not to mention expensive. So make up your mind!" Nancy knew that she was being ungracious and probably rude to the man, but she just couldn't help herself.

"Yeah, all right," said the man. As Nancy carefully threaded the next reel of the *Times* for him, the man watched closely, saying "Oh, I see!" and "So that's it!" as he observed her technique. When she was finished, she turned to him and said, "It's ready for you to use. When you're done, I want you to call me. Under no circumstances are you to touch anything but this little handle here, is that understood?"

"Yes, ma'am," said the subdued man, who thanked her politely and closed the door behind her.

Nancy brooded about the incident for the next ten minutes, casting worried glances over to the microform carrel where the man sat. Finally, when she had a moment, she arose and walked down the hall to the office of Pat Broughton, the library's director. Explaining the incident to Pat, Nancy asked her if there was any way to keep people who couldn't work machines away from them.

Pat told Nancy that she, too, was concerned for the safety of the microforms and their necessary hardware, but that she felt it important to give mentally impaired people every opportunity to lead lives as normal as possible. If that meant entrusting them with valuable equipment or materials sometimes, well, so be it.

Nancy agreed with Pat in principle, but worried aloud that one day there would be a problem involving costly replacement or repair of library materials, and then what?

"Then we'll just have to accept it and deal with it," said Pat. "I just can't tell you to deny or refuse service to a patron based on what might happen.

"I suppose you're right," said Nancy, returning to her desk.

When she got back to the newspaper area, she took a look into the microform booths. The young girl was still using her machine, taking notes from the pages she was consulting. The man's booth yawned open, however, and Nancy could see something dark and formless lying beneath the machine. On closer investigation, she found that the man had left hundreds of feet of microfilm twisted into something resembling a large, black, plastic pretzel. The little yellow reel that had held the film was lying asymmetrically and broken on the floor, and about eighteen inches of film dangled jaggedly out of the take-up reel where it had been torn or ripped apart.

Nancy spun around and ran back into the reference room in search of the tall man with the pronounced limp, but he was nowhere to be seen. Furiously, she reentered the carrel and gathered together the remnants of what had once been *The New York Times* for May 2 through May 7, 1963.

After thinking about it for a few moments, she composed herself and walked once again into the office of Pat Broughton, who was bent over a filing drawer, humming to herself. Pat looked up with a smile. "What now?" she asked.

"Pat, if I were the kind who said 'I told you so' what do you think I'd be telling you now?" said Nancy, striving to keep her voice light and bantering.

Questions for Discussion

1. How can a library staff accede to the wishes of retarded or disabled patrons to do things for themselves without jeopardizing important materials or equipment?
2. As Nancy, would you have given in to the man's initial request when he pointed out that you had just let another patron handle her own films and service? If not, what would you have said to the man in denying his request?
3. Do you feel that Nancy's display of irritation was inexcusable in this case?
4. As Pat, what would you say to Nancy, now that she is telling you that her grim prophesy has come true?
5. What should the future attitude of the library towards this patron, or others like him, be?

Resources

1. Bennett, Janet M. "The Library: The Retarded Person's Alternative." *Catholic Library World* 45 (April 1974): 420–22.
   Discusses the role of the public library in attempting to mainstream mentally retarded patrons and raises potential problems.
2. Berry, John. "Crazy Willie, the Problem Patron." *Library Journal* 103 (November 15, 1978): 2279.
   An editorial urging greater understanding of the harmless but "different" people who frequent public libraries.
3. Newberry, William F. "The Last Unserved." *American Libraries* 11 (April 1980): 218–20.
   A plea for extra attention, asking that the public library consider the retarded patron as any other patron, as an individual with special needs.

A recent book containing numerous valuable chapters and bibliographies on the subject is: Thomas, James L., and Carol H. Thomas, eds. *Library Services for the Handicapped Adult*. Phoenix, AZ: The Oryx Press, 1982.

Case 15
I'm Not Drunk, but Some
Thinkle Peep I Am!

In the gathering gloom of an early winter's evening, the electric front door of the River Bend Public Library swung open to admit a large man who lurched from side to side as he tracked snow on the vestibule carpet. Muttering to himself, the man stood, indecisively swaying, and then stumbled into the Reference department, where he literally fell into one of the easy chairs over by the window, and fell again, this time into instantaneous and noisy sleep.

His snoring and sprawling caused everyone near him to take notice, and the sharp reek of cheap whiskey began to permeate the atmosphere of the room as he exhaled through his gaping mouth. Irwin Rossiter, the library's custodian who doubled as evening security guard three times a week, shook his gray head in disgust as he spied the man sleeping in the chair. Irwin had seen his share of drunks in his time, both on the job, he conceded, and in his own shaving mirror, but now it bothered him greatly that people could have so little pride in themselves as to become blind, staggering drunk in public.

Carefully, Irwin watched the sleeping man for a while. Other than the snorts and whistles of his alcoholic slumber, the man was doing nothing to upset anyone. He had probably just run out of money at some corner tavern and had gone out into the frigid night to return to his bed, if he *had* a bed. The man's clothes were grimed and crusted with filth and stains, and Irwin thought it a good bet that the man might be a vagrant as well as a drunk.

Irwin further guessed that the man, on his aimless or deliberate walk through the snowy streets of downtown, had suddenly become aware of how cold the evening had grown and had shuffled into the library to escape the north wind for a while. Seemingly, he had just made it to the armchair he now occupied before his intoxicated brain had shut down. What he needed was a chance to sleep it off, and Irwin was torn between the desire to pitch the damned drunk back into the snow from whence he had come and wanting to just ignore him for the rest of the evening.

Whatever happened to the man, however, he couldn't be allowed to sleep so noisily. His snores brought to Irwin's mind a sawmill he had once worked in, and several people were staring pointedly at him, obviously distracted from their work. Nudging the man gently on the upper arm, Irwin said softly, "Hey! Buddy! Wake up, willya?" The man's jacket was so frayed and soiled that Irwin really didn't want to touch him any more than was necessary.

Nothing happened. Irwin poked the man, more sharply this time, with a leathery fingernail. "C'mon, pal. You know you can't sleep it off in here, so why don't you just get on home, whaddaya say?"

"Got no home," the man muttered in a moment of understanding, and then fell back asleep, snoring even more loudly than before.

"Want me to call the police and tell them that we got a vagrant here? You won't like it in the drunk tank, pal. I know."

The man opened one red-rimmed brown eye and regarded Irwin blearily. "At least it's warm."

"Why do you lousy drunks have to wander in here and flop?" said Irwin in a loud, aggrieved tone of voice, trying to embarrass the man into alertness.

"Not a drunk," muttered the man.

"Hell, you're not! You're a worthless, lousy drunk, and if you got no home, you're worse than worthless."

"Not a drunk, I said," repeated the man, trying to sit up. "Had a few, maybe, but that don't make me no drunk. Don't you be callin' me no drunk or I'll mess up your face."

The possibility that the man resented being called what he was and was feeling belligerent about it was just too much for Irwin, who had long ago conquered a similar problem and now led a life of exemplary temperance. With one fluid motion he seized the man by both his shoulders and jerked him to his feet. Going behind him and wincing at the powerful smell of mingled sweat and booze, Irwin began propelling him, none too gently, in the direction of the front door of the library.

Without warning, the man took a swing at Irwin. A powerhouse right, but wildly thrown and mistimed, it missed Irwin's jaw by a good six inches. Quickly deciding that enough was enough, Irwin began shoving and pulling the man toward the door, saying nothing further, but grunting with exertion and rage. The man offered no further resistance, allowing himself to be pulled along, and muttering to anyone he saw that he was not a drunk and that it was a free country, wasn't it?

Pat Broughton, the library's director, had been working late over some accounts payable, and she couldn't miss hearing the noise of the men's confrontation as they walked past the conference room where she was working. Alarmed, she pulled open the door and saw Irwin locked in a sort of awkward embrace with a disheveled and disreputable-looking patron.

"Irwin," she called out to the older man, "would you mind stepping over here for a moment?"

"In a minute, Pat," he growled back, "I'm a tad busy just now."

"Irwin?" said Pat, somewhat more forcefully. "Now!"

Nodding his understanding, Irwin let go of the other man, who slumped uncaringly against the inside front wall of the building and seemed to fall asleep. Irwin trotted over, looking annoyed, and inspected his uniform for signs of dirt he might have picked up through contact.

"What is going on?" Pat came right to the point.

"Lousy drunk," responded Irwin gruffly. "Got a skinfull and thought he'd come in here and sleep it off. Strictly against the rules, isn't it? I'm sending him packing. Let him go to the bus station or someplace else. He doesn't belong here, that's for sure."

"I just heard on the radio that it's currently seventeen degrees in town, going down to around ten tonight," said Pat, meaningfully.

"Yeah, I know. But why does he have to come in here with his problems? I don't want him to freeze out there, Pat. I just don't want him in here with his whiskey breath, his snoring, and his filthy, lousy clothes!"

"If he goes out into the night and passes out in an alley, he could be dead by morning, Irwin. Do you want that on your conscience if you read about it tomorrow in the paper?"

"No, I suppose not, It's just. . . ."

"I can understand your feelings, but I want you to do something for me." She fished briefly in her jacket pocket and withdrew a couple of coins, giving them to Irwin. "Go down into the basement and buy the man a cup of hot, black coffee from the machine down there. Then try to get it into him. Take him into the staff room and wait for me. I'll make a few telephone calls and join you there. Understand?"

"Yeah. Sorry, Pat. I just got carried away, I guess. Drunks really get me steamed. I don't want anything bad to happen to the guy. He just reminds me of what I was like once, and it makes me sick, that's all."

"Sure. Now get some coffee for the man and help him back to the staff room. I'll see who's available at this time of day to come get him."

Looking somewhat chastened, Irwin strode over to the slumped man and began trying to get him back on his feet. A crowd of curious children had gathered by the door to watch the goings on, but one snarl from Irwin and they dispersed. Pat went into her office and found a battered copy of the latest River Bend *Directory of Community Services*. Selecting a number, she began dialing.

Questions for Discussion

1. How can a public library avoid becoming a refuge or shelter for drunks, addicts, vagrants, and others who are drawn by the free atmosphere of such a facility?
2. How can a library staff balance the needs of one patron against those of all others present at the time of such an incident?
3. If you were Irwin, how would you have handled the situation in question?
4. As Pat Broughton, whom would you call first to come and take care of this man?
5. As Pat, what would you say to Irwin in the aftermath of this incident to keep him from such impulsive behavior next time?

Resources

1. Cherry, S. S. "The Library: Fortress of Dreams." *American Libraries* 13 (February 1982): 112.
   Results of a survey of public libraries and how they handle people who fall asleep in the building.
2. DeRosa, Frank J. "The Disruptive Patron." *Library & Archival Security* 3 (Fall/Winter 1980): 29–37.
   Discusses ways in which a library's security force may deal with drunks and other classes of nuisance patrons, in terms of the New York State Penal Code.
3. Griffith, Jack W. "Of Vagrants and Vandals and Library Things." *Wilson Library Bulletin* 52 (June 1978): 769+.
   Points out that librarians are not social workers, psychiatrists, or police, but that occasionally they are called upon, in the line of duty, to act in those capacities.

Case 16
Captain Ripoff

The annual chore known as inventory pleased nobody on the staff of the
River Bend Public Library. As the saying went, however, "it's a dirty job,
but somebody's got to do it." A recent review of the shelf list versus the
shelves in the Science and Technology department had revealed an interesting and alarming fact: at least fifty of the library's reference titles in
science, including every volume of the *McGraw-Hill Encyclopedia of
Science and Technology,* were missing since last year at the same time.
Once notified of this fact, department head Bob Castlebury had turned the
problem over in his mind and decided that such gaps in the collection did not
represent random thefts. He believed strongly that most of the disappear-
ances were the work of a single thief, and he had devised a plot to try to
figure out who it was.

For several days, Bob had instructed the pages and clerks in the
department to make unscheduled walking tours of the reference stacks and
to report to him anyone who spent a great deal of time consulting certain
multivolume sets of science and technology information. Ginny Christopher, who worked after school as a page, had quietly discovered that one
particular man, elderly and bespectacled, spent long hours out in the
reference stacks and that he took his briefcase with him when he entered the
area. This would not have been unusual, since anyone who left an expensive leather briefcase unattended was almost asking to have it stolen, yet
Bob Castlebury felt sure that he had now identified the man as the source of
all the unexplained removals of valuable reference books, and today he put
his plan into action.

First, he alerted Irwin Rossiter, the custodian and security guard, to be
standing by the front door between 4:00 and 5:00 p.m., the customary time
at which the man was known to leave the building. Irwin agreed but
questioned the likely result of such a stake-out. The library had installed a
magnetic alarm system at its exit expressly to prevent such theft. A thin
magnetized strip of metal placed down the spine of each library book was
designed to trigger the alarm and simultaneously lock the gate in the event

that anyone tried to take an unchecked-out book from the building. This procedure had replaced the time-worn practice of having security guards stationed at the doors and was seen as more cost-effective.

Even Irwin, however, had to admit that it would probably take an observant patron only a few moments to figure out how the security system worked and a few more to beat it. Therefore, the system was not foolproof, and in any event, a person who really wanted to could steal books in several ways, such as sailing them through open washroom windows into the bushes below and retrieving them when outside, to give just one method as an example.

Still, Bob assured Irwin that he was certain that that day they were going to catch the old man red-handed with a book or two in his briefcase. Nervously, Bob watched the man, although he tried not to stare or be obvious in his surveillance. Finally, at about 4:30, the man came out of the stacks, put on his coat, snapped his briefcase shut with a loud click, and began to make his way downstairs to the main door. That was the moment Bob had waited for, and he called Irwin at the front door to be ready. After delivering his message, Bob scurried downstairs, wanting to be in at the denouement of this dramatic moment.

As Bob arrived on the first floor on the elevator, he saw that the elderly man was walking slowly through the swinging gate of the security system, which was not activated by whatever he carried in his briefcase. As the man smiled and said "goodnight" to Irwin, Irwin quietly took him aside and asked him to open the briefcase. Bob, his eyes glittering in anticipation, watched avidly.

"Why do you want me to open the briefcase?" asked the man, looking puzzled.

"Probable cause," growled Irwin, whose two sons were policemen.

"And if I refuse to open it?"

"Then I'll have to ask you to wait here while I call the police."

"Look here," said the man, "I walked through that gate and nothing happened. What is it that you're accusing me of?"

"I am accusing you of nothing," said Irwin. "Just open the case, and I'll be satisfied once I've looked at what you've got in there, all right?"

"I know my rights, you know. There are laws against illegal search and seizure."

"Sure there are," said Irwin patiently. "Now I ask you again. You going to open the case for me or for the police? The choice is yours."

His head down, the man handed Irwin the briefcase, muttering something unintelligible.

"What was that?" asked Irwin.

"I said I was going to bring them all back eventually," the man said, beginning to sob softly.

Inside the briefcase, Irwin found two volumes of *Van Nostrand's Scientific Encyclopedia* from the Science and Technology department, a lined notebook, a pair of reading glasses in a brown vinyl case, some cookies in a plastic bag, several pencils and pens, and a small folding umbrella.

Bob Castlebury walked forward and asked, "Why do you steal our books? You know that you're free to use them anytime."

"I was going to bring them all back when I had everything," came the mumbled response from the man who was studying his scuffed shoetops through tear-filled eyes.

"But what is the purpose of stealing them?"

"I'll tell you the truth. I don't know."

"And what else do you have of ours?"

"I don't know. Couple dozen other books. The whole McGraw-Hill set. Few other things. You can have them all back. I wasn't going to keep them. . . ."

"It's like a game to you, isn't it?" Bob checked the two books he was holding and saw that the magnetized metal strips had been removed.

"I guess so. Say, you're not going to tell the police about this, are you? I never planned to keep the books or sell them. I only wanted to *have* them at home for a little while. Then I was planning to bring them all back in the same condition as they left here. Please let me off and I'll bring everything back first thing in the morning!"

Irwin and Bob exchanged glances. Irwin then asked the man for identification, and the man silently handed over a leather wallet containing the usual cards and a considerable quantity of money.

"Mr. Weed, it says here. That you?" asks Irwin.

"Yes. George Weed. I didn't steal that wallet or the money. And the books are in good condition. I just did it for the hell of it, you know? Didn't you guys ever do anything just because it was there and so easy? I don't know why I do it, honestly. I can afford to buy most of the books I want, and the library, as you say, has the rest for me to read or consult. But please let me off this time and I'll never do it again. If my daughter and son-in-law ever found out that I was doing this, they'd die of embarrassment, and I'd never get to see my grandchildren anymore. Please? Can't you give me a break? I promise. My right hand to God, I'll have every book I took back here at 9:00 tomorrow morning."

Irwin was nodding sympathetically by this time, but Bob was wondering if the man were an accomplished con artist in addition to being an unprincipled thief or a kleptomaniac. When Irwin hinted that the library might be willing to overlook the thefts if he could accompany Mr. Weed to his home and retrieve all library property in his possession, Bob remained silent. With a nod of gratitude, the man led the way to his car. Irwin followed along with a look of compassion on his seamed face. Bob watched them go, torn between outrage and pity. Finally, he turned to go back to his department, saying to himself, "What the hell, it *is* Christmas time."

Questions for Discussion

1. Do you think that the library employees have the right to ask patrons to open their packages and briefcases when they are suspicious of theft?
2. As Bob, would you have insisted that Irwin call the police and let them handle the matter?
3. What do you think of Irwin's implied offer to overlook the thefts if the man will return all the materials he has stolen from the library?
4. Assuming that all materials are returned in good condition, would you, as the library's director, be willing to consider the matter closed now?
5. If this patron is a true kleptomaniac and the man is only caught but not cured, how can the library take steps to ensure that he will not be up to his old tricks again in the near future?

Resources

1. Bahr, Robert, and Alice Harrison Bahr. "Throwing the Book at Library Thieves." *Parade Magazine* (April 8, 1979): 10–13.
   Explains how some libraries have begun getting tough with those caught stealing materials.
2. "College Librarians Nab Major Book Theft Suspect." *American Libraries* 12 (June 1981): 303.
   The case of the infamous James Richard Shinn, who stole 73 rare and expensive books from three major research libraries, having a total value of over $30,000. Shinn's method involved removing the magnetized strips from the books.
3. Flagg, Gordon. "Librarians Meet to Fight Book Thieves." *American Libraries* 14 (November 1983): 648–50.
   Describes Oberlin, Ohio conference attended by librarians, booksellers, lawyers, and law enforcement agents. Issues discussed include the importance

of theft reporting, visibly marking all library materials, dealing with the law, and the pros and cons of closing stacks.

4. Griffith, J. W. "Library Thefts: A Problem That Won't Go Away." *American Libraries* 9 (April 1978): 224–27.
   Echoes the sentiments of Thompson's lament (below) but lists a few preventive steps a library may attempt to reduce chances of loss.

5. Thompson, Lawrence S. "New Reflections on Bibliokleptomania." *Library Security Newsletter* 1 (January 1975): 8–9.
   The author theorizes that things don't change much and that book thieves will be with us as long as we have libraries.

Case 17
The River Bend Flash Strikes Again

Despite the fact that the city of River Bend was geographically located in an area marked "temperate" by climatologists, winter could be very harsh as the winds off the great prairies came screaming across the plains, bearing snow and freezing rain and battering the city with frightful storms. With the coming of spring, the city greened up rapidly, and the nasty conditions of winter were forgotten. People moved outdoors, and the long, hot summer days were spent, by a large segment of the population, under the midwestern sky.

The River Bend Public Library seemed to have its seasons, too. The library building, like virtually all similar structures, was occasionally prey to persons who came inside not for any appropriate reason, nor even just to get warm in wintertime, but for bizarre and deviant purposes of their own. At least one man in recent years seemed to have in mind whatever enjoyment he could get from scaring the wits out of people and had thus created quite a problem for the library staff.

Specifically, this man liked to creep up on young girls in the library's stacks when no one else was near. As several upset, angry, or frightened witnesses had reported, the man would make some sudden sound, such as clearing his throat loudly. When the victim looked up or turned around to locate the source of the noise, she was obliged to see that the man had lowered his trousers to the level of his knees and was furiously working his hand up and down.

By the time the screaming girl could get out front to tell someone in authority of her shocking experience, the man was typically nowhere to be seen, seemingly having evaporated into thin air.

Over the past two years, eleven such incidents had been reported to library staff members, who then forwarded them to the police. Frustratingly, descriptions by the victims of their assailant were fragmentary and sometimes contradictory, and, to date, no arrests have been made. The

River Bend Police Department had therefore been unable to do much about this man, whom the local press had dubbed "The Flash," because of his *modus operandi*. All they could be reasonably certain of is that these outrageous acts were very likely the work of one man, a Caucasian somewhere between twenty and forty years of age, with nothing terribly unusual in his appearance or attire. Each time he had struck, he had created terror in his victim, always a young female who had been alone at the time of the incident and who had been badly frightened but otherwise unharmed.

If there were any common thread running through all eleven accounts, it was that each person he accosted was so unnerved by her experience that she wanted no part of anything like it again, and that she was unable to recall more than a sketchy description of the man and his tactics. During the long, dark winter days, staff members grew jittery when out in the stacks alone, and some members of the public had made it clear that they were avoiding certain parts of the building until the man was caught and stopped. A female police officer, who had hung around in the stacks for days, pretending to browse, had been unsuccessful in causing the man to take the bait and, with winter coming on again, the library was bracing itself for the reappearance of "The Flash."

On a blustery day in early November, Hilary Brewer, a page in the library's Circulation department, was pushing a booktruck laden with recent returns slowly through the stack aisles behind the desk area. Thinking wistfully about someone she hoped to see at school the next day, Hilary was poking along, replacing books in their Dewey Decimal order on the shelves when she heard a loud noise of someone clearing his throat coming from the next stack aisle. Without thinking about it, she peered through an opening in the shelves of books and saw the exhibitionist engaged in his favorite pastime.

All at once, Hilary remembered what had happened last winter. She had seen the panic on the faces of several girls her age or younger who had had brief encounters with a man such as this, and now she realized that it was happening to her. Fighting down terror and revulsion, she looked again, to make certain that it really was what she thought it was, and not just somebody doing something innocent in the gloomy stacks. Once she was sure that the flasher was indeed . . . well, flashing . . . she walked deliberately and rapidly to the stairway and, once safely inside, ran down the stairs to the basement, her heart beating wildly.

Irwin Rossiter, the custodian and security guard, was just polishing off his fourth cup of coffee of the afternoon in his office when young Hilary burst unceremoniously into the room. She quickly explained the situation, her words cascading over each other in her excitement and fear.

"Did you see what the guy was wearing?" Irwin asked her.

"Wearing? No. Wait. Yes. Let me think," said the confused girl.

"Take your time," murmured Irwin, soothingly.

"I remember!" Hilary smiled at the unexpended memory. "I was so grossed out by what he was doing that I forgot what he had on for a minute, but I remember it now. A tan coat and dark trousers. I don't know what color pants for sure, but they were dark. That I remember."

"Good. Now maybe we can get this guy," said Irwin, abruptly jumping up and pushing Hilary ahead of him through the door to the custodial office.

"Where are we going?" she asked, breathlessly.

"To the front door," he explained curtly. "If we haven't missed him, we've got him. He's got to leave that way, and when you point him out to me, the bastard is mine." Irwing grinned wolfishly at the thought of what he'd like to do to the perverted prowler who had once again staked out a claim to the library's stacks as his winter hunting grounds.

"You mean I have to identify him?"

"Look, Hilary, all you have to do is stand next to me and watch men as they leave the building. You watch them and I'll watch you. When you nod your head at me, I'll know that you've spotted the guy who did this thing, and I'll nab him. Also, I'll tell who's ever on the circ desk to have a police unit outside, and we'll hustle this psycho off to jail so fast his head'll swim."

"I don't know, Irwin," said Hilary, nervously. "It was dark out there and I only saw him for a moment, and my attention wasn't really on his clothes, you know what I'm saying?"

"Yeah, I do." Irwin regarded her thoughtfully. "You're saying that you're scared, aren't you?"

Hilary nodded. "See, what if he saw me finger him to you, and he came back some day. . . ?" Her face showed extreme anxiety at the thought of such a man bent on revenge with her as the target.

"Hilary, you just trust old Irwin to protect you, you hear? Now, all you got to do is nod your head and I'll do the rest. You don't have to say anything or stick around, and he probably won't even see you. Does that help?"

"Yeah," she said, "I guess."

They arrived at the front door and took up stations in such a way that Hilary could see anyone who was leaving, while Irwin could look at her while appearing to be gazing out the glass doorway. Carolyn Harada, working the circulation desk that afternoon, had been told to summon a police car and have it wait unobtrusively outside. All was in readiness, and Irwin and Hilary waited and watched for the man they were sure must come past them.

They waited for two hours. Anticipation gave way to boredom and disappointment, while dozens of men fitting the general description of the flasher passed them and went out into the cold evening. One of the men wearing a tan raincoat and dark trousers turned out to be the father of Hilary's best friend, Susie Cameron, who nodded and stopped to pass the time for a moment. In all, at least fifteen men dressed as Hilary remembered the stack assailant to have been left the building while they stood there, but no one triggered her memory or seemed to look very much like the person she had seen.

At precisely eight o'clock, the door swung open and a uniformed police officer whose nameplate identified him as "Hodges" walked in and strolled over to Irwin and Hilary.

"Ah, Rossiter, we're kind of busy tonight and the desk sergeant said that I should come in after two hours if you didn't bring me anybody to take downtown."

"Yeah, I hear you," said Irwin, despondently. "Guess we missed the guy while Hilary, here, was coming to tell me about it. He may still be in the building, but I'm coming to doubt it. Go on in, Hodges. Sorry we wasted your time."

The policeman shrugged and turned to leave. "Better luck next time," he called over his shoulder. "I'd really like to put guys like that away, man. I have daughters of my own," he added, for Hilary's benefit.

Hilary felt depressed. Irwin had asked her dozens of times over the past two hours whether this man or that one might be "the one" but she had been unwilling or unable to commit herself in each case. All in all, it had been an unnerving afternoon, and now that it was evening, she just wanted to go home. Gratefully, she accepted Irwin's offer of a ride home and, even though he casually waved off her apologies, she felt that somehow she had failed him in not being able to come up with the culprit, who would, no doubt, roam free to catch other unwary women alone in the stacks.

"It's going to be a long hard winter," said Irwin, as he led the way to his car after the day's work ended. Hilary thought of this, and the image of that horrible man out there in the stacks every afternoon while she was shelving books made her want to turn in her booktruck and quit her job.

Questions for Discussion

1. How can a library guard against people who wander around the building seeking to gratify themselves at the expense of the unwary patrons or staff members who encounter them?

2. When such a person is caught, what should be the library's role in dealing with him? Is it strictly a police matter or should security guards be given the authority to apprehend him? Can it be assumed that he is not physically dangerous or aggressive?
3. What can be done, in general, to make remote stack areas of large buildings safer for staff and patrons?
4. As Irwin, how would you devise a strategy designed to catch this man?
5. As Hilary, how might you seek to make your job (and those of your co-workers) safer?

Resources

1. Groark, James J. "Assertion: A Technique for Handling Troublesome Library Patrons." *Catholic Library World* 51 (November 1979): 172–73.
2. The Schenectady County Public Library's "Problem Patron Manual" (see Case 1) has a section (page 35) dealing with the library's response to sexual deviants, girl/boy watchers, flashers, etc.

See also Kantorowski, D. S., and Davis, P. W. "Meaning and Process in Erotic Offensiveness: An Exposé of Exposeés." *Urban Life* 5 (October 1976): 377–96, a study of the reactions of women who have encountered male strangers engaging in what is referred to as "exhibitionism" or "indecent exposure."

Case 18
Grand Mal

There is something extremely depressing about an all-day rain in August. All over town, people must cope with the literal washout of their plans: barbecues, garden parties, swimming days, and ball games must be postponed, and children have to be entertained indoors. Even those who had planned to work on their lawns and their tans must accede to the inexorable will of the weather. When such things happen on Saturday, it's even worse.

Saturday, August 18th, was one of those days in River Bend. The rain slanted in from the southwest, rendering umbrellas almost useless, while those wearing raincoats sweltered in the sultry heat. The riverfront parks, the tennis courts, and the outdoor pools stood abandoned under gray, lowering clouds, and people all over town stared dismally through their windows at the rain-swollen streets and gutters and lawns, wondering what to do with their time.

A good number of them elected to come to the public library. In fact, Carolyn Harada, one of the circulation clerks, couldn't ever remember seeing so many people in the place on a summer Saturday afternoon. Well, they had to be someplace, and the library had always seemed to appeal to those with time on their hands, in ways both good and bad. Carolyn was busy checking books out for a straggling line of raincoated and umbrella-toting citizens, wondering how many rainy Saturdays it would take to boost circulation over the million mark for the year, when the sound began.

It began low, reminiscent of one of those air-raid sirens placed on the tops of city buildings and rose slowly through the scale to a fairly high note that was sustained for a moment before falling off to a sort of sob. It took a few moments before Carolyn could sort out what she had heard and classify it as having come from a human throat. Open-mouthed patrons in the check-out line reflected her surprise and alarm, and, for a while, they all just stood and stared at one another in wild surmise.

Then Carolyn sprang into action. Calling into the back room for Althea Jackson to take over the desk for a moment, Carolyn raced around the curving circulation counter and into the reading room, from which the sound had emanated. She could see nothing as she entered the room, due to the large knot of people that had gathered to surround whomever or whatever was lying on the floor in their midst.

With considerable effort, Carolyn shouldered her way through the throng until she had reached the center of the circle they had formed. There, lying on the floor, was a woman of indeterminate age, seemingly unconscious, her lower jaw working up and down rapidly in convulsions, and her booted feet beating a soggy tattoo on the linoleum. Her breathing was very loud and her flushed face showed distended veins as though she had exercised strenuously for hours. While her eyes were tightly shut, Carolyn could see that her eyeballs were racing right and left beneath their lids.

Carolyn knelt by the woman's side, wondering what to do. Suddenly aware of the crowd pressing forward on all sides, she bellowed "Get back! Please get back and give her room to breathe!" The inner members of the circle retreated a little, having to shove the second row of onlookers backward to widen their perimeter. "Is anyone a doctor here?" demanded Carolyn, hopefully. No answer. Carolyn looked down at the writhing woman. A superficial check of her condition revealed that there seemed to be no obstructions to her breathing, although the woman's inhalations and exhalations were irregular and somewhat ragged. Uncertain as to whether she ought to touch the woman, Carolyn hovered unsteadily over her until she reached a decision. Then she opened the woman's blouse, uncomfortably conscious of the eyes of the onlookers, and fumbled out a tag that was hanging around her neck. On its steel surface was an engraved inscription:

> My name is Louise DeBold. I live at 29 Fountain Avenue, River Bend 66616. I am an epileptic. In the event of a *grand mal* seizure, try to keep me warm and comfortable and away from crowds. Just let me breathe and I will recover. No hospitalization is necessary. Thank you.

Shaking her head, Carolyn decided to obey the instructions on the tag and hope that she wasn't committing a fatal error by not summoning a doctor right away. As Irwin Rossiter, the guard in charge of security on Saturdays, came puffing up, Carolyn asked him to keep the crowd of curious bystanders away, and as they fell back, in response to his commanding growls, she bent again to examine the woman.

Carolyn seemed to remember something concerning the danger that epileptics might swallow their tongues, but she hesitated to place any of her fingers inside the woman's mouth, which was furiously working up and down, her teeth clacking together in her seizure. Something about a washcloth occurred to her, but she knew that there were no washcloths in the library restrooms, and besides, the woman might gag on anything placed in her mouth.

Hoping for the best, Carolyn decided to do nothing about the poor woman's breathing unless it seemed to become labored. She concentrated instead on such things as listening for pulse, heartbeat, and other general signs, as she noted with relief that the outward symptoms of the *grand mal* seizure were diminishing quickly. Making her as comfortable as possible, Carolyn sat at the woman's head, watching carefully for any problems that might still emerge. Louise DeBold's purse, which had fallen at the side of the stricken woman, was handed to Donna Campbell for safekeeping behind the circulation desk, and Irwin was doing his usual job of keeping people back by virtue of his intimidating and commanding voice. All seemed to be under control, and Carolyn was congratulating herself on the way in which things had been handled when she noticed that the woman on the floor had opened her eyes and was regarding her with an expression which seemed to combine embarrassment and concern.

"Ohhhhhh," she groaned, and Carolyn bent over her to catch her words. "Not again!"

"I'm afraid so," she responded, "but you're all right now."

"My purse. . . " the woman's eyes darted around frantically.

"We have it. It's safe."

A sigh of relief. "I want to thank you, Miss. . . ."

"Harada. Carolyn Harada, and no thanks are necessary."

Louise struggled to sit up, and Carolyn applied gentle pressure to her shoulders to keep her lying flat on the floor. "Just take it easy for a little while, why don't you?" she said. "When you're ready, I'll help you into the staff lounge and fix you a nice cup of tea, if you like."

"You're very kind," said Louise with a smile. "Tell me, did I scream? Was it very disturbing?"

"Well, yes, you screamed, and no, it wasn't disturbing. It got people's attention, all right, but pay them no mind. Now, are you sure you don't need a doctor?"

"No. In fact, I feel much better now. I'm fine, really. This has happened before. I think things are okay. Look, Carolyn, (may I call you that?) I am really much improved, and I've taken up enough of your time, so why don't I just nip out into the stacks and get what I came here for, and you can get back to your desk?"

"Well, if you're quite sure. . . ."

"Sure. Don't worry about me. Things like this have happened to me all my life. As long as I don't fall down in front of a bus, I'll live a long, statistically normal life. And thanks for the offer of tea. Another day, I'd love to. Today, I'm on a pretty tight schedule. My daughter will be out of her ballet lesson in," she consulted her watch, "twenty minutes."

"I can stay right here, if you need me," said Carolyn, torn between concern and duty. Around her, people were returning to whatever else they had been doing, spurred on by Irwin's rumbles that the show was over and that they must have better things to do.

Gently but firmly, the woman declined offers of further assistance, and, rising unaided, she went over to the desk, retrieved her purse, and then moved off into the stacks, looking little the worse for her experience. Carolyn, however, felt shaken and as though she was a ball of nerve endings.

As she watched her go, Carolyn said with admiration to Donna, whom she was relieving at the desk, "There goes one tough little lady!" Donna agreed, smiling, and then indicated to her that the woman was on her way back to the desk. Carolyn turned around and watched her approach.

"Do you like chocolate chip cookies with big raisins in them?" asked Louise DeBold.

"Er. . . yes. Sure. Who doesn't?"

"Then expect a surprise on Monday morning." Louise was brushing a few spots of debris off her raincoat which had been under her when she had fallen down.

"Oh, you don't have to. . ." began Carolyn, flustered.

"I know it. I want to."

"Fine, then. I'll share them with my crew, here."

"See you then." Once again, the woman made her way toward the stack area.

Carolyn returned to her duties, noting unobtrusively several approving comments that those who had witnessed the incident were making about her quick thinking and decisive actions. Within herself, however, she was not so sure. Everything had turned out all right, but Carolyn knew that she had wasted precious seconds while she was paralyzed with indecision, and she knew that she, and the whole staff, for that matter, could do with some simple training in first aid and emergency procedures on the job. Just being a mother and well acquainted with Band-Aids and Mercurochrome didn't prepare one for the shock and suddenness of a *grand mal* seizure, that was for sure.

Thinking these thoughts, Carolyn was startled to hear another loud commotion, out in the stacks, from the sound of it. She sprinted nimbly around the desk and took off at a dead run, finding her way blocked on a couple of occasions by ubiquitous rubberneckers who seemed to gather from nowhere like sharks or piranha do at the slightest taste of blood in the water.

When she got into the stacks she swerved left in response to the noise of the crowd and burrowed forcefully through the crowd until she was again kneeling at the head of Louise DeBold, who lay, for the second time that afternoon, gasping and wriggling on the library floor. "Hang in there, Louise," she shouted into the contorted face of the struggling woman, "Carolyn's here!"

Questions for Discussion

1. What kinds of instruction and information should be given to library staff members concerning methods and procedures for dealing with sudden illness or injury in the building? How can new staff members be made aware of such information?
2. As Carolyn, would you have insisted on calling for medical assistance for the woman, despite her protestations that she was feeling fine after her initial attack?
3. Now that Louise has had a second epileptic episode, what would you do for her this time?
4. On a related matter, do you see any ethical problems with library staff members accepting gifts of food, or the like, as rewards for favors rendered?

Resources

1. Henderson, John, M.D. *Emergency Medical Guide*, 4th ed. New York: McGraw-Hill, 1980.
   A copy of this or any other convenient and inexpensive medical guide for the layperson should be handy at every desk or department in the library. Such guides treat fainting, heart attacks, epileptic seizure, etc., and prescribe interim treatment until a physician or paramedic can be summoned.
2. Pettit, Katherine D. "Emergencies and Problems: A Procedures Manual for Trinity University Library." Trinity University, San Antonio, Texas. 1981. 73 p.
   This manual, while specific to a particular (academic) library situation, has application to any library whose staff must deal with sudden emergency situations.
3. Timko, Lola C. "Teaching Communication with Problem Patrons in Emergency Situations." *Journal of Education for Librarianship* 18 (Winter 1978): 244–46.
   This author stresses methods by which library staff can be better prepared to deal with emergency and unexpected situations with a minimum of panic and confusion.

Case 19
The Breather

"History and Travel department," said Burt Stone into the telephone, "may I help you?"

"Yes. Good afternoon. I would like to speak to Mrs. Parsons, please." The man's voice was cultured and had a trace of a central European accent.

"Certainly, sir," replied Burt. "Please hold on and I'll tell her."

"Thank you very much," he heard, as he pushed the hold button on the phone.

Walking back into the staff room of the department, Burt called, "Emilia! Emilia!" fighting to be heard over the din of the jackhammers that were tearing up a section of the drive outside the building.

"Over here, Burt," she responded from behind a range of shelving.

"There you are. Telephone for you."

"Do you know who it is?"

"No. Want me to ask?"

A shrug. "Never mind, I'll get it." Emilia rose and went out into the reading room to answer the telephone. A few moments later, Burt heard a sudden sound like a mouse's squeak, followed by the clatter of the telephone receiver dropping to the floor. Racing out into the reading area, he beheld his friend and colleague Emilia Parsons standing next to the reference desk, her hands to her mouth, trembling. Several library patrons were staring at her, their expressions mirroring curiosity or concern.

Without even thinking about it, Burt threw a protective arm around the waist of Emilia and pulled her gently back into the workroom and out of public view. "What happened?" he asked.

Burt had worked with Emilia for over two years, and despite the difference in their ages, he felt something like romantic love for her. She, a quiet widow of forty-two, had always been kind to him, especially when his temper or awkwardness had gotten him into trouble with other members of the staff, and Burt, at twenty-six, was devoted to her, although he had never betrayed his true feelings to anyone else. The sight of Emilia pale and trembling now moved him to protective concern for her, and he felt outrage that someone might have upset his favorite person.

"It's just this man . . . on the telephone . . . he won't leave me alone," she finally managed to say.

"What man?"

"That's just it. I don't know."

"What does he say to you?"

"Nothing, really. He calls me every afternoon, and once he's sure that it's me on the phone, he just starts breathing heavily, louder and louder. . . and then I hang up."

"Does he say anything dirty to you? Talk about sex?"

"No. I'd know how to handle that. A couple of years ago, there was one of those sickies who used to call here whenever he got bored. He'd talk to anybody female who answered the phone and say disgusting things about what he wanted to do to us. I admit I was pretty nervous about it for a while, but then Barbara Jordan (oh—that's right—she left before you got here) recognized his voice. He was just a businessman who got his thrills calling the library on slow afternoons and throwing a scare into women. So Barbara and I went over to him one day while he was reading a magazine and told him that if he didn't stop bothering us, we'd tell his wife. He pretended that he didn't know what we were talking about, but you know what? Those calls stopped immediately. And it was all a bluff, anyway. We didn't have any way to call his wife, or even find out if he had one." Emilia took a long, shuddering breath and went on in a more somber tone of voice. "But this man, whoever he is, is different. Evil. He scares me, Burt. He got my home telephone number and I hear from him most evenings now. At home, he doesn't even have to speak. He just starts breathing into the telephone. Of course, I hang up right away, and lately I've taken my phone off the hook at night, but I have to tell you, I'm scared."

Clumsily, Burt patted her arm. "C'mon," he said. "We're calling the police about this."

"I did," she explained, wearily. "Just like it says in the telephone directories, I called the police. They made me feel foolish, though, when I had to confess that the caller had neither threatened me nor said anything obscene."

"So, they did nothing for you?"

"Well, they advised me to get an unlisted number and to call again if this creep ever started saying things to me. Big comfort that was. I called the phone company. D'you know what it costs just to get a new number? Forty-five dollars just to change numbers, and a monthly charge for the unlisted one. And besides, how do I get an unlisted number here at the library? Shall I refuse to answer the phone?"

She stood glaring at Burt, frustrated and angry. He wanted to calm her down. "If I ever get my hands on this guy. . . ."

"You'll do nothing. Hear me? Nothing. Look, I don't want this guy beaten up. He's probably just some disturbed and pathetic person who has only one way to make an impact on people's lives. I just want him to stop doing this to me and to turn himself in for psychological help."

"Emilia, is there anything I can do? I could come over and stay with you for a few days. I'd sleep on your couch. Answer the phone. Whatever."

"Thanks for the offer, Burt. I mean it. But I suppose that the police are right. He hasn't done anything to me or shown his face, and I hang up at the first breath when he does call, so I guess I just have to endure it until he gets tired of his nasty little game."

"And you're all right?"

"Sure. Never better. It just gets to me sometimes."

"Okay, but I'm around if you need me. Let me answer the phones when we're on duty together."

"Nonsense. I just had a bad moment, that's all. Forget about it, all right?"

"Forget about what?" asked Burt, smiling at the old joke.

"Good," said Emilia. "Hey, it's quitting time in ten minutes. You flash the lights and I'll make the announcement and we can both go home."

"Sounds good to me," said Burt, relieved to see Emilia herself again.

Two days later, as Emilia was on her way home, Burt watched her as she left the department. After saying goodbye to him, she detoured to a corner table on her way out and dropped a small sheet of notepaper in front of Mr. Knopka, a smiling and perennial visitor to the History and Travel section of the library.

The graying, heavyset man in the tweed jacket glanced curiously at the note, frowned, and read it more carefully. As Burt watched, he arose and shuffled slowly up to the reference desk, the note clutched in his large hand. "Young man," he asked, "do you haff any idea vy dat voman vould leave such a message vit me and choost run avay like dat?" Burt looked quickly at the handwritten note that Emilia had dropped in front of the man on her way out that evening. It read:

I know who you are and I know what you're doing. Stop it now, or you are going to be very sorry. You need help.

Alarmed, Burt looked up at the man standing before him, trying to think of something to say.

Questions for Discussion

1. What should be the response of librarians to threatening or anonymous telephone calls?
2. How can one tell whether such a caller is a harmless crank or dangerous?
3. Given the refusal of the police to assist you in this problem, how would you, as Emilia, try to deal with this person?
4. As Burt, what would you say to the apparently puzzled man who is now standing before you with Emilia's note in his hands?
5. In general, what can libraries do to discourage or dissuade those who make annoying or frightening telephone calls to staff members?

Resources

In addition to several previously cited articles (e.g., Schenectady (Case 1), Easton (Case 6), Samet (Case 6), and Elliott (Case 13), there are several good articles on dealing with obscene callers found in popular magazines. Among these:

1. Furlong, William Barry. "What You Can Do About those Obscene Telephone Calls." *Good Housekeeping* 165 (September 1967): 82.
2. Olendorf, Donna. "Handling an Obscene Phone Call." *Cosmopolitan* 182 (March 1977): 150–54.
3. Putrosky, Stephanie. "Dial H for Help." *New York* 14 (June 8, 1981): 38+.
4. Star, Jack. "Heavy Breathers and Other Strangers." *Chicago* 27 (March 1978): 138–41.

Case 20
Jimmy and Me, We Fall Down a Lot

"Jimmy and me, we fall down a lot," said the young girl to Gretchen Schroeder, who was on duty in the Children's department that morning in January.

"But how does it happen that you *both* got bruises around your eyes at the same time?" Gretchen was more than just curious. She was beginning to be alarmed. She had noticed the pair in the children's room before and had helped them find books to read a few times. Gretchen liked the little girl, who reminded her somewhat of a favorite niece. The boy seemed remote, however, and rarely spoke to anyone other than his sister. Gretchen's concern arose from the realization that the children had both been bruised the last time she had seen them, and the time before that.

"Well, see, there was a lot of ice around yesterday," the girl began her explanation, occasionally putting her small, dirty hand to her left eye. "And my brother and me," she indicated the silent boy standing beside her, "we thought, like, it'd be really good for sliding, you know? I mean, cold enough so it don't turn into wet slush, but sunny and no wind, so you can stay outside a long time. Well, Jimmy said he could slide farther than me, and I. . . ."

"What's your name?" interjected Gretchen quickly when the girl paused for breath.

"Susie."

"Susie what?"

"Just Susie. My last name don't matter. I'm twelve, and this here is Jimmy, my brother. He's eight."

"Won't you tell me your last name? Mine's Schroeder," Gretchen persisted.

"Do I have to?"

"Well, no. Not if you don't want to. But it would make it easier for us to get to know each other better."

"I don't want to tell you my last name."

"Well, what is Jimmy's last name then?" asked Gretchen, figuring that it was worth a try.

"You must think I'm pretty stupid, don't you?"

Gretchen sighed. "Sorry, Susie," she said. "I just want to know more about you and your brother, that's all. And I don't think you're stupid. I just want to be friends, and I want to know a few things about you."

"But you ask so many questions!"

"Just trying to help."

"Well, don't. It won't do any good whether you do or you don't, anyway."

"What are you so afraid of, Susie?"

"There you go again. If we're going to talk you gotta stop asking me so many things."

"If I knew your last name, I could talk to your parents about getting you and Jimmy into a reading program. Would you like that?"

"No," said Susie, looking frightened.

"But you love to read. I can see that."

"Please, ma'am. Leave my parents out of this. Please?"

Gretchen nodded and smiled, changing her tack. "So you were telling me about yesterday in the snow and ice."

The girl looked relieved. "Yeah, right. So Jimmy and me slide along the ice down to the corner but then we couldn't stop and we slid smack into the fence at the end of the sidewalk. Splat!"

"And that's how you got those black eyes? Both of you?"

"Yup. First Jimmy slid into the fence goin' real fast. And he fell down and started to scream, holdin' his eye and cryin' his head off. When I tried to help him up, the same thing happened to me. It was real slippery, you know, and we just couldn't stop."

"And what did your mother do when you got home?"

"Gave us hot soup and told us to lie down with washcloths on our faces."

"I see," said Gretchen, not seeing at all. "And where was your father, while this was going on?"

Gretchen thought that the girl looked nervous at that point. Jimmy had wandered over to a picture book display on the other side of the room, but Susie just stood there in front of her, blinking rapidly and looking frightened.

"Uh, what?"

"Where was your father when you and Jimmy came home with your eyes all banged up," Gretchen persisted.

"Where? Nowhere. I mean, out. He was out."

"Out where?"

"I dunno. Just out. How should I know?"

"And when you told him about your accidents, what did he do then?"

"I dunno. Nothin'."

Seeing that Susie's answers were getting increasingly terse and evasive, Gretchen risked one further question. "Wasn't that you who came in here last fall with your arm in a sling?"

"Yeah, I guess. Look, we gotta go, okay?" Susie walked rapidly over to her brother and wrestled him into his coat. In seconds, they were gone, leaving Gretchen frustrated and deeply frightened for them.

As they had passed her desk on the way out, Susie had turned and opened her mouth to say something, but then had shrugged and turned to leave with her smaller brother meekly in tow. Gretchen was more certain than ever that she had just had an interview with a victim of child abuse and that the two children were in deep trouble. But what could she do if the girl wouldn't even tell her her last name? Thoughts of rifling through Susie's purse or following the children home flitted through Gretchen's mind, but she knew better than that.

Still, as a concerned, caring person who worked with children all day, Gretchen knew also that she could not just go home and eat dinner and forget this matter without a course of action of some kind. Something had to be done or the next time these children might not get off with only token shiners as evidence of having angered someone, possibly someone in their home. The problem, as Gretchen Schroeder saw it, was not whether to do something on their behalf, but what to do and how to proceed.

Questions for Discussion

1. What procedures should a librarian follow when child abuse is suspected but not admitted by the child?
2. As Gretchen, if you could determine the names of the children, would you deal first with the school authorities or call a social service agency or even the police? What do you think of talking to the children's parents as a first step in your plan?
3. Discuss possible consequences for Gretchen and for the library if the librarian's suspicions turn out to be unfounded.
4. Can you see adverse results of failure to report such suspicions, aside from possible further injury to the children involved?

Resources

There are no items in the literature of librarianship that specifically and exclusively treat child abuse as a problem. The following recent articles, however, provide useful information for the library staff member, as well as for members of the general public who suspect that a child is being abused at home:

1. Bridgeman, Anne. "Schools Joining National Fight against Child Abuse." *Education Week* 3 (17) (January 18, 1984): 1, 16–17.
   Includes a list of signs of child abuse that teachers and others who come into regular contact with children should know. Also provides a directory of the 50 state agencies that handle child protective services.
2. National Committee for Prevention of Child Abuse. P.O. Box 2866, Chicago, IL 60690.
   Provides information on preventing child abuse, including a $3.00 booklet, *The Educator and Child Abuse,* by Brian G. Fraser, and a free information package.
3. Wilson, Jean, et al. "The Silent Screams: Recognizing Abused Children." *Education* 104 (1) (Fall 1983): 100–03.
   Describes types of child abuse and neglect and how to report child abuse.

Section 2

Nuisances
Cases 21–40

Case 21
Close, but No Cigar!

There are some people who just wouldn't look quite right without cigars stuck in their faces. Winston Churchill was one, and George Burns comes readily to mind. A certain type of man seems inseparable from his cigar, and there is a whole ceremony attached to smoking one. First, the cigar is taken from its wrapper or humidor and passed slowly beneath the nose of the smoker, so that he (it's rarely a she) can enjoy the tobacco aroma before combustion begins. Then, but this is a matter of personal preference, a clipper may be used to trim one end of the cigar for more even burning. Finally, the cigar is set afire, and the smoker may chew eagerly on it or remove the cylinder of smoking leaf and stare at it in admiration from time to time. Curiously, cigar smokers seem to derive almost as much personal pleasure from an extinguished cigar as from one that is lit, and a true, habituated cigar smoker will not discard his smoke just because it has gone out.

Such a man was Harry Gaines. A small, cheerful fellow of perhaps seventy years of age, Harry just didn't feel comfortable without a cigar in the corner of his mouth. His doctor allowed him one a day, and Harry began to feel guilty only after his sixth or seventh. Harry was retired, and his principal passions were card playing, cigars, and the public library, although not necessarily in that order. Unfortunately for him, there were city and state ordinances that prevented him from smoking while using the library. These he cheerfully disregarded whenever he could by sneaking a smoke during his perusal of three daily newspapers and several magazines.

Harry's ability to sneak puffs on his cigars, however, was limited by the fact that everyone within several rooms in any direction could smell them within seconds of their being lit. Harry was partial to a brand of cigars that emitted thick, noxious black smoke, apt to sting the eyes and cause the nose to twitch at a distance of fifty paces.

Irwin Rossiter, the security guard and custodian of the River Bend Public Library, was onto Harry's game. He had greeted Harry on occasions too numerous to count with the stern injunction that smoking, and especially cigar smoking, was not permitted in the building and that if he caught

Harry with a lit cigar he would oblige him to leave the library at once. An elfin man of unflagging good spirits, Harry merely smiled on such occasions, had elected to make a game out of his contest with the security guard. He seemed to have challenged Irwin to catch him at smoking and, to Irwin's intense frustration, he rarely had done so.

Typically, at some hour in the afternoon, usually just after Harry returned from going out for lunch, the penetrating, acrid aroma of a strong cigar would permeate the building. Irwin would seek out Harry Gaines in the stacks or reading rooms and swoop down on the small man with a speed and grace that were surprising, given his large and bulky frame. Yet while Harry may have reeked of cigar smoke and was, on occasion, enshrouded in a cloud of it, Irwin had almost never caught the man in *flagrante* (Irwin thinks of it as *fragrante*) *delicto*.

There were days when Irwin tolerated Harry as a benign prankster, and he even entered into the game: Irwin hid in the stacks, or attempted to sneak up on the man silently in the postprandial period during which Harry fancied a little smoke. Having rehearsed the triumphant ''Gotcha!!'' that he would shout, Irwin relished the future moment of pleasure in daydreams. After that, however, the future was muddied. What was to be done with such a man? Should he be thrown out of the library for smoking in violation of various rules? Might he be frisked for cigars upon entering the building after his lunch? Would finding cigars upon his person justify such a search? Irwin was sure that library staff had no legal grounds for action, other than their right to evict the smoker if and when he was apprehended in the act.

When Irwin had spoken to the man about his habit, he had cited chapter and verse of the city and state fire codes; had appealed to Harry's consideration for the noses, eyes, and lungs of the rest of the building's occupants; and had threatened to bar the smoker and his smokes from the library permanently. Such entreaties and threats had met with amused grins, and Harry had even on occasion chirped ''what cigar?'' with an expressive shrug of his narrow shoulders. Irwin, therefore, alternated between saying ''I'm going to catch that guy if it's the last thing I do,'' and muttering, ''To hell with it. I give up.''

The fire marshall, however, was insistent on this point. No smoking in the library means NO SMOKING in the library, as he had said over and over, pointing out the presence of hundreds of thousands of books, periodicals, people, and other combustible items. The last time he had said these things, he had spoken them to Irwin, personally, and given him the mission of ensuring that the cigar-smoking malefactor be told, in no uncertain terms, that smoking in the library except for the central foyer where ashtrays are provided is strictly forbidden. Irwin, therefore, had renewed his dedication to the task of catching Gaines redhanded and persuading him somehow to stop his childish, obnoxious, and unlawful behavior. Maybe if I caught him dead to rights, he'd listen to reason, Irwin mused, but even if I did, what the hell could I do with the guy (or to him) to make him stop smoking in the building? And first, I'd have to catch him!

As he stood by the front door, lost in thought, Irwin heard a cheerful "How're ya doin?" and saw that Harry Gaines stood before him, smiling broadly, and patting his vest pocket significantly. Furiously, Irwin vowed to redouble his efforts to apprehend the man and set off at a brisk pace to follow him wherever he might go.

Questions for Discussion

1. At what point does a harmless prank become a serious nuisance or even a dangerous activity in the library?
2. Suppose that Irwin actually catches Harry smoking a cigar in the library building. What should or can he do about it so that no laws are broken and yet the man is dissuaded from coming back and doing it again?
3. Do you think that Irwin and the library staff should be more assertive, taking sterner measures in enforcing the fire marshall's ordinance? How?
4. Assuming that no one really wants to bar Gaines from the premises, what alternatives to such extreme action seem to you feasible and sound in this case?

Resources

1. Caputo, Janette. *The Assertive Librarian*. Phoenix, AZ: Oryx Press, 1984.
   See especially Chapter 2 where Caputo examines the rights and concomitant responsibilities that library patrons and library employees have.

Manuals of procedure and policy such as the Schenectady one listed in Case 1 normally provide clear advice on how to deal with those who smoke in violation of laws or rules. See also the following two articles: "Cigars without Guilt." (column) *Forbes* 131 (February 28, 1983) 115–16. (Expresses the point of view of the smoker whose rights are being abridged by new ordinances that forbid smoking in public places.) and Langway, Lynn. "Showdown on Smoking." *Newsweek* 101 (June 6, 1983): 50+. (Deals with the confrontation between those who seek to ban all public smoking, and those who feel that it is the right of the people to choose.)

Case 22
A Matter of Balance

The River Bend Public Library was founded on the principle that all points of view deserve a representation in a publicly supported facility. Through the years, Library Director Pat Broughton and her staff attempted to resist all attempts to restrict or remove material that did not meet with the approval of individuals or pressure groups, and such resistance was generally approved by the library's board. The morning mail, one day recently, brought a letter of complaint that put Pat's principles to the test. As she read it, she noticed that the writer had thoughtfully furnished a copy to each member of the board, and she knew that this would be an issue which would not go away and that had to be confronted squarely.

The letter came from a Mr. Luther Scadden, co-owner of River Bend's biggest hardware store, and claimed to represent not only Mr. Scadden's views, but also those of the entire congregation of Fundamentalist Protestants. In it, he said that he had visited the library recently, and, going out into the stacks and using the card catalog, he had done a small-scale unobtrusive survey of the library's collection of books. To his shock, he said, he found a grossly distorted collection in the area of religion in favor of what he chose to call "secular humanism," which he did not bother to define. He wrote:

> I counted 57 books on evolution and the origins of man but there were no books on creation science or on anything relating to the competitive theory of world origins which rejects the notion that apes swung down out of the trees and gradually were evolved into men.

> The vast majority of members of this community attends church and believes in the word of God as literal truth. To have almost five dozen books which dispute Genesis while having no books whatsoever that endorse the Creationist explanation of how we all got here is totalitarianism which would put Soviet Russia to shame!

I enclose a list of books in the area of Creation Science for you and your staff to use in selecting materials for future purchase which will remedy this gross distortion of the "balance" you boasted about in a speech last year to the Rotary Club. Please use it to buy a fair representation of titles in substantiation of the Creationist view of our world, and shelve them, when they arrive, with the other books your library has in the science area, not with religion. To do otherwise, Ms. Broughton, is not only an affirmation of my perception that the library is one-sided on this important question, but could leave you and your board vulnerable to a lawsuit which I am being urged to bring against you. I sincerely hope that such drastic legal action will not be necessary and that you will quietly use the list I am pleased to enclose to remedy previous deficiencies in your library's holdings."

The letter rambled on, but Mr. Scadden's point was not lost on Pat because of an excess of verbiage. Charging misuse of public funds to support one point of view at the expense of another (he called it propaganda), Scadden sought voluntary change and threatened to get action one way or the other.

Pat figured that the library could (and probably should) accommodate Mr. Scadden and his congregation by purchasing a few of the titles on the booklist he had supplied, together with prices and publishers' addresses, but she was not too sure that such books belonged in the science classification, rather than the one for religion. She took half an hour after lunch and checked the card catalog, finding, as Mr. Scadden had alleged, that none of the sixteen titles on his list was currently owned by the library.

She conceded that the man had a point and made a photocopy of the list for the order department, checking in red marker each of the titles she thought they might try to purchase. There were six in all, when she was done, and she noted that they were all from publishers she had not dealt with before, and whose materials were probably not available through discount wholesalers. Sighing, she put the book requests through, figuring that fair was fair, after all, and six titles in "Creation Science," whatever that was, might mollify those who complained about bias in the collection and possibly avert further trouble with Scadden and his supporters. She would worry about how and where to classify them after they were received, she figured, wondering how serious a matter it would be if they became part of the religion collection, rather than being placed in science which seemed somehow wrong to her.

As an afterthought, she wrote up a summary of her actions and views, to be distributed to the board members at the upcoming meeting, hoping that her response would satisfy them and absolve the library from unfairness or bias in book buying.

Questions for Discussion

1. What obligation does a public library have to its community to present all sides of controversial issues, especially as regards matters of religious belief?
2. As Pat, how would you defend the library against charges that it is guilty of censorship by neglecting books that endorse the Creationist viewpoint?
3. Is it a requirement of "balance" in a collection that approximately equal numbers of books on both sides of delicate questions such as this must be purchased and made available?
4. How would you deal with the further request of the complainant that all Creationist books purchased for the collection be displayed alongside works in the area of science? Whose decision is it, and how shall it be made?
5. Whatever you decide, Mr. Scadden is waiting for an answer from the library and will not forget about this matter. Would you call him or write him, and what would you say to him?

Resources

1. For an endorsement of the various aspects of intellectual freedom for libraries, see the *Intellectual Freedom Manual* (2d ed., 1983) of the American Library Association's Office for Intellectual Freedom. This is a roundup of positions and arguments which make it easier for a library to resist attempted censorship from any sources or pressure groups. This 1983 paperback is available from the American Library Association, Office for Intellectual Freedom, 50 East Huron Street, Chicago, IL 60611 and should be in all libraries.
2. The best way to keep informed on censorship disputes and how libraries (and other communications agencies) are dealing with them is to read regularly the bimonthly *Newsletter on Intellectual Freedom*, available by subscription for $15.00 from the American Library Association, 50 East Huron Street, Chicago, IL 60611.
3. Thomas, Cal. *Book Burning*. Crossway Books, 1983. 158 p.
   This book presents the other side, alleging that libraries have systematically and intentionally ignored and suppressed certain types of religious literature for generations. Thomas is vice president for Communications, the Moral Majority.

Case 23
La Strega

The little old woman in black clothing was a mystery to the clerks at the circulation desk of the library. Several times a week she would be seen entering or leaving the library, and yet none of the staff could ever remember seeing her with a book in her hands. She would enter, nod stiffly to whomever was behind the desk, and proceed upstairs or out into the stacks. Just before dinnertime each day, she would leave, empty handed, with the same little curt nod. No one had ever heard her speak, and she didn't appear to be using the library for its intended purposes, but since she never caused trouble or for that matter approached anyone in the building about anything, there was never any need to worry about her. Still, the circulation staff were a social group, admirably suited to working with the public, and they all took note of the tiny woman wrapped in black woolen clothing, summer or winter.

Donna Campbell, one of the circulation staff, was therefore surprised when the woman came up to her one afternoon at the circulation desk with a question. "Scusi," she said in broke English, "How I getta dis book outta da library?"

Donna smiled and reached into a drawer for one of the library's borrower's card applications. "Just fill out this form, and you may borrow books this afternoon, if you like."

"No. You don' unnerstan'," said the woman, excitedly. "I don' wanna take this book home for reading. I wan' di book not be inna library no more."

Donna realized that the woman was holding out a copy of Mario Puzo's *The Godfather* and that she was referring to it when she said that she wanted to take a book out of the library, meaning that she wanted it removed from circulation. Giggling nervously, she said, "For that, you'd have to speak to our department head, I'm afraid."

"An whosa dat?" asked the woman, refusing to surrender the book she was carrying.

"Miss Bondanella," replied Donna.

Sudden pleasure lit the face of the elderly woman. "Ahhh, Bondanella!" she repeated, letting her tongue linger lovingly on each syllable, "Bon-da-nel-la. Yes, lemme talk to Meese Bondanella, please."

Grateful to be doing something that pleased the patron, Donna slipped down from the high stool on which she had been sitting and went into the back room where Freddie Bondanella was seated at her work station, checking order slips against a shipment of books that had recently been received by the library. "Freddie," she said, "there's an old woman out there who's asking for you."

"Who is it?" asked the department head.

"Don't know. She seems to have some kind of problem with that book, *The Godfather*. Remember a couple of years ago, when we had that trouble with the Italian-American Anti-Defamation group? Well, it might be about that again."

"Did she say what she wants done about it?"

"Well, she kind of said that she wanted to get the book out of the library, but it wasn't clear. She has this thick accent, and I might have missed something. Then when she heard your last name, she brightened up. Must've figured that she could explain better to somebody Italian."

"But I'm about as Italian as you are or Althea is," said Freddie, alluding to a Black member of the staff. "Did you tell her that?"

"No. I thought I'd let you tell her, yourself."

"Thanks a bunch," groaned Freddie as she stood up and walked behind Donna out into the public area where she saw the little old woman standing, her head just barely topping the height of the circulation desk.

I'm Miss Bondanella," she smiled down at the woman. "Would you like to tell me what the problem is?"

"Miss Bondanella," the woman smiled at her through gapped teeth. *"Parla Italiana?"* she asked hopefully.

"Sorry, no. I was born in St. Louis and my mother is Irish. My father's people were from Italy, but a long time ago."

"No matter," said the woman. "You're Italian, so you gonna understand when I tell you thata dis book don' belong here. Itsa not gooda for Italiana people. So many killers, so mucha murder. Please. You take. You read. Then get ridda this book. Instead, get sometin' tells about how we build uppa da cities, make fine church in America, worka hard. You know. You Italian like me. You understan', nice girl lika you, right?"

"Ma'am, I sympathize with what you're saying, but I don't have the authority to remove any book because someone doesn't like it."

"Whosa gotta dis autority?" asked the scowling woman.

"Well, it's a committee. A selection committee. Now, I can get a form for you to fill out, and at the next meeting of the committee, I can bring up your case and put it on the agenda for review."

"An' how long dis take?" the woman asked suspiciously.

"The next meeting should be in a couple of weeks. If you like, I can check for you." As Freddie turned to consult the calendar she kept pinned to a bulletin board at the side of the desk, she became aware that the woman had just torn the book into small pieces and was now grinding the dismembered pages and covers into the floor with her thick black heels.

"Dats for a couppla weeks," she shouted. "Dis booka no good. Somebody gotta do sometin bout no-good books. Here's what I do." For emphasis, she stirred the pile of small pieces of the book with the toe of one of her tiny shoes.

Freddie sighed audibly and told Donna to summon Irwin Rossiter, the security guard and custodian, from wherever he might be in the library. Donna picked up the microphone of the public address system and paged Irwin tersely. In thirty seconds, he came puffing up to the circulation disk and was looming over the small but defiant old woman who was fishing in her purse for a match to set afire the pile of pieces of what had until recently been a library book.

"Lady, you're going to have to leave the building," he said, "but first, we need your name and address so we can bill you for destruction of library property."

"Eh, *signorina* Bondanella," the woman had lapsed back into her native language in her excitement and anger, "*Puoi spiegare questo per me?*"

"I'm sorry, I don't understand," said Freddie.

"*Si!* You Italian, you understan'," insisted the woman. "Splain."

"Come along, now," rumbled Irwin, gently taking the woman by her arm and guiding her in the direction of the library's administrative offices.

Without warning, the woman broke free of Irwin's massive hand and fled, shouting a string of invective-filled words in Italian at them all as she scuttled out of the building.

"Want me to go after her?" asked Irwin of Freddie as they watched her run down the walk to the street.

"I guess not," she replied, "it was only one book and we have plenty of copies. Let her go. It's generally not worth it to try to chase down these crazy ones. Just let her go, Irwin."

"What was that she was sayin' when we were standing here watching her leave? I mean all that Italian she was spouting when she was doing that stuff with her hands?" Irwin tried to imitate the old woman's gestures, as he waved his right hand under his chin and flicked one gnarled fingernail against his teeth.

"Like I told her, I don't really speak any Italian. We never spoke it at home, you see. What I did catch, however, were the words *biblioteca,* that means library, and *maledizione.*"

"And what does that mean, if you please?"

"Well, it means 'curse'." Freddie grinned nervously. "She put a curse on the library, I think."

"What rubbish!" shouted Irwin. "There's no such thing as a curse."

"Of course there isn't!" agreed Freddie, unenthusiastically.

"Besides, the whole thing was over a fifteen dollar book. Boy, the wacko people we get in here," said Irwin in parting, as he went back to his rounds of the building.

"Ain't it the truth?" agreed Freddie, grinning fondly at the avuncular security guard as he disappeared from sight.

The following day, Irwin sprained his ankle as he stepped down from a bus on his way to work, Donna was sent home with severe stomach cramps, and Frederica Bondanella accidentally sliced her finger open with a razor blade while she was opening a package of books from a wholesaler. These unrelated incidents were recalled by Freddie that evening while she was changing the Band-Aid on her finger prior to going to bed. "Hmmmmm," she said to herself. Later, after tossing and turning without sleep, she called her father at his home in St. Louis.

After apologizing for awakening him, Freddie explained the reason for her call. She asked him what he knew about curses placed on people by angry old women, and he recalled that there had been a similar woman in his neighborhood when he was a boy. Everyone had called her *"La Strega,"* which meant "The Witch," and had given her a wide berth on the street and in the market.

"And could she really call down curses on people?"

"I just can't answer that, Fred," her father said. "I don't think of myself as a superstitious man, but I remember how everybody sort of stayed out of her way and how Mamma would shield us with her skirts when we met her in the street."

Finally, Freddie explained what had happened at the library the previous day and told of the accidents which ensued. Then she came to the point of the whole conversation. "Dad," she asked her father, "not that I believe any of this 'curse' stuff for a moment, but if I did, how would I get such a person to lift the curse from me and my friends?"

"Beg her forgiveness is all I can think of," her father responded. "Beg her forgiveness and hope for the best."

The following day, when three more minor but painful on-the-job accidents befell staff members of the library, Freddie became really frightened. Feeling foolish just for bringing it up, but experiencing a growing sense of alarm, just the same, Freddie walked into Pat Broughton's office and stood in front of her director's desk. "Got a minute, Pat?" she asked, hoping that she wouldn't get fired or institutionalized for what she was about to say.

Questions for Discussion

1. How should requests for the suppression or removal of library materials be handled by staff members when the request is made by someone with very strong beliefs who will not comply with established library procedures?
2. As Freddie, what would you have said to the angry woman upon seeing her tear the offending book to bits?
3. In your opinion, did the library staff members handle the case correctly by asking the woman to pay for the destroyed book and leave the building immediately?
4. How can a staff member differentiate between an irrational patron and one who is simply annoyed with an aspect of the library's policy or procedure?

Resources

1. The American Library Association's *Intellectual Freedom Manual*, mentioned in the resources section of Case 22, contains sample forms to be used in discussions with patrons who request reconsideration of library materials, along with helpful strategies for dealing with angry or irrational patrons who demand that such materials be removed from or restricted in the library.
2. DeRosa, Frank J. "The Disruptive Patron." *Library & Archival Security* 3 (Fall/Winter 1980): 29–37.
   DeRosa, a police officer for 21 years who turned security guard after retirement, has seen it all and provides sound and cautious advice on dealing with irrational, irate, or temporarily deranged patrons in the library.
3. "The Problem Patron: Sioux City Briefings." *Library Journal* 105 (December 16, 1980): 2536.
   This is a report of a workshop given by Gardner Hanks, former head of the Mental Health In-Service Training Project at the Oshkosh (WI) Public Library. Hanks deals with effective countermeasures to bizarre or angry behavior inside the library in a variety of situations.

Case 24
A Quiet Place to Study

The River Bend Public Library attempted to be many things to many different types of people. For the senior citizen, it could be a recreational center, as an alternative to a dreary day of watching television or staring at the wall. For a small child, it could be wonderment with its thousands of picture books, supplemented by story hours and special programs. For everyone in between, it served many functions—answering questions, circulating materials, and providing cultural and intellectual enrichment of many varieties. One of its important functions was that it served as a quiet place to study, away from the noise and distraction of one's family, when papers or examinations required that school-age patrons exercise intense concentration.

In an effort to make the library such a place, a curious balance had to be found. The old days of "shushing" librarians and "SILENCE" signs on the walls were gone forever, at least at the River Bend Public Library, and yet those who required concentration and tranquility also had to have a sanctuary from noise. River Bend's main library was neither exceptionally large nor exceptionally small. Its size was too small, however, for its staff to set aside a dedicated room for its clientele needing silence, which included the meditator, the serious scholar, and the high school student who has a chemistry final the next day.

Instead, there was sort of an unwritten law concerning excessive noise. Too much noise and one was asked politely to hold it down by whichever staff members were at hand. "Too much" was not defined by decibels, or measured in any precise fashion, but was situational, depending on the expressed or perceived reactions to it of those in the room. If no patrons were around, or if no one seemed to be bothered, the library staffer had a great deal of latitude in whether a loud patron must be told to be quiet and in what happened next should he or she fail to do so.

The rule had worked fairly well through the years in reducing the sound level of the occasionally noisy patron, most of whom were not aware that they might be annoying others in the vicinity and who were embarrassed to learn that they had done so. The past few weeks had posed a problem concerning the younger visitors to the library in the late evenings, and no one on the staff had yet come up with an ideal solution to that problem.

Public libraries everywhere attracted teenagers who showed up on weekday evenings to study. They also came to socialize, to talk, to see and be seen, to flirt, to make arrangements for later, and to stroll from table to table, just "checking out the scene." For the most part, they were a pretty well-behaved bunch, as they came to be sociable, not to cause trouble, and incidents in which people had been harmed to threatened were few. The noise level, however, was appalling sometimes. Dozens of enthusiastic young people in the same room, carrying on their social commerce and occasionally conferring over school assignments, could make a considerable amount of noise. Once in a while, someone complained. Last Tuesday evening, for example.

Larry Green and Virginia Watanabe, two librarians on duty in the library's Performing Arts department, were having their usual busy night. They took turns on the desk, one answering questions in person and by phone, while the other one floated through the department, helping people find things and making sure that no one was dripping Big Mac sauce on any of the valuable art prints. Food, of course, was forbidden in the department, but Larry and Virginia tried to be tolerant of a little eating or drinking, as long as it didn't seem to threaten the library's materials. Larry, who had been an Air Force sergeant before going to library school, had an easy way with the young people and seemed to be able to keep them in line pretty well. Virginia, despite her diminutive stature, had a quiet dignity which had more than once faced down a hulking, athletic young person bent on fighting or verbal abuse in the library.

As Larry sat at the desk, enjoying a brief respite from the run of telephone reference calls he had had in the last half hour, a middle-aged woman appeared in front of him, having come from the far corner where study tables were arranged in rectilinear rows. "Excuse me," she said.

"Evening," said Larry, companionably. "May I help you?"

"Don't you think it's rather loud in here?" the woman came right to the point.

"Loud?" Larry stopped and considered the question. Come to think of it, it *was* loud in the room tonight, although Larry, through years of practice, had learned to screen the din of so many young voices out. "Yeah, I guess so. It's a nightly event around here," he said to the woman, wondering what she wanted him to do about it.

"What about the rights of those of us who came in here to read in peace and quiet?"

Larry didn't like the way this conversation was going.

"I know what you mean, ma'am. I hear it, too," said Larry, "But I really can't feature myself going around shushing everybody who speaks above a whisper."

"Still and all," the woman continued, "I can't hear myself think over there in that corner. I'm trying to take some notes on those Skira books of reproductions for my art appreciation course at the university, but the constant stream of chatter has me going crackers. Won't you come over and tell them to be quiet? You're a big man, and maybe you could succeed where I seem to have failed. They stop for a few seconds and they they start up again, louder than ever. It's like throwing a rock into a bush full of crickets. Soon they're at it again."

"We sympathize, ma'am," said Virginia, who had walked over to hear the conversation. "Maybe if you could come around in the mornings, we can get you some peace and quiet. Every morning until about noon, you can hear the proverbial pin drop in that corner. Tonight? Forget about it." Virginia's entrancing smile wavered and then fell when she saw that the woman was not to be jollied out of her anger.

"Do you mean that you and this big man here are powerless to stop the barrage of noice coming from those kids over there. What if I summoned that guard with a face like a bloodhound? Do you think he could enforce the rules where you can't?"

"We've tried, and the guards try," said Virginia wearily. "But these kids are having a good time, and they're off the streets. Some of them are even studying. And frankly, we just don't know what to do about them. Couldn't you try us in the daytime?"

"But I'm here tonight. I work in the daytime." said the woman.

"How would you suggest we achieve and enforce silence?" asked Larry, trying to sound polite.

"I don't know. Find out who the ringleaders are and have a talk with them. The rest will follow their lead."

"Ringleaders? What ringleaders? Everybody comes here to talk or read or both. That's the way evenings go. There's no organization, no leadership, no structure to it. We just let them enjoy themselves, because some of them check out books or consult encyclopedias, and the library thinks its doing a good job when somebody checks out a Renoir or a Picasso for a few weeks to take home."

"And you're not going to do anything to shut up their adorable little mouths so that I can hear myself think?"

"What do you suggest?" asked Larry innocently.

"Oh, I give up!" the woman cried in exasperation. "Will you give me your name, please? And yours?" she said, turning to Virginia.

"Mr. Green. And this is Mrs. Watanabe, spelled W-A-T-A-N-A-B-E. What are you planning to do with that information?"

"You'll see tomorrow, young man. Bright and early. Just remember: if you're not helping with the solution, you're part of the problem. Good night!" Angrily, she rushed over to her coat, put it on, and departed casting one last angry glance at Larry and Virginia, who stood together by the desk.

Larry uttered a four-letter expletive. Virginia nodded her head in sympathy, saying "One hundred minutes and we can go home." Both were suddenly aware of the waves of noise breaking over them as perhaps twenty happy students discussed matters related to work and play.

Questions for Discussion

1. Do you feel that a "quiet room" is essential to a modern "full-service" public library?
2. How can you reconcile the needs of those who require peace and quiet with those of patrons who wish to talk, laugh, move around freely or make unnecessary noise?
3. As Virginia and Larry, what would you have done to attempt to comply with the request of the woman who needed quiet to do her assignment?
4. Do you think that, in the situation described, it is worthwhile to try to identify ringleaders to talk to in order to sway the whole group?
5. If you were Pat Broughton, the library's director, and the woman complained to you about the unhelpful attitude of Larry and Virginia on the previous evening, what would you say or do?

Resources

1. DeRosa, Frank J. "The Disruptive Patron." *Library & Archival Security* 3 (Fall/Winter 1980): 29–37.
   DeRosa takes a legalistic approach to the problem, saying that those who disturb others in public buildings are in violation of state legal statutes.
2. Jordan, Peter. "Behaviour in Libraries." *Library Literature Five: The Best of 1974*. Metuchen, NJ: Scarecrow, 1974. (Also in *New Library World* 75 [January 1974]: 11–13.)

Jordan, a British librarian, discusses ways and means of keeping order and a semblance of quiet in a library, proving that the problem of the unruly patron is far from a uniquely American phenomenon.

3. Savage, Noël. " 'The Troublesome Patron': Approaches Eyed in N.Y." *Library Journal* 103 (December 1, 1978): 2371–74.
A report of a conference in which several experts on security offer tips on dealing with the usual run of distractions and dangers confronting the public library staff member.

Case 25
Hizzoner the Critic

Herbert Clemons had been mayor of River Bend for a dozen years, and the office seemed to fit him like a comfortable shoe. A big, handsome man of fifty-five, Clemons affected a flashy image, featuring a Stetson hat, numerous rings, loud ties, and brightly colored trousers. Despite his jaunty appearance, he was possessed of a deep streak of conservatism, which manifested itself in his policies of fiscal restraint and local boosterism.

Regarding the public library, Clemons had generally taken a *laissez-faire* attitude, rubber-stamping the appropriations made by the city council and staying out of Library Director Pat Broughton's hair. At least he liked to read, Pat noted, and the mayor would either appear in person or send an aide to the library about once a week to check out westerns, do-it-youself repair books, and books discussing Communism, which seemed to be one of his obsessions.

The mayor had posed a serious problem for Pat three years back, when reference librarian Bob diMarzo had accidentally run across evidence to link George Clemons, the mayor's younger brother, with slum housing on the city's south side. The mayor had become extremely angry with Pat and her reference staff for "stirring up trouble," but Mayor Clemons had managed somehow to distance himself sufficiently from his errant sibling, and no political damage had been done to his administration. In time, the whole affair had blown over, and by now was officially forgotten.

This year, a sweeping tide of austerity had descended from the state level decision makers to the local communities, and River Bend, to put it bluntly, was financially strapped. The newspapers in the area carried daily threats by the city administration that services deemed "inessential" would be severely curtailed, and Pat knew that her library was in deep trouble.

At a press conference, Herb Clemons, resplendent in his coordinated western costume, and affecting a drawl not common to those born in Milwaukee, stated to the assembled reporters that all city agencies would be obliged to share in the pain of fiscal cutbacks until the city could balance its budget. He went on to detail several necessary economies that had been agreed upon by the board of fiscal review, which he chaired. Among these was the revocation of a hard-earned eighteen percent increase in the library's materials budget for the coming year.

Pat Broughton had worked and lobbied hard for that increase, and one of the reporters present at the news conference knew it. "Mr. Mayor," asked Eleanor Garwood, a reporter for the *Herald*, "isn't it true that just last year you expressed satisfaction with the increased spending the library was able to get? And didn't you praise Patricia Broughton for her steward-ship of the library at the annual budget hearing?"

"Well, yes," said the mayor, "but that was then; now is now."

"But the increase affords the library a chance to purchase thousands of new books for its general collection, and that benefits everybody, doesn't it?"

"Now, Miz Garwood," Clemons said with an indulgent smile, "that library down there is full of junk and trashy novels. Hell, *I* could select books better'n those people do."

Eleanor Garwood leaned forward. "Does that mean, sir, that the library's share of the fiscal crisis we now face is partly attributable to poor selection practice by the library staff?"

The mayor thought a moment. "All I'm sayin'," he said slowly, "is that whenever I go to that library, I see a whole mess of books critical of our government and our traditions. Then there's sex in so many of the novels and books that tell you how and where to get an abortion or buy drugs. Why, I could pick books better than that! A lot of the books down there just pander to public taste and sensationalism. It's not what kids need today, and it's a damn waste of good money, besides!"

"Mr. Mayor," asked Ed Samuels, a veteran reporter for a local television channel, "even if you could influence the selection of books for the library, I fail to see how it would save money. Can you explain that?"

"Gladly," said Herb Clemons, with his winningest smile. "If Pat Broughton, who's a friend of mine, mind you, left off buying smut and junk and tasteless indictments of our national leadership, that alone would save plenty of money. And the library could buy better books with half of what we'd save and the city could use the other half for other purposes."

"No disrespect intended, sir, but could you define for us, ahh. . ." Samuels consulted his note pad, "smut and junk?"

"Eddie, I'm not about to get into a war of words over this thing," said Clemons. "I just want to point out the waste I see in this agency of city government, in the hope that y'all will see where we can and must make our cuts." He looked up for a few seconds, seemingly seeking inspiration from the room's ceiling. "We are doin' the best we can, friends. Somebody's gotta bleed if this body's going to survive. The library's only one example of where economies are possible. Now, turning to the sanitation department. . . ."

Pat Broughton was at home that evening with her husband, nervously awaiting the ten o'clock news, at which time the highlights of the mayor's press conference would be revealed. A phone call at 8:15, however, brought her the news in advance. Eleanor Garwood read to Pat some of the mayor's pithier comments concerning the library, especially the ones about selection of books and asked her if she'd like to respond for the record.

After a moment's hesitation, Pat told Eleanor that she was grateful for the advance word and that she would have some remarks to make the following morning, if she could be called at the library after 9:00 a.m. Going over to her rolltop desk, Pat selected two sharp pencils and a large pad of legal-size paper. Moving into the kitchen, she began fixing a large pot of strong, black coffee to get her through the night.

Questions for Discussion

1. How should a library administrator react to reporters who quote provocative statements by city officials and demand reactions?
2. As Pat, what would you say for publication concerning the mayor's indictment of your selection policies?
3. Would you call the mayor directly to discuss the matter before you went public with your own remarks?
4. How do you see this potentially damaging issue being resolved so that the library does not come under scrutiny by numerous self-styled "watchdogs" of the public welfare and purse?

Resources

The following representative articles will show some of the ways in which the press, seeking newsworthy stories, can sometimes cause conflict and difficulties between public libraries and local elected officials:

1. "Director's Remark at Press Preview of New Library Shakes Officials in Iowa Town, Stirs Deeper Issues." *American Libraries* 7 (November 1976): 612.

An unfortunate remark to a TV newsman by a library director brought a firestorm of criticism from both citizens and City Hall.

2. "Houston Public Facing Huge Cuts; Mayor Whitmire Calls for $2 Million Slash from $3 Million Materials Budget Now under Revenue Sharing." *Library Journal* 108 (September 1, 1983): 1628–29.

3. "Mayor Locks Library Door: Finesses Opening." *American Libraries* 9 (April 1978): 187–88.

4. "Plight of Boston Public Deplored by 'Boston Globe.' " *Library Journal* 108 (July 1983): 1303.

Case 26
The Plungers

To the library staff, Ernie Manners was an interesting enigma. He had been coming to the library for years on a regular basis, yet details of his life, such as where he lived, and how he lived, were unknown to everyone on the staff. Ernie wore old, shabby clothing which, while always clean, seemed to be in imminent danger of shredding or rotting away from excessive use. A few called him a bum, but that was unfair. Bums have no visible means of support and normally panhandle people for contributions. Ernie never did. Despite his shabby and unkempt appearance, he had never to anyone's knowledge asked anyone in the library for a dime, and he seemed rather content to be wearing clothes that looked as old as he did.

The unusual thing about Ernie, and the thing that set him apart from the usual run of vagrants, derelicts, and transients who find the public library to be a convenient base of operations six days a week, was his hobby. Ernie played the stock market. Each day at 9:00 a.m. sharp, Ernie would be among the first people waiting to get into the building when it opened. Walking briskly to the stairs, he would head straight for the Reference department where he would hang around impatiently until the morning edition of the *Wall Street Journal* was ready for viewing.

As soon as it had been slotted on sticks and placed on its rack, the newspaper would be swept away to a table by Ernie who would spend the rest of the morning going through it and making entries in pencil in a small blue notebook he always carried in his pocket. It was his routine, and Ernie was more predictable than the City Hall clock.

Through the years, a sort of mystique had grown up around Ernie. Because no one knew anything with any certainty about the man and how he lived, everyone liked to play the speculation game, and numerous conflicting theories about him were in existence. Some said that he was an eccentric millionaire who enjoyed dressing the part of a vagrant and hanging around the library. Their fantasy ran that he would leave the building in the late afternoon, walk several blocks, careful to see that he had not been followed, and enter a waiting limousine where he instructed his chauffeur to take him to the club for billiards and drinks with his friends.

Others figured that he actually invested heavily in the market and that he lived off the "system" he had developed, but he shared it with no one. Once, when Bob diMarzo, one of the reference librarians, had kidded him gently about the system he was keeping in his little book, Ernie's smile had vanished abruptly. "You don't know anything about my system," he had said rather loudly, "and I'll thank you to keep silent about things you don't understand." Bob, who hadn't intended to anger the old gentleman, apologized, and nothing more had ever been said.

After that, however, Bob had watched silently and had observed that Ernie had a few regular stock companies that he followed avidly. When he was in a good mood, he might chirp happily to Bob as he passed his desk, "Sears is up one and three-eighths, today," or "How about that? Pfizer preferred split three-for-two!" Bob had learned that as long as he didn't attempt to pry into Ernie's methods or strategies he could get the man to talk about investments, although on several occasions Ernie had said smilingly that he owned no stocks personally but just liked to keep track of them for his friends. Whatever it meant, Bob reflected, none of Ernie's friends had ever been seen, going back as long as anyone on the staff could remember.

Still, Ernie Manners was just another part of life's colorful cavalcade at the River Bend Public Library, thought Bob. A little weird, but harmless and actually one of the more interesting people who went into a typical day in the reference department. As long as Ernie derived satisfaction and information from the library's copy of the *Wall Street Journal,* Bob was content that the man was innocuous. Bob imagined Ernie spending the night wherever he did, going over both short-term and long-term trends in industrials, services, and commodities, and figuring out hypothetical investments for the future. Hey, thought Bob, it gets him through the night and keeps his vitality up, so what could be bad?

Then one sunny morning at about 11:00, Bob was jolted out of his own reading at the desk by the sound of angry voices, one in English, the other in Spanish. Two men were obviously yelling at each other, and it sounded like it was coming from the area adjacent to the newspaper desk. Bob ran quickly around the corner and stopped, stunned by the astonishing sight of Ernie Manners locked in armed combat with a small, dark man—each of them brandishing newspapers on sticks.

For a moment, Bob just stood and watched the two men attempt to strike each other over the head with their makeshift weapons, noticing that, as long as he had been watching, not a single blow had connected. A small crowd of people had gathered and were laughing, shouting encouragement to one man or the other.

Bob stood there, feeling his own laughter coming, and unsure as to whether to do something about the fight or call up everybody he knew to come and see. Then the little man feinted a jab with his stick and managed to deal Ernie a rather healthy blow to the top of the head. The old man doubled over instantly, holding his head, and Bob, moving to prevent the other man from hitting him again, noticed that all of the fight seemed to have left both contenders.

In a second, Bob had disarmed both men, and he gave Stanley Lewis, the page on duty in the department, both newspapers to be inspected for damage. Then grabbing both of the diminutive pugilists by their elbows, Bob brought them unprotesting along to his small office adjacent to the reading room. When he had closed the door behind them, he regarded Ernie and the other man with a look meant to be fierce and reproving.

"Mind telling me what the hell that was all about?" he addressed Ernie, not sure at that point if the other man spoke English.

"Gladly," said Ernie, putting his fingertips occasionally to the crown of his head and examining them for possible blood, "just keep this maniac away from me, that's all."

"I am no maniac," said the dark man, in heavily accented English. "I am Carlos Fuentes, and I have a right to read the newspaper like any other man."

"That's true enough," said Bob. "So what happened?"

Fuentes opened his mouth as though to answer, but Ernie Manners interrupted. "Bobby," he said. "You know me, right? I never bother anybody. Twenty years, more than that, I been coming in here every morning, and I read the *Wall Street Journal*. It's what I do. It's what I live for. I take a few notes, read some articles, and I'm out of here. Nobody complains about me. Nobody bothers me, isn't that so? All I want is my *Journal* and a place to sit and write. So today I'm reading along, like usual, and I have to go to the bathroom. Happens, you get old. I really had to go, you know? So I did a little trick so I wouldn't have to take the *Journal* and all that lumber in there with me. I kind of slid it under the *Cincinnati Enquirer* so it'd still be there for me when I came back."

"Yes, he hide it. He hide it so no one can get it," Fuentes broke in, excitedly. "But I watch. I wait and I watch. When he no has it no more, I take. Is fair, no? Your law say 'possession is. . . .' "

"Nine-tenths of the law, I know," said Bob, beginning to see how the men had come to blows over this newspaper. "So you watched and waited and when Ernie here put down the *Wall Street Journal,* you grabbed it up."

" Si! I take. It's my right. I no keep it long. Too many time I want to see it and thees man have it all morning. Thees once, I take it. Feefteen minute an he have it back. Okay?"

"Bobby, will you tell this *foreigner* for me that I always am first on the *Journal*? Every day since you were running around in diapers, I come in here and grab the paper first. By eleven, eleven-thirty, I'm usually done with it and I put it back nice and neat for the next one. But I gotta get to it in the morning or my system don't work. Just tell him that. Please!" Unwilling to wait for Bob or Mr. Fuentes to say anything, Ernie continued his explanation. "So this morning, like always, I get the *Journal* as soon as the kid puts it out, and I sit down to plug yesterday's quotes into my system."

"How it works, thees system?" asked Fuentes, hopefully.

"Forget about it. Just never mind. You expect me to perfect a system over twenty years and then give it away to a. . . ."

"Ernie," growled Bob, warningly.

"Yeah, right. Anyway, it's my system and I'm not about to share it. Could've made me millions. Millions! Only I just do it for fun. So anyway, I come out of the john and this . . . guy is using my *Journal*. I asked him real nice if I could have it back but he said no and went on reading like I wasn't there. Made me so mad, I picked up the *Enquirer* next to him and I gave him a good whack on the shoulder with it."

"He say it 'his' *Journal*!" interjected Fuentes. "It not his. Library newspaper belongs to everybody. Tell heem!"

"He has a point, Ernie," said Bob.

"After I'm done, I don't care if everybody in Mexico reads it, but I gotta get to it early. Can't you see it that way?" sighed the old man, imploringly. "Twenty years, I get it before anybody, even when I was sick and had fever. Now a man can't even go to the bathroom without some Spanish guy comes and steals his paper."

"Colombia, no Spain!" said Fuentes. "No Mexico, Colombia!" "And I no steal anything my whole life. You put it down, I pick it up. And when you hit me, I defend myself. I gotta right!"

Finally, after everything had been said, Bob used all of his influence and charm to get the two men to shake hands and agree not to fight over library materials. As he ushered them out of his office, however, he heard their final exchange. Carlos Fuentes told Ernie that he had better be quick about getting to the newspaper desk every morning, because he was going to try his best to get there first. Ernie's unhelpful retort was "Damned foreigner!" Shaking his head, Bob went back to his desk and opened the library's policy and procedure manual, wondering if the take-a-number system they used in bakeries would work for his newspapers.

Questions for Discussion

1. Should time limits ever be set for use of library materials?
2. Is there any justification for making exceptions to the first-come, first-served rule in such matters?
3. As Bob, how would you seek to handle the situation such that repetitions of the fight do not occur?
4. When hostilities break out, what should be the criteria for deciding when security personnel (or police) are to be called?
5. How can staff be trained to deal effectively with sudden but nonlethal outbreaks of hostility between or among patrons?

Resources

1. Brashear, J. Kirk; James J. Maloney; and Judellen Thornton-Jaringe. "Problem Patrons: The Other Kind of Library Security." *Illinois Libraries* 63 (April 1981): 343–51.
   A survey of all types of Illinois libraries reveals that a written policy covering various types of problem behavior is an important prior step.
2. Driscoll, Alice. "A Dilemma for Today's Public Librarian: The Problem Patron." *Southeastern Librarian* 17 (Spring 1980): 15–21.
   Tackles specific problem behaviors including disruptive behavior and recommends plans of action for dealing with each.
3. Grotophorst, Clyde W. "The Problem Patron: Toward a Comprehensive Response." *Public Library Quarterly* 1 (Winter 1979): 345–53.
   Discusses an overall strategy for increasing the competence of library staff members in dealing with the occasional disruptive event. Adherence to coherent rules and guidelines is stressed.

Case 27
The Editorialist

Libraries attract readers, and it stands to reason that those readers will form opinions about what they read. Usually, those opinions are kept private, reflected Bob Castlebury, head of the River Bend Public Library's Science and Technology department. When they are not, they are made manifest by a variety of means. And when the method of telling people what you think of a book extends to mutilation or defacement, groaned Bob inwardly, you are a nuisance at best, and a criminal at worst.

Recently, someone, or a number of people, had been defacing the books and magazines in his department, and Bob, for one, was outraged. Magazines found on tables at the end of the day might have articles neatly razorbladed out of them, or perhaps the editorialistic reader had written comments next to the text, expressing his or her opinion of the author's contentions. The same thing was going on with the book collection, and desecrations ranging from marginalia to outright removal of pages were becoming common.

When such practices had been brought to Bob's attention, he had uttered several choice remarks to himself on the state of intellectual freedom and the general intelligence of the people who came to the library. After some weeks of investigation, however, he discerned an important fact: at least ninety percent of the mutilations and comments were to be found in books and periodicals dealing with one subject area: feminism and the women's movement, in general. This deduction caused Bob to rethink his previous position that there was a general wave of crime affecting the reading materials his department had to offer. The subject specificity of the acts of destruction that he had found persuaded him that he was viewing the work of one person, or at least a small band of persons sharing a single point of view on the subject.

Bob had instructed the circulation clerks to call to his attention any science and technology materials that had been returned with mutilated pages or written comments. As he sat at his desk, he fanned a sampling of the plundered books and magazines around him and looked at them again. Each had something to do with a feminist point of view. Picking them up one at a time, Bob sadly read the remarks written in the margins:

"Completely untrue!" read the first.

"Unfounded generalization." "Rubbish!" "This is just plain silly!" said others. One comment was a vernacular term for bovine excrement, scribbled all over several pages of a book entitled *Our Bodies, Ourselves,* which had been written by women for women, and contained some rather angry references to the present "male-dominated" society. One comment even read, "Thou shalt dash them in pieces like a potter's vessel!" written in an enviable gothic hand, probably the work of a religious fanatic.

Somebody had evidently taken personal charge of becoming a one-person truth squad, Bob reasoned, and was systematically reading and annotating the library's books that had a feminist point of view. The handwriting on all the samples before him was sufficiently similar in structure that it could have all been the work of one person, and whoever was wielding a razor blade to achieve censorship of antithetical ideas to his or her own was very adroit at neat, square cuts. All of this persuaded Bob that he was after one culprit, and he began considering ways that he might succeed in finding out the identity of the malefactor and putting him or her out of business. It *was,* after all, destruction of city property, and a crime by any definition. Furthermore, it was a method designed to remove from public view certain ideas found unacceptable by one citizen or, in the case of the marginal comments, to deride and refute them. Such a person was clearly bent on reading and rendering "safe" for public consumption every book dealing with women's rights in the library, and that gave Bob an idea.

It stood to reason that, since the censorious but unknown reader was plowing through all the books and periodicals with a feminist viewpoint, a certain number of books and magazines as yet untouched by his or her fell hand might be identified as likely candidates for future plundering. These, Bob hoped, could be used as bait. True, it would expose still more materials to the depredations of such a destructive person, but it might then be possible to figure out who it was from circulation records and possibly catch the mutilator of books before he or she finished the task.

This plan seemed much preferable to some sort of surveillance in the building, which didn't seem terribly effective in catching malefactors in the act of committing their crimes, and which required plenty of staff time spent in patrolling the reading rooms and stack area of the large building. Smiling at his ingenious scheme, and fantasizing about a ceremony in which the mayor and the library director would confer upon him some great honor for having saved the library thousands of dollars and much senseless damage to the collection, Bob trotted off in the direction of the circulation desk to explain his baited trap concept to the clerks who worked there and why it was important that they go along with it. The way he figured it, all the library would have to do would be to match up vandalism on previously inspected books and magazines with the identities of the most recent borrowers. Confronted by the evidence, the one who had been messing around with the materials dealing with sexual equality would have to admit to his or her misdeeds. Threatened with possible fines and other penalties, including imprisonment, he (or possibly she) would come clean, promise never to do it again, and become a model of borrowing decorum in the future. Ah, yesss! Bob could see it all clearly.

Visions of the crime, the punishment, the threats, the confession, the pleadings of the felon, and the magnanimous clemency recommended by himself filled Bob's head as he walked up to Frederica Bondanella, head of the Circulation department, and explained his scheme. When she told him of a firm library policy that borrower's records are strictly confidential, Bob felt frustrated, depressed, and very angry. As he mentally watched the crumbling of his dream, he wheeled and walked rapidly in the direction of Pat Broughton's office, hoping that Pat would be able to see the importance of granting a variance to the rule this once, due to the significance of the goal and the simplicity of the means.

Questions for Discussion

1. Do you agree that it is important that the person (or persons) who is writing in the books and cutting out the articles should be caught? Or, is it more important merely to stop the defacing and mutilation without necessarily identifying the perpetrator? Can you think of any ways that such behavior can be stopped without identifying anyone?
2. What do you think of Bob's plan to use certain books and magazines as bait and then consult circulation records in order to apprehend the guilty party?
3. If the person who's been doing these things were caught, how would you, as Bob, handle the situation?
4. Can you see any implications for materials selection arising from this case?
5. As Pat Broughton, the director, what would you say to Bob when he came into your office demanding that the rules which preseve borrowers' confidentiality be overlooked to assist in catching this individual?

Resources

1. "Crime Risk Revealed." *American Libraries* 11 (September 1980): 474.
   Stating that "crime in and against public libraries is becoming a serious problem," this news article reports that "over 80 percent of the responding libraries [to a Massachusetts survey] reported intentional book damage."
2. Garfield, Eugene. "Highly Cited Articles: Human Psychology and Behavior." *Current Contents* (Social and Behavioral Sciences) 7 (1975): 5–11.
   Details the reasons why some library materials disappear or are defaced. Two types of perpetrators are identified: those who wish to own the information without buying it, and those who wish to conceal the information from others.
3. "Periodical Mutilation Zooms." *Library Journal* 100 (June 15, 1975): 1172.
   Indicates the nature of the problem, despite the general availability of inexpensive copying machines open for use by the public. Cites reasons for such vandalism, ranging from laziness to censorship.

On the topic of user record confidentiality, the recent literature of librarianship teems with articles. Especially germane and recent is: "Bruce Defies Secret Service, Protects Library Records." *American Libraries* 15 (January 1984): 6+. This article details the fight of one librarian to preserve confidentiality of borrowers' records, despite threats by the U.S. secret service to "make life difficult" for her if she refused. Here the issue wasn't one of mutilation of materials, but was much more fraught with menace: a book had been found containing written threats against the life of President Reagan.

Case 28
A Weekend for Two

The calls would begin coming into the library's reference department just after 10:00 a.m. on weekdays. At that hour, a barrage of trivia questions, asked by people in obvious great haste to have the answers, would flood the department's staff members. It didn't take very long for reference librarians Nancy Groves and Bob DiMarzo to figure out what was happening: a local radio station had begun offering prizes for prompt responses to trivia questions as a boost to their ratings and as a promotional inducement to advertisers.

Nancy and Bob, along with their colleagues, had grown used to the *modus operandi* of the callers. A typical question received between 10:00 and 10:30 a.m. would consist of a breathless, impatient voice, a rapidly asked question, a stressed urgency for haste, and a curt farewell, with or without thanks, once an answer had been provided. Presumably, those who received such nuggets of informational trivia hung up quickly so that they could dial the number of the radio station, blurt out the answer as quickly as possible, and win a prize, currently "a luxurious weekend for two at the fabulous Lantern House Inn and Restaurant," according to the disc jockeys who asked the questions.

Nancy and Bob were unaware of how many couples they had sent on such fun-filled holidays as the result of their scrupulous provision of reference service, but they were pleased that the library was becoming known as a "trivia mine" and the first place to call when one sought accurate, speedy information. Maybe it wasn't the most important thing for a library to be famous for, but it was a start. Nancy's only complaint was a joking reference to the fact that, despite over a dozen people who had won weekends thanks to her good work, no one had ever asked her to be the other half of the couple who were to take advantage of the prize. Of course, considering some of the men who came into the reference department, she reflected, that might be just as well.

Still, it was a positive thing for the library that so many people turned to the reference staff when seeking answers, even if it were for help in remembering all of the names of Walt Disney's seven dwarfs. Bob and Nancy were proud of their contribution to the knowledge pool of the community and actually looked forward to the phone calls each morning.

One morning, when Bob was on duty, the switchboard telephone buzzed with what he figured would be another trivia question, judging by its timing. Happily, he went to the reference phone and said into it, "Reference. Bob. How may I help you?"

"Yeah, right," began a gruff man's voice, showing the usual haste. "I need to know right away who played the role of Marshall Dillon on the radio show "Gunsmoke.""

Bob was overjoyed. This was a piece of cake. If there was one thing he knew, it was Gunsmoke, which he had watched faithfully on television for most of its twenty-year run. Since early childhood, he had watched the show and followed the adventures and discussions of Matt Dillon, Doc Adams, Miss Kitty, and Festus in the Long Branch Saloon in old Dodge City. This reference question required no pawing through volumes of forgotten lore: he knew the answer, and could send this man to the Lantern House Inn with no delay.

"You've called the right place, sir," he said into the phone. "I used to think of Dodge City as my home town. Now, you want the name of the man who played the marshall, right?"

"Jeez!" said the man with a tone of scornful impatience, "I just said so, didn't I? Save the garbage! Who, already?"

Rude, wasn't he? Ah, well, thought Bob, when there's money riding on it, one is probably justified in wanting to dispense with the amenities and get on with it.

"Okay, sorry," said Bob. "The actor who played Dillon was James Arness, and he. . . ." Bob was suddenly and uncomfortably aware that he was speaking into a dead telephone. The man had gotten what he needed and had severed the connection with dispatch. Just the same, Bob congratulated himself on another feat of instant vacation provision and pictured the man phoning in the correct answer and being told that he. . . .

Wait a minute! Wait a minute! Bob shifted in his chair, as a sudden chill passed through his central nervous system. Hadn't the man said *radio* show? Bob played the brief conversation over in his head and shuddered. He *had* said radio show! And that meant. . . .

Groaning audibly, Bob shot out of his chair and raced for the staff lounge, where he startled several of his fellow employees who were enjoying a coffee break. Grabbing the small portable radio from its place on the shelf, he hurriedly flipped the dials until the contest-question station was coming in loud and clear. To his horror and chagrin, he was just in time to hear the buzzer sound that radio stations associate with wrong quiz answers. "Ohhhhhh, too bad!" came the maddeningly cheerful voice of the usual morning disc jockey. "We're sorry, but the answer isn't James Arness. He was the *television* Matt Dillon. On radio, where you could use your imagination, they used Bill Conrad, a short, portly actor with a deep voice. Remember William Conrad? He played *Cannon* in his own television series? But anyway, we want to thank you for playing our game, Mr. Evans, and better luck next time, hear? Bye, now."

With a sinking feeling approaching intuition, Bob was certain that the next call he would get at the reference desk was going to be from somebody named Evans, and that he was going to be very angry. Resignedly, Bob trudged back to his chair, waiting for the phone to ring, wondering how he could have blown such an easy one. Time pressures, he figured, and unpleasant and harassing patrons.

Bob was wrong. When the telephone did ring, the caller was Pat Broughton, the library's director, who asked Bob in a neutral tone if he would mind stopping by her office when his shift on the desk was over. Bob agreed to be there in twenty minutes and hung up the phone, after which he sat very still for a while, trying to figure how his reference accuracy could have taken such a nosedive. Dismissing such speculation, he considered appropriate lines of defense, should he be accused of poor or slipshod reference service. Pat would back him up, he told himself. She had to!

Questions for Discussion

1. What can public library reference departments do to reduce the amount of erroneous or inaccurate information they give out?
2. How can a librarian best deal with urgent requests for immediate answers without either being rude to the questioner or being stampeded into making careless mistakes?
3. Do you see any problem with libraries responding to reference questions in which the information provided may help one patron at the expense of others?
4. As Bob, assuming that Mr. Evans has lodged a complaint against you, charging that he suffered loss of his prize as a result of your actions, how would you explain or defend yourself in this case?
5. As Pat Broughton, how would you seek to balance the traditional "customer is always right" philosophy of a manager with your intuitive feeling that Bob made an honest mistake brought on by the urgency and time constraints of a somewhat frivolous reference question?

Resources

1. Angoff, Allen. "Library Malpractice Suit: Could It Happen to You?" *American Libraries* 7 (September 1976): 489.
   This fictional treatment of a possible problem for the library asks what you would do if the information your staff gave out caused injury or property loss, or both.
2. Crowley, Terence, and Childers, Thomas. *Information Service in Public Libraries: Two Studies*. Metuchen, NJ: Scarecrow Press, 1971.
   These two dissertation topics measured public library reference service unobtrusively and found it to be sorely deficient in both accuracy and completeness.
3. Shuman, Bruce A. "A Charge of Malpractice." Case 15 in *The River Bend Case Book: Problems in Public Library Service*. Phoenix, AZ: Oryx Press, 1981.
   Another fictional portrayal of a reference transaction that causes someone (this time a corporation) to lose a considerable amount of money due to faulty information provided by the reference staff.

Case 29
I Wanna Go Home!

Saturday can be rough in the children's department of a public library. It is a day for story hours, film programs, special events, and, normally, vast crowds of noisy children and their parents. Barbara Prell, a children's librarian in the River Bend Public Library, once estimated that she walks between eight and ten miles on a typical Saturday, in addition to playing nursemaid, referee, surrogate mother, and reader's adviser to hundreds of young people. Toward the end of this gruelling fall day in the library, Barbara was pleased to note that the time had passed quickly enough and that soon she would be on her way home to a hot bath, a new dress, and a dinner date with Roger.

That's what she thought.

At a quarter to six, as Barbara was halfway through her normal preclosing routine, she looked up to see Billy Jo Macklin, one of the most industrious of the department's pages, standing in front of her holding the hand of a very young, very small girl. "Miss Prell," said Billy Jo, "this is Marcie. She says that she doesn't know where her mother is, and I brought her to you for help."

Marcie was a rather pretty little girl with soft brown hair and huge brown eyes brimming with tears. She was wearing a thin yellow sweater over a patterned shortsleeved shirt and faded jeans over well-worn red sneakers. Billy Jo's face showed concern.

"Kid here says she was dropped off by her mother about ten this morning. The mother had some shopping to do and Marcie likes to look at the picture books. Her mom told her to stay in the department, and she'd be back at lunchtime to take her to McDonald's." Billy Jo paused, looked down at the girl, and shrugged eloquently. "It's after five now," she said, her voice trailing off. "Soon it'll be six."

Barbara gave Marcie a closer inspection. The girl looked worried but not terrified. Her day's experience in the library might have been anxious but had not been traumatic. Now, however, it was almost closing time, and a very real problem of what to do with the girl had arisen. "Hi, Marcie," she said, smiling, noticing that the girl had clutched to her frail chest a small blue doll wearing a white floppy cap.

"Who's your friend?" she asked, gesturing at the doll.

"Clumsy," said Marcie, showing the doll to Barbara with a trace of a smile.

"Clumsy? That's a funny name for a doll. It's a Smurf, isn't it?"

"Yes. Clumsy *Smurf,*" said the girl with a trifle of impatience in her voice, as though everyone knew that.

"I see." Clearly a bright child, which made her easier to talk to. "Well, how do you like our library?"

"Fine. But I wanna go home! Where's my mommy? She said she'd be back for lunch."

"And she said she'd meet you right here? In the children's room?"

"Yes, right here. Over by the picture books."

"How old are you?" asked Barbara. "I'd guess . . . about five." Marcie giggled and held up four fingers. "Four? Well, I was close. Now tell me your last name."

Marcie tried, but three repetitions could only help Barbara to pin it down to Harris or Harrison, or maybe Maris. She tried another line of investigation.

"When did your mother say she was coming back for you?"

"Lunchtime. She was going to take me to McDonald's."

"And you haven't seen her since early this morning?" Marcie shook her head negatively, and for a moment, she looked as though she might cry. Suddenly, Barbara was struck by another thought.

"Are you by any chance hungry, Marcie?"

A delighted smile.

"Because I have these two delicious chocolate cupcakes I was saving for later, but I think you need them more than I do." Barbara held a packet of cupcakes out to the small girl, who neatly stripped off their cellophane wrapper and began devouring them down to the last crumb. As she ate, Barbara and Billy Joe exchanged worried looks. After her hunger was satisfied, Marcie allowed Barbara to wipe her smeary face with a disposable towelette and looked reasonably happy. She didn't know her telephone number, unfortunately, and there seemed to be nothing in her pockets or elsewhere on her person that might provide a clue.

It was now nearing 6 o'clock, and Barbara and Billy Jo held a brief and hushed conversation out of the child's earshot. "What are we going to do with her?" asked the younger woman. "She can't stay here after closing time, can she?"

"Certainly not. And I would be afraid to let Marcie just hang around outside the front door after we've all gone home until her mother gets here from wherever she's gone."

"She could come home with me!" In her enthusiasm, Billy Jo seemed scarcely older than some of the children Barbara had been dealing with all day. "I can call my mother and Marcie can play with Rita, my kid sister, until her mother reads the note we'll leave on the front door and calls, and. . . ."

"No. Sorry, but it's my responsibility as department supervisor, at least on Saturdays, to see this thing through. It's lovely of you to offer, but I will have to see to it that Marcie is safe and sound with her family . . . somehow."

Just at that moment; the amplified voice of one of the circulation clerks came over the PA system, informing them and everyone else that the library was now closed and wishing all who heard it a pleasant weekend.

Putting on her jacket, and seeing to it that Marcie's sweater was buttoned all the way up, Barbara instructed Billy Jo to put a note on the library's front door informing anyone who came for Marcie that the girl was at the police station one block away, and she made preparations to walk over there with her. Roger would have to be very understanding tonight, she thought, because this might take a while and this was important. As Barbara and Marcie left the building, Barbara checked to see that the note was correctly worded and securely taped to the big glass front door of the library. Then, chattering away gaily, she took the hand of the girl and led her slowly down the street in the direction of the city's main police station.

By the time that Barbara Prell and little Marcie walked up the steps of the police station and squeezed through the front door, a typical River Bend Saturday night was already in progress. In a corner, one man was ineffectually daubing at a profusely bleeding gash on the head of another, while a uniformed desk officer interviewed them both. In another corner, two brightly clad women were arguing vociferously, and sometimes profanely, with a second officer, who was trying to write something down on a form held on his knees. Two men in baggy suits and loosely knotted ties seemed to be extremely upset about something, and a handful of people in the room added their voices, in a number of languages, to the general din.

Barbara tightened her grip on Marcie's hand and walked purposefully up to the desk sergeant, whose creased and weathered face showed strain as he spoke rapidly into a telephone, while another one at his side shrilled insistently.

"Yeah, who's next?" said the sergeant, gruffly regarding the woman and the girl standing before him.

"I guess we are. My name is Barbara Prell, and I work down the street in the children's room of the public library. This little girl here, Marcie, was left there by her mother this morning, and when we closed, about ten minutes ago, the mother hadn't returned."

The sergeant's stern face softened somewhat at this news, and he smiled warmly down at Marcie. He was about to ask her something, when the door burst open to admit two men, one in a police uniform, screaming at each other in Spanish. As Barbara pulled Marcie gently out of their way, she saw that one man was handcuffed behind his back, and she was glad that neither she nor Marcie could tell what he was shouting at the officer. Clearly, this was no place for a small child, she thought, but she stood her ground.

In a few moments, the two noisily abusive men had gone past the desk and had disappeared somewhere back in the building, and she felt that she could speak to the sergeant again.

"Please, sergeant?" she asked.

"Huh? Oh, excuse me, miss. Saturday night, you know how it is. So your problem is that this little girl is temporarily alone and has misplaced her mother? Do you have the parents' names?"

"Well, no. She's a young girl, and rather frightened.'

"I understand, miss. Look, here's what you do. There's a lot of paperwork involved in this sort of report, so why don't you take one of these 1505s and," he reached under the counter and probed for something, "a 1084, and go sit down over there and fill it out as best you can. One's a lost child report, the other's a missing person report on the mother."

"Yes. I will. Thank you." Barbara turned and led Marcie over to a vacant wooden bench. Oh, sergeant," she called, when there was a lull in the room's noise level, "just out of curiosity, what happens when the forms are completed?"

"Normally, miss, I'd call an officer from Juvenile Hall to come down here and take Martha, here. . . ."

"Marcie," said the girl, in a clear, high voice.

"Sorry," said the sergeant, grinning, "*Marcie* to an overnight shelter. Then, in the morning, someone will call the county welfare authorities. Only tomorrow's Sunday . . . it may take longer than that. But in the meantime, parents usually call in, so it may not be so bad."

Barbara looked down at the small child and thought of Marcie spending a night, maybe two, at the Juvenile Home lockup, alone and terrified, with only her Smurf doll familiar to her. She waited while the sergeant talked urgently to someone on the telephone who seemed to require repeats of everything he or she was being told. Finally, he put the telephone down and turned to her.

"I'm sorry. We have a 'shots fired' report, two, no, three robberies, an aggravated assault, and a family disturbance. Then there's a big fire on the west side, and officers are needed for crowd control. Two officers are out with the flu, and my back is killing me, but you don't want to hear my problems."

Barbara smiled sympathetically. "Sergeant, is it possible for me to complete these forms and then take the girl home with me for the time being? I just can't leave her here and go about my business."

Once the forms are filled out, you'd only have to sit here and wait. Maybe for hours. Sure, why not? Take her home. Just leave the address and phone so the parents can get to her, will you?" He paused to consider. "That's if that's what Marcie wants, of course. Do you want to go home with this nice lady, Marcie, or hang around here?" His gesture took in the panorama of noise and confusion in the huge precinct room.

"With her," said Marcie, without hesitation. Barbara finished the forms to the extent she could, leaving out anything about Marcie or her parents she didn't know and guessing at things like height and weight for the girl. She placed the forms in front of the sergeant, again deep in telephone conversation, and walked out with her unexpected new responsibility.

"C'mon, Marcie. Just let me write something to your Mommy on that note we put on the library's door, and then you're coming home with me. On the way we can get some ice cream. Do you like chocolate or vanilla, or maybe chicken mint?"

The girl's laughter reassured Barbara that nothing bad had happened yet and, with luck, nothing would.

Questions for Discussion

1. What is the best way for a library staff to monitor unsupervised children on busy days, to keep them both safe and out of mischief?
2. Can you think of ways that libraries can deter or discourage parents from using children's areas as free babysitting services?
3. Do you think that Barbara Prell acted correctly in deciding to leave a note and take Marcie to the police station?
4. Do you think Barbara Prell acted correctly in offering to take Marcie home with her?
5. What steps should Barbara take on Sunday morning, assuming that no one has come to claim the child during the night?
6. When the mother does show up, what would you, as a library staff member, say to her about incidents of this type?

Resources

Several public library policy and procedure manuals deal with the problems of unsupervised and temporarily abandoned children in the building. Among these are those of the Pacific Northwest Library Association (Haley, from Case 2) and Schenectady (from Case 1). Most libraries have clearly defined rules for dealing with such situations.

Case 30
Moron!

The trouble with working in public libraries, Althea Jackson mused to herself while standing behind the circulation desk, was that anybody, just *anybody* could walk right in and make himself or herself comfortable. Like the moron. Now there was a case where something ought to be done. There was one sick little man who ought to be set straight about the library as a place to practice his sickening hobby.

The man probably wasn't a moron in any clinical sense, of course. Althea and the other women at the circulation desk had reacted with varying degrees of disgust when they had become aware of him, but so far no one had figured out a really effective way to keep him from doing what he did. He was probably breaking no laws (although Althea figured that someday, somebody ought to check on that) and was creating no serious disturbances. What the moron seemed to love best was to sidle around the library until he had positioned himself directly across from a gaggle of young girls in plaid jumpers, the uniform worn at St. Catherine's School for Girls, which was three blocks away.

Then, thought Althea, with a shudder of distaste, he would wait until one or another of the young girls would forget to keep her feet on the floor and her knees together, and he would bend down or squat and peep up her skirt. The police called men like this "voyeurs," she knew, but she knew them by other names, all the way from Peeping Toms to perverts, and she found them loathsome.

When she had first become aware of the moron and his habits, Althea had summoned all the will power at her command to keep herself from bringing the heaviest book she could find crashing down on the man's head while he squatted and peeped in the reading rooms. Stifling her desire, however, Althea had turned to Freddie Bondanella, her department supervisor, for guidance on how to deal with this irritating patron.

"Even if what he is doing were ruled illegal, we'd still have to be able to prove in court that he was doing it," explained Freddie, who had already talked informally with the police about this problem. "And the man could simply say that he was looking somewhere else and we erroneously assumed that he was trying to look up skirts. Forget about it, Althea. There's nothing we can do, really, unless or until he molests somebody.''

''Well, there are a couple of things I want to do,'' said Althea, looking off into the stacks from which the man had recently emerged. ''First, I'm going to talk with Irwin about watching this creep wherever he goes. Then, maybe I'll have a chat with some of those girls who insist on giving this degenerate free shows. How's that?''

The next morning, Althea asked Irwin Rossiter, the library's custodian and part-time security guard, to keep a special eye on the activities of the man, and she described the moron as best she could. Irwin said that he had his afternoon rounds to cover, but that he would keep him under surveillance if he could and send him packing soon enough if he caught him eyeballing the young girls in jumpers and knee socks from St. Catherine's.

The second step of her ''prevention program'' was that she, when not charging out books at the circ desk or otherwise busy, decided to follow the man around the building, making sure that he knew of her pursuit, until he became so uncomfortable knowing that she knew that he would leave and go find girls to gape at elsewhere. Step three involved having straight-from-the-shoulder talks with some of the girls, telling them that, while they innocently read or talked or slumped in the library's chairs and sofas, someone had been ''stalking'' them.

Althea tried this approach, and every girl she buttonholed said that she was shocked and embarrassed at what had been taking place and that she would remember to sit decorously from now on. Intentions, however, have a way of going astray, and Althea found it necessary several times in the next few days to reprimand one or more girls for her posture or position.

At night, as she lay awake next to her gently snoring husband of thirty years, Althea turned the problem over and over in her mind, seeking a solution to the vexing dilemma. Then one night she had it, and smiling, she dropped instantly into a deep, comfortable sleep. The next day, she waited until the little man arrived, on schedule, and watched him as he circled the circulation and periodical areas, cruising slowly. Silently trailing after him, she put her new plan into operation, relishing its success in advance.

Rounding a corner in the current periodicals shelving area, she found her quarry, who had spread several magazines around him on the carpeted floor and was pretending to scan them, while his eyes kept straying to a table across the floor where three young St. Catherine's students took their ease while tackling homework and conversation.

Taking down a book at random, and opening it to a point near the middle, Althea took a deep breath and began her offensive, standing no more than three feet from the man, yet careful never to look directly at him. "Moron!" she hissed, passionately.

The man stirred, looked briefly at her, then looked away again.

"Pervert! Loathsome reptile! Sickie!" These epithets were released from between Althea's clenched teeth and, even though she spoke them to her book, her meaning and implication were manifest.

Finally, the man spoke in an unexpectedly erudite tone. "Are you talking to me?" he said, softly.

Althea started, but returned to her shammed perusal of the book, which seemed to be a special issue of a popular travel magazine. "Pederast! Revolting criminal!" she seethed, her voice dripping with scorn and condemnation.

"Because if you're talking to me," the man continued, not appearing to be ruffled in the slightest degree, "I think I'd better advise you that there are specific and clear legal remedies for slander and other forms of verbal abuse, and I wouldn't hesitate to resort to them." He smiled, disarmingly. "That is, of course, if you are addressing such epithets to me. If not, I shall then assume that you are either temporarily deranged or exceedingly whimsical, talking to a book as you seem to be."

Clearly, this was not your basic, common garden-variety Peeping Tom. All pretense of reading abandoned, Althea put the book in her hand back on the display shelving and stood goggling at the man. He took a single step toward her, and she noticed that he had quietly and quickly replaced all of the magazine issues he had spread out on the floor. "Or perhaps you addressed those words to some third party in this area whom I am presently unable to see? Is that the cause of our misunderstanding, perhaps?" His grin was so free of obvious malice or calculation that Althea felt herself wanting to return it.

Flustered, wondering what had gone wrong with her scheme, Althea bolted headlong out of the magazine stacks and returned to the circulation area, quivering with tension. After two aspirin and a quick glass of iced tea, she felt better, but her encounter with the man in the stacks had done nothing to allay her worries. Whether he was a degenerate member of the hard-core unemployed or a skilled and celebrated member of the legal profession, Althea was sure that the man was a peeper, and that such men had to be stopped. "Great," she told herself. "You've defined the problem." Now the important question was going to be "how?"

Infuriatingly, the very man she had been thinking about rapped loudly on the circulation counter at that moment, saying a cheery, "Good morrow to you, madame!" and tipping an imaginary hat in Althea's direction as he strolled past her and out the door.

Questions for Discussion

1. Since voyeuristic activity is demonstrably difficult to prove, and not, strictly speaking, dangerous, how can a library discourage the activities of Peeping Toms without leaving themselves open to legal problems?
2. If such a voyeur were observed conducting his activities in your library building, how might you first attempt to deal with the problem: by addressing yourself to the voyeur? the intended victims? the library's security force? or the police?
3. As Althea, what would your next move be, now that the man has clearly thwarted your plan to embarrass or distress him?

Resources

1. Dumaux, Sally. "The Voyeur Observed: Taking a Long, Hard Look at Peepers." *News Notes, California Libraries* 72 (1977): 21–26.
   Dumaux makes it clear that voyeurs represent a serious and demoralizing form of harassment in the library.
2. Easton, Carol. "Sex and Violence in the Library: Scream a Little Louder, Please." *American Libraries* 8 (9) (October 1977): 484–89.
   Examines various aspects of the library's ongoing struggle with problem patrons, especially those who threaten women.
3. "A Low Blow." *Library Security Newsletter* 1 (March 1975): 10.
   Cheap opaque screens installed on low shelves were used by one library to deter and defeat troublesome voyeurs.

Case 31
Draft Registration Resistance

Randy Gardner was satisfied. Since coming to the River Bend Public Library, he had developed the provision of reference services, he thought, to a fairly high degree of precision. His Information and Referral desk had been written up in the city's newspaper, with favorable comments from reporters and the public alike. Finally, Randy had received a small increment over and above the usual raises given library staff at the end of the year which was, he was told, a merit increase for services beyond the call of duty.

Yes, Randy was satisfied, and so evidently was River Bend. Take the Information and Referral desk. This service, designed to go substantially beyond conventional look-'em-up reference work, was billed and advertised as a place where a citizen could get more than information; it was a place to get help. In the two years of its operation, Randy's desk had dealt with such problems and situations as rent strikes, finding out the qualifications for Aid to Dependent Children, sexual counseling, bankruptcy hearings, and social clubs for the elderly. The procedure was flexible but usually involved Randy's contacting of agencies, governmental bureaus, and associations for the purposes of developing a file of "who does what" for metropolitan River Bend. He kept this file on a floppy disk for use on the library's microcomputer, where it could be stored, added to, altered, and accessed. In his time at the desk, Randy had formed a database of over 100 organizations that could be used for referrals. In addition to the names and numbers stored on his software, Randy prided himself on the personal contacts he had built up. He now knew, as a result of his pioneer efforts for the I & R desk, dozens of people in helpful agencies by their first names and felt confident that he could refer a client to most of them, saying "tell 'em Randy sent you" and rest secure that such a handoff wouldn't lose anybody in the shuffle.

Of course, there had also been problems connected with the desk. The delicate problem of advocacy had arisen several times, seemingly forcing the library, while serving as advocate or ombudsman for one or a group of citizens, to place itself in an adversary situation relative to a social agency, or to other citizens, or even—Randy remembered with a slight *frisson* of distaste—to the mayor's younger brother, who had operated tenements in the city's slums without regard for the building code or the welfare of his renters. That had been a bit of a near thing, and Pat Broughton, Randy's fair-minded but politically savvy library director, had received plenty of heat from the mayor's office over that one.

Randy fancied himself a sort of Don Quixote figure, helping in his small way to right wrongs, speak for the downtrodden, get a fair deal for minorities, and generally do what was right. He was not blind to the facts concerning achieving one's goals by going with the flow or how to compromise with vested interests for the betterment of all parties concerned. He was however, young, idealistic, and perhaps a bit conceited and felt that where there were good guys and bad guys his hat was invariably the whitest in the territory.

Currently, in Washington and in other capital cities of the world, tensions had been escalating. The "Cold War," which had gone on without interruption since Randy was born, and even before that time, had begun to warm up, such that it became once again necessary for all young men to register for the Selective Service. Draft boards were dusted off and set to running again, and compulsory eighteenth birthday registration was the law of the land.

Shortly after the news carried that story Randy Gardner in his capacity as I & R librarian began receiving telephone calls concerning alternatives to draft registration from young men who were obviously unwilling to go through with it. While their private reasons might vary widely, and the degree of articulateness ranged from very high to very low, at least eighteen of the city's young people asked Randy for any information he might be able to provide on alternatives to draft registration.

Randy had always been a conscientious young man. He took his job seriously and believed that any service he provided must and should be in the best interest of the client or patron. Librarians didn't swear anything like the physician's Hippocratic Oath, but Randy tried to live by a professional code which had certain similarities to one. This meant that he did his level best for anyone who asked him to help. And Randy's level best was an impressive level of service, as many residents of River Bend could testify.

Therefore, Randy gave numerous young men a little talking to, in which he presented them with options ranging from going through with draft registration to taking extreme measures to avoid it. Even though he took great pains to avoid actually advocating any of the alternatives he laid out for the clients he counseled, he felt that he would have been remiss if he didn't mention the fact that many Americans had moved to Canada, where they were beyond the reach of the Selective Service System and had found jobs, homes, and even citizenship there.

Each young man obviously dealt with Randy's services differently and, even though he told each one that he was not giving advice, some must have construed his words as such or else the trouble would never have occurred, he thought. Just before his shift on the I & R desk on Tuesday, October 15, Randy was asked to step into Pat Broughton's office. Complying, he found Pat seated behind her large oak desk while an angry-looking man paced before it.

Hastily, Pat introduced Randy to Colonel R. P. Jeffries (Ret.), who served River Bend as the founder and organizer of its chapter of the Veterans of Foreign Wars, as well as holding several prominent offices at the state level in the American Legion. Colonel Jeffries cleared his throat and came right to the point.

"Gardner," he began, "do you know the name Richard Jeffries? He likes to call himself Rick."

"Can't say that the name connects with a face, Colonel, sorry." Randy, careful to keep a smile on his face, had not missed the obvious fact that the Colonel was asking him about someone who had the same last name as his. This was getting scary.

"Think now, son. Rick Jeffries. Tall, rugged boy, just turned eighteen. Looks like a football hero and, as it happens, he was. Clean cut lad, the kind you'd want your sister to marry."

Randy didn't have a sister, but he felt intuitively that no good would come of his pointing that out. Suddenly, an image swam into his consciousness. A kid fitting Jeffries's description had come to him for counseling and had been seriously concerned about his impending eighteenth birthday and the consequences it might bring. The young man, whether Jeffries or not, had spoken eloquently about his militaristic family tradition and had sworn that he would not have anyone's blood on his hands. Randy couldn't be certain that he had been the Jeffries boy because he made it a matter of principle and practice never to ask anyone's name when giving I & R service. Since he was not protected like priests or attorneys by legal statutes respecting confidential or privileged information, Randy made it a point to ask as little as possible about a client, just in case he might be required to testify later about any incident concerning legal proceedings. It might not be the right thing to do, he reflected, but it inspired trust in the client who was confiding in Randy, and it worked.

Now he stood in respectful silence as the Colonel, clearly in a state of agitation, waved a post card under his nose, informing him that it had arrived that day from Montreal and had been sent by Rick Jeffries to his grandfather. "I don't know if this will mean very much to you, son," the Colonel went on, "but the Jeffries family's military tradition runs back through this country's history to the battle of Shiloh." Rubbing his long nose with trembling fingers, the Colonel meditated a bit and then told Randy that Rick Jeffries had just missed nomination to West Point and was expected to make his career as an Army officer after college as had his father, the Colonel's son. "And now," the lean and erect old man spat out, glowering at Randy from beneath huge and shaggy eyebrows, "my grandson, a Jeffries, writes from *Canada*, for God's sake, telling me that he is running out on his country, his family and our traditions—and it's all your fault!!" The Colonel swept forward one lean arm which clutched the post card, so that Randy could read it clearly. The last line read, "Don't hate me for this, Grandfather. I am acting consistent with my honor as you have always done with yours. Respectfully, Rick. p.s. Please thank Mr. Gardner at the library for his help. I couldn't have done it without him."

Shocked, and unable to assimilate what was going on and the implications of it all, Randy looked first at the furious Colonel Jeffries and then at Pat Broughton. She looked concerned but was making unobtrusive calming motions with both hands, signalling with her eyes that she would have more to say to him later.

Questions for Discussion

1. In your opinion, is absolute privacy and secrecy essential to effective I & R service?
2. When it begins to appear that the library might be taking a position of advocacy in a matter of controversial nature, what do you think ought to be done?
3. As Randy, given the Colonel's anger, what would you say or do now?
4. As Pat, how would you deal with this matter, both before and after the Colonel leaves your office?

Resources

1. Croneberger, Robert, Jr., and Luck, Carolyn. "Defining Information and Referral Service" (in two parts). *Library Journal* 100 (November 1, 1975): 84–87; 100 (January 15, 1976): 318–19.

Two good, if somewhat dated, sources on information and referral services both deal with the delicate problem of advocacy.

2. Shuman, Bruce A. ''Advocacy and the Mayor's Brother'' Case 39 in *The River Bend Case Book* Phoenix, AZ: Oryx Press, 1981.
   This case is referred to by Randy in the present situation.
3. Suvak, David. ''Registration & The Draft: Sources for Libraries.'' *Library Journal* 107 (April 15, 1982): 790.
   Provides an excellent bibliography on the subject matter of the case.

This case turns on the ethics of providing full and complete information to patrons on demand. For an interesting slant on reference ethics, consult Hauptman, Robert. ''Professionalism or Culpability? An Experiment in Ethics.'' *Wilson Library Bulletin* 50 (April 1976): 626–27.

Case 32
Attention Must Be Paid!

Martha Forsch, the head of the Reference department at the River Bend Public Library, was not too busy on a rainy April morning recently, and, since few people came in or called, she felt herself lazily beginning to drowse over the weekly statistical summary she was preparing. "Excuse me!" someone said, making her jump.

There before her stood a short woman of about her age, dressed in a somewhat severe suit with a plain white blouse under it. Smiling, Martha said, "Yes?"

"I was wondering if you could recommend a good book for me to read," the woman said, smiling in return.

"This is the Reference department. The books here are mostly used for finding bits of factual information, not for pleasure reading. Besides, none of the books in this department circulate, which means that you couldn't take one home even if you found one you liked."

"Oh," said the woman softly, looking disappointed.

"Tell you what," Martha tried to sound encouraging, for this woman looked to be in need of some cheering up, "Why don't you go down to the circulation department? Ask for Miss Bondanella. She's the lovely young woman with shiny blonde hair. The thing of it is, she takes home a stack of recent novels just about every night, so if anyone can steer you to a book you're going to enjoy, she can."

"Yes, I'm sure she can," said the woman.

"Is there anything else I can help you with?" Martha noticed that the woman was making no attempt to follow her suggestion.

"Look, may I level with you?"

Martha stared into her eyes for a moment. "Please!" she said.

"Yes, I came in here with the hope of finding a good book or two to drive away my loneliness for a while, but what I really crave is someone to talk to. See, the women in my building are sort of, well, shallow, I guess. Soap operas and gossip and coupon clipping from the Wednesday paper are their chief preoccupations, and I need someone educated, someone cultured to talk to." She paused, then added, "Someone like you, I think."

Martha frowned, then smiled. Casting a glance through the big windows of the room at the pattering rain and then around the nearly deserted room, she said, "Well, don't just stand there! Sit down and introduce yourself and let's get to know each other. I'm Martha Forsch." The painful truth was that she had been lonely also and could always use a friend with similar interests. Then, too, on a slow, dismal, morning, what could better pass the time then a getting-to-know-you chat with an obviously interesting new friend?

The woman said that her name was Beatrice Hiller and that she had just moved to town from Milwaukee after the death of her husband the previous year. From that, their conversation moved from topic to topic, and Martha noted agreeably that the morning had passed delightfully as they exchanged life stories and personal philosophies in the virtually empty reference room. By noon, they seemed like two old friends, comfortable with each other, and they made plans for lunch.

They went out for lunch together, and Bea came back with Martha to the library for the afternoon. Occasionally, the phone rang with a reference question and, towards 3:00 p.m., the usual gaggle of schoolchildren came in with typical assignments to do and problems to solve. Bea seemed unwilling to turn loose of her for even a moment, as Martha handled the various reference transactions of the afternoon, and Martha found gradually that her enthusiasm for her new friend was tempered somewhat with the first hints of irritation at the woman's omnipresence in her department.

At 5:00, when her day was over, Martha exchanged telephone numbers with Bea and said that it had been a pleasant day but that she couldn't afford to take it easy all the time and that on the next day she'd have double work to do. Bea said that she quite understood and promised to drop in again for conversation and lunch one day the following week. Saying that she'd be looking forward to it, Martha said goodnight and went home.

The next day, Thursday, was her late day at the library, so Martha busied herself around her apartment in the morning and did some much-needed food shopping just before noon. At 1:00 p.m., she strode out on the floor of the Reference department, relieving Randy Gardner, her young co-worker, and wished him a good lunch. As she sat down and sharpened a couple of #2 pencils, she looked up to see that Bea Hiller was approaching the desk.

"Well, Bea," she said, smiling uncertainly, "back so soon?"

"Couldn't wait to see you again, Martha. I woke up this morning, and I just felt good all over, having a friend is so wonderful, at last. So I got over here this morning. When the nice young man who just left told me that you wouldn't be here until 1:00, I figured maybe I'd go on downstairs and see that Miss Bon. . . Ah, you'll have to help me.''

''Bondanella,'' supplied Martha.

''Right. Bondanella. And she did what you said she could do. She asked me a few questions about what I like to read about and came up with these.'' Beaming, Bea displayed two novels she had been carrying.

''Good. I'm glad it worked out.''

''It certainly did. And now, I just thought I'd sort of . . . you know . . . hang out with you for the rest of day, or at least until it gets dark. I don't like wandering around outside in the dark. You never know who's out there, you know.''

''Bea,'' said Martha, fearful of giving offense, ''Do you remember yesterday, when I dropped everything so that I could devote most of my attention to you? How I said that I'd have that much more to do today? Well. . . .''

''Say no more,'' said Bea, laughing softly. ''I'll just sit here by the desk and you won't even know I'm around. Then, when there's a lull in you day, I'll be here and we can continue our chat.''

''Yeah, well. . . .'' Martha couldn't see much point in telling the woman to go away. She *did* like her, after all, and it might be nice to have someone to talk to when things got slow in the time period between the late afternoon crush of young students and the evening's contingent of high schoolers. ''Stick around and we'll see.''

The following day found Martha returning to a nine-to-five schedule, and she was not even surprised when, about a half hour into her morning, the door opened to admit Bea Hiller, who walked cheerfully over and dropped down in the chair adjacent to Martha's desk and began telling her a long, sometimes interesting, chronicle of her life as a young girl growing up in Fresno, surrounded by grape arbors.

By noon, she begged off from Bea's luncheon invitation, pleading a headache, which was real enough, and wandered back into the staff lounge where she knew Pat Broughton would be eating her daily carton of yogurt and avidly reading several current periodicals.

Easing into a chair opposite her director, she sighed, slipped off her pinching shoes, and groaned, ''Pat, I've got a problem.''

''So what else is new?'' Pat smiled, sympathetically.

''No, really. This one's a pip. Did you ever befriend a patron and find out to your horror that the person just won't leave you alone?

''Couple of times. Why? Happen to you today?'' said Pat around her spoonful of strawberry yogurt.

"And yesterday. And the day before that."

"Tell me about it," said Pat, having finished her dietetic luncheon and now settling herself back in her chair to listen.

Martha complied, and when she had told it all, including her liking for the woman, her neglected workload, and the alarming fact that Bea was actually kibitzing her reference questions now, Pat stopped laughing and grew serious.

"Martha, I can't tell you what to do," she began. "I don't even know what you ought to do, frankly. About the best I can do for you is to tell you what I think I'd do in your place."

"I guess that's why I laid this long story on you, Pat," said Martha. "So give. What would you do about this problem?"

"I'd sit her down someplace private and tell her everything you've just told me. Tell her how much you like her and how much you're afraid of hurting her. But tell her gently but firmly that the library pays you to work, not to socialize, and that you don't have the time to sit and shoot the breeze all day with her. Emphasize your concern and, if you feel like it, arrange to see her evenings after work or for lunches. Just tell her the way you told me that this situation has gotten out of hand, that's all."

"Oh, but she's *so* lonely, Pat!" exclaimed Martha. "I know what that's like. When my Harold died, I thought I wouldn't last out the year, I was so depressed. And Bea says she's become so much happier since she's found me and had someone to talk to. She's alone and scared and depressed. Did you ever read Miller's *Death of a Salesman?* It's like that thing that Willy Loman's wife says to their son about his father: 'Attention Must Be Paid!' Do you remember that line? Well, I don't want Bea Hiller to wind up like poor Willy did, Pat! I can't live with that on my conscience!"

"So, what are you going to do, let her trot along after you as you go through your day?"

"No. That won't do, and you know it."

"Precisely," said Pat Broughton, nodding sagely as she began cleaning the remains of her lunch off of the staff table. Bidding Martha a pleasant afternoon, she arose and walked swiftly from the room.

Questions for Discussion

1. What can librarians do to discourage lonely and chatty patrons from becoming oppressively time consuming, without unduly hurting their feelings?

2. As Martha, and having entered into a personal relationship with Bea, how would you break the news of your need for distance to her with a minimum of pain to both of you?
3. Would you, if a polite attempt at dissuading Bea from hanging around failed, resort to sterner measures? What would you say or do if she didn't appear to be taking the hint?

Resources

1. Bernikow, Louise. "Alone: Yearning for Companionship in America." *New York Times Magazine* 131 (August 15, 1982): 24+.
   Explores the dimensions and effects of lonely people.
2. "Disturbed Clients." *The U*N*A*B*A*S*H*E*D Librarian* 44 (3) (1982): 16.
   Among other topics, treats the handling of "the elderly and the lonely."
3. Schenectady County Public Library's *Problem Patron Manual* (page 25, see Case 1 for citation) has a section dealing with "Chatty Patrons Who Distract Staff Members."
4. Sonnichsen, C. L. "A Real-Life Gothic: Dracula in the Stacks." *Wilson Library Bulletin* 51 (January 1977): 419–23.
   "Dracula" refers to those the author terms "vampires" whose inquiries make excessive demands upon the librarian's time.

Case 33
A Matter of Sects

Michael Ross, assistant director of the River Bend Public Library, was really nervous about today's budget hearing. He was scheduled to make a presentation this afternoon which could, if favorably received, result in more funding from the city council for database searching terminals and some software enhancements for the library's microcomputers. The problem, however, was not in what he had to say: that was solid and well-supported by facts and figures. The problem was that Mike, since childhood tended to stammer at critical moments. He didn't think that being glib and silver-tongued was an absolute necessity today in winning council support for his proposal, but he felt that a good presentation helped a lot in persuading members of the council who might balk at "all this new computer stuff" and who tended to believe that all a library really needed was more books and better books.

So lost in worry and thought was he as he pulled open the big front doors of the library and entered that he was completely unprepared for what happened next. A young, pretty girl, wearing an old-fashioned, long print dress, swept out of a corner and deftly pinned a flower to his lapel before he could speak a word. Stepping back, she smilingly admired her work, and said "God bless you, sir!" up into the astonished face of the speechless Mike.

So surprised was he that the very stammer he had feared emerged from his mouth. "Wha-wha-what is this all about?" he asked the smiling girl.

"The New Harmony Church wants you to have this flower and, if you have the time, to stop a moment and consider God's message." She smiled again, winningly, and stood there expectantly, holding a colorful leaflet in her hand.

"Oh. You're Har-harmonists, is that it?" stammered Mike.

"Harmony is at once our goal, our method, and our founder's church's name," said the girl, reciting the singsong rejoinder with practiced ease. On closer inspection, she didn't seem to be much older than 16.

"Uh-huh. And I'm supposed to give you m-m-money for this fl-flower?"

"Only if you choose. Any contributions are gratefully accepted, but the flower is yours, in any case. A gift to you from our church. And here's some literature for you to ponder as you go through your day," she said, thrusting the small, expensively turned-out pamphlet into Mike's hand. He looked it over briefly, seeing several pages of question-and-answer interview dialog with the Reverend Clement Harmony, whose smiling face was displayed at no fewer than three places in the eight-page booklet.

"Wait a minute," said Mike, as his normal thought processes and his normal speech pattern returned to him gradually, "Aren't you people supposed to confine your solicitations to places like the airport and the train station?"

"Well, that was the judge's initial ruling in the state. But recently, our church leadership has decided to challenge that decision, and that's why Lee Ann," she indicated another girl of similar age, who was attempting to buttonhole a bustling woman with a leather briefcase who had just entered the library's vestibule, "and I are here. Sort of a test case."

"What is it you stand for, anyway?" asked Mike, more puzzled than angry. He had heard about the Harmony Church and its flamboyant leader, their mass-marriages, and some rumors of their aggressive and possibly illegal methods for winning converts among the nation's populace. Still, he realized that he knew nothing concrete about their aims, beyond their continual collections of money in public places.

"Oh, we are doing all we can to accomplish the work of God through Reverend Harmony and our organization. Your willingness to purchase the flower you're wearing would assist us in reaching our goal for the month."

"Yeah, right," said Mike, reaching for his wallet. He was unsure as to whether he was doing the right thing, but he had always believed strongly in paying for services received and hated the idea that there were people who took and felt no responsibility to pay. After all, he told himself, he had received a flower.

Fumbling in his wallet's bills compartment, Mike found two singles and dropped them into the hand of the young girl, feeling a mixture of embarrassment, resentment, pity, concern, and confusion. "What'd you say this money goes for, again?" he asked as she thanked him.

"To do God's work and to assist the Reverend Harmony in bringing the Kingdom of Heaven a little bit closer for all of us," she said piously and from rote.

"I see," said Mike. "But I don't think we can let you stand here and solicit contributions from our clientele as they come through the door."

"Oh, you work here?" said the girl.

"Yes. Assistant director, as a matter of fact."

"Then please let us use the vestibule here as a place to sell our flowers. We won't go inside and bother people as they read or study. Just here."

"But why don't you just go outside and sell flowers on the street corners or in traffic lines as cars wait for the lights to change like those other people do?"

"The Mantra Consciousness Society?" she prompted, helpfully.

"Yeah, them. Why here in the library?"

"As I told you, we've decided that we want to test the law. We hope that you won't deny us the right to stay here. It is awfully cold out today, and we really don't want to stand out in it."

Mike looked thoughtfully through the glass doors behind him and saw that the wind of early springtime was blowing hard, causing the bare trees to bow and dance. Looking back at the girl, he could see that she was wearing nothing but a light, waist-length jacket over her long dress. He had daughters of his own and felt a rush of concern for this frail, spunky, and persuasive young person.

"You'll both stay here in the doorway area and stay out of the reading rooms and stacks?"

"Promise!" said the girl, beaming.

"You understand that I'll have to make several phone calls about this, to establish the legality and possibility of letting you and. . . ."

"Lee Ann. And I'm Peggy," said the girl, ingratiatingly.

"You and Lee Ann, then. If you are going to sell your flowers I want to find out if it's possible, fair, and appropriate. Otherwise. . . ." He didn't finish his sentence, letting the threat dangle.

"Otherwise, you'll call the police to have us removed?" Strangely, Peggy seemed hopeful that that might be necessary.

"You w-want me to call the police?" asked Mike, startled.

"Not necessarily," said Peggy, "but it is the quickest way sometimes to determine the legality of an action."

"Who sent you here?"

"The Harmony Church, as I told you."

"I know, but who's your superior in the organization?"

"Frank Jenner. You can call him at 555-2362. Or leave a message on his machine and he'll get back to you."

Carefully, Mike withdrew a small notebook from his jacket pocket and a ballpoint pen from his shirt, and wrote down the name and number the girl had given him. "One more question," he said at last.

"Sure. Ask away!"

"Why the library?"

"Why not the library?" said the girl, slowly. "It's public, for one thing. It's centrally located, it gets lots of pedestrian traffic every day, it cuts across economic lines in its clientele, and you can come here without being urged to buy something or identify yourself. Why not the library?" she repeated, smiling her dazzling smile. "Besides," she added, "it's warm."

"Okay, I'm going to my office to make some calls," said Mike as he pushed open the inner door of the library, "One way or the other, you'll be hearing from me again."

"So we can stay?"

"For now. That seems to be what I have said, yes." Mike waved goodbye to Lee Ann, the other girl, and smiled at Peggy, who was likeable and intelligent, whatever her religious beliefs and affiliation. "Good luck!"

"And to you, sir. May God bless you!" said the girl, turning her attention to an elderly couple who had just walked in, her hand already clutching a red flower and a straight pin.

Shaking his head, Mike walked slowly over to the elevator. When he got to his office on the second floor, Marge Strazinsky, the administrative secretary of the library, greeted him with the news that two patrons had already been up to complain about being panhandled on the library's premises, and that a third one, a Mr. Martin, was so upset and angry about it that he had vowed to come back and insist that the library administration put an immediate stop to such practices or he would be calling his friend, the mayor.

"His friend?" moaned Mike weakly. "Did you say 'friend'?"

"Yeah, I did,"said Marge, sympathetically. "Says he's known Mayor Clemons since childhood. The whole bit. Guess you'd better do something, Mike, before Hizzoner gets all exercised over this bunch of religious fanatics on our doorstep."

"Wish it were that simple, Marge," said Mike. "Tell you what. Put a call through to Pat at home and tell her what's happening down here while she's taking a few days off. Then hold all my calls and keep line 7126 clear. I have a few calls of my own to make, I'm afraid."

"Right, Mike. I'm just glad that it's you who has to deal with this mess and not me."

"It's what they pay me for, I guess," said Mike, walking into his office and throwing his hat and coat on a chair. "Call Pat right away and see if she knows what to do about these people. I'll call our attorney and then this guy," he fingered a slip of paper from his pocket, "Jenner, he's the local honcho of his church for the River Bend area. I'll see what he has to say about sending his people down here to sell posies."

Questions

1. Do you think that Mike acted correctly in allowing the solicitors to remain in the building pending the outcome of his investigation?
2. As Mike, what would you say to Frank Jenner about the presence of the girls in the building's entryway?
3. How would you handle the complaints of those who have already been "sold" flowers by the members of the Harmony Church?
4. If publicity is what the Church wants, what are the pros and cons of giving it to them by having the solicitors arrested?

Resources

1. "FAA Sets Airport Soliciting Rules." *Aviation Week* 112 (June 2, 1980): 23.
   Sources 1 and 2 are news items in which the members of various religious groups have created test cases of their right to proselytize and solicit contributions in public places.
2. "Krishnas, Moonies and the State," (editorial) *New York Times* 130 (July 10, 1981): 22, section A.
3. See Schenectady County Public Library's *Problem Patron Manual* (page 32, see Case 1 for citation) which has a section entitled "Panhandlers or Solicitors on the Library Premises."

Case 34
Restraint of Trade

The small rectangular card was red with black printing. Centered on its face was a large almond-shaped eye which featured an enlarged black pupil. Above the eye the print spelled out

Madame Olga—Seer, Adviser.
Sees all! Tells all!
Palms read, Tarot, Phrenology.

Beneath the eye was an address and a telephone number.

Martin Ellis, a librarian in the Science and Technology department of the River Bend Public Library, had just retrieved the card from a woman who was seated in the department taking notes from several periodical issues. She had been lost in thought when a tall, spare woman wearing gypsy robes and several pounds of gold jewelry around her neck had dropped the card in front of her and moved on to the next patron in the department. As Martin watched, the gypsy deposited one of the red cards in front of each occupant of the room (himself excluded) and promptly left the department, turning left into the corridor beyond. Shaking his head, Martin handed the card back to the patron and quickly went to the telephone, where he called his friend Randy Gardner in the Reference department.

"Randy? Marty. Listen, have you seen that gypsy woman all done up in costume today?" he asked.

"You mean Madame Olga?"

"The same. She's been up here again passing out her business cards, and some of the people here resent it."

"I've been trying to discourage her for years," said Randy, "but she just mutters something about how it's her livelihood and keeps on doing it."

"Isn't it illegal, this soliciting business in the library?" asked Martin.

"Well, technically, yeah. But she's in here every once in a while distributing her cards and I just kind of look the other way, you know?"

"Randy, I admire your laid-back style, but several people have complained about her, and I think it's time that we did something about her soliciting."

"It's not as though she's a hooker, you know, Marty. Just an old woman trying to pick up a few dollars. Let it go. Tell the complainers that you'll talk to her and then don't. They can't be too upset about a little red card dropped on their books while they read, now, can they?"

"Yeah, I suppose. Okay, thanks. See you at lunch."

"Right. Your turn to buy the beer."

Martin hung up the telephone feeling that Randy was probably right and that it just wasn't worth it to the library to hassle the old woman who was a fortune teller or something and pretended to know the future. Couldn't get too much money that way, he mused, or she'd be out at the track picking winners every race. Just then, he looked up to see that the woman from whom he'd borrowed the card earlier was standing in front of him.

"Young man," she began, "I really have to ask what you and the library intend to do about that gypsy. I'm in here three times a week and every time I am accosted by that woman with that card. If you don't put a stop to her activities, everybody with something to sell, including drug peddlers, prostitutes, and salesmen, will be walking from room to room in the library, calling out their services and importuning your patrons to buy!"

Martin agreed that the woman was right. Enough was enough. After all, the library maintained a community billboard in the lower-level foyer, and those with things to sell or swap were permitted to advertise by means of index cards on the board. There were of course limits as to what could be offered for sale, but the board seemed to be a popular service, and no one to date had tried to use if for improper purposes. Martin had even found a guitar for sale through one of the cards on the billboard and had obtained it from a young woman for a very advantageous price.

Therefore, her complaint had merit and just to satisfy himself, he looked into the library's policy and procedure manual to see if it treated the question of solicitation. Sure enough, under the heading of "Panhandlers and Solicitors," he found the unmistakable injunction that such practices were expressly forbidden on the library's premises. While Martin wasn't too sure that panhandlers should be equated with solicitors, especially since the woman in question was not asking charity but rather offering a service in exchange for money, he now had the answer he had sought: according to policy what she was doing was not allowed.

Martin kept a sharp lookout for the gypsy woman, and the next time he saw her enter his department with a pocketful of her red business cards, he drew her aside immediately and told her that her activity was not permitted by the library's rules and that she would not be allowed to distribute her cards in the building any longer.

"Who says so?" the old woman challenged him.

"The library's manual of policies and procedures says so," said Martin, offering to quote chapter and verse to her, if she wished it.

"Look, sonny boy, I hurt no one. I help people. I see things. Told one woman she was going to inherit big money. Next week she gets phone call. Uncle died. Eighty thousand dollars, she gets. Bought me this." She held up one of her gold necklaces for Martin to admire. "Other time. . . ."

"That's all fine, ma'am, and I'm happy that you are successful in predicting people's futures," said Martin, who didn't believe in fortune telling at all, "you're welcome to do it anywhere you like, but you just can't do it in the library. The rules. . . ."

"Rules? What rules? I do this for three, four years now. Nobody ever says anything. Now you tell me that I can't do it any more? Feh! You try to keep old woman from making a living." She paused, eyeing him speculatively. "Tell you what. You come around to this address," she held out a card, smiling broadly. "I make you full treatment. Read your future in the cards, your hands, your stars. Don't cost you anything. Just let me be."

Martin didn't take offense at the obvious bribe attempt, but he held firm. Madame Olga would have to take her cards somewhere else, somewhere not on library property.

"But who is hurt if I go around and give people cards?" she protested.

"A woman complained just this morning, and others have done so before. Now please be reasonable or I shall be forced to ask our security guard to come up here and escort you out the door."

"No need, no need," said the old woman, sadly. "I go. Only where am I going to get business? Sign in window not enough. Newspaper want too much money. Wintertime I cannot stand outside long time and give away cards on street. You tell me: where I go to get business?"

"I sympathize, madame, but you can't do it here. You might put one of your cards downstairs on our community billboard."

"Yeah, yeah. Downstairs." The woman shuffled out of the department, her gold necklaces softly clanking together. Martin felt a pang of guilt, but he reassured himself that rules were there for a reason, and this one made sense. Returning to work, he dismissed the woman from his mind. A week later, Martin returned from lunch to his department and, while walking through the reading room on the way to the back room where he would hang up his coat, he beheld the familiar sight of Madame Olga plying her trade again, tiptoeing daintily among the reading patrons and depositing a small red card at each place.

Questions for Discussion

1. Martin clearly is within his rights to uphold library policy, but can you justify looking the other way in this one special case in which a senior citizen is trying quietly to make a living?
2. As Martin, what would you do now that you see that Madame Olga is going to keep coming back with her cards, despite your warning and explanation?
3. Whose position do you tend to favor, Randy's philosophy that one may sometimes look the other way or Martin's idea that rules are made to be enforced?
4. Are "panhandling and soliciting" so clearly different in definition and scope that they deserve separate sections in a library's policy and procedure manual?

Resources

1. Jaynes, Gregory. "Urban Librarians Seek Ways to Deal with 'Disturbed Patrons.' " *New York Times* 131 (November 24, 1981): A16. Includes the problems attendant on an increase in panhandlers, solicitors, beggars and thieves, arising from difficult employment conditions.
2. See Schenectady County Public Library's *Problem Patron Manual* (page 32, see Case 1 for citation), which offers a section dealing with "Panhandlers and Solicitors on the Library's Premises." This manual states that both are strictly prohibited.

Case 35
A Clove a Day

"Now take garlic," said the old gentleman, chewing reflectively as he spoke. "Garlic is cheap, it's natural, it's available just about everywhere, and it needs no refrigeration."

Randy Gardner was having another one of those days. First, his car wouldn't start, and he'd had to call a tow truck to boost its battery. Then, arriving at work late, he'd dropped the *Encyclopedia of Bioethics* on his foot in his haste to answer a telephone reference question. Finally, at lunch, he'd consumed something that didn't agree with him, causing his stomach to roll disconcertingly all afternoon. Now this old guy had come through the door just reeking and was trying to engage him in protracted conversation. Randy loved to talk, and people were his hobby, but this old man spouting a melange of fact and opinion about healthy living was driving him up the wall with his breath.

"Garlic," the man continued, "is good for you, son. I can't begin to explain the ways to you that it adds to your life."

Don't. Please don't, thought Randy, but out loud he said a noncommittal, "Is that right?"

"Sure is!" It wasn't so much that the man was boring or that Randy had a whole lot of other things to do on this particular afternoon, but the man's exhalations were enough to knock a buzzard off a tree, and the old guy seemed unaware of it. As Randy watched in fascination and horror, the man withdrew from his pocket a small clove of garlic, polished it on his shirt as though it were a red apple, and popped it into his mouth, smiling.

"Not only is it good for whatever ails you, but it actually will keep you from getting. . . ."

"Excuse me, sir," Randy blurted out, trying to hold his breath at the same time, "but what about the . . . er . . . side effects of eating all this garlic?"

"Side effects?" The man looked genuinely puzzled. "How d'you mean?"

"Well, your breath, for instance."

"Oh, that!" The man laughed softly. "Well, hell, I don't notice it anymore, and other people can get used to it or not, it's up to them."

"Yeah, but there are maybe seventy-five people in here tonight, and. . ."

"Anybody else complaining?"

"Not yet, but. . . ."

"Then it's really my business, and not theirs, isn't it?"

"Yes, but. . . ."

"Yes? Go on."

"Sorry. Nothing. Let's forget about it." And the matter was dropped as the pleasant but aromatic man drifted into the stacks to choose a book to read. Randy supposed that there was nothing he could do about this problem, if it was indeed a problem to anyone but himself, and couldn't see the point of bothering the man further about his choice of foods or medicines.

The problem stayed with him that evening after work, however, and Randy, after eating a quick dinner, called his sister Janice. Janice was a self-styled health authority, and she read widely and with retention in the area of natural health and dietary regimens.

"Jan," he asked her, "what do you know about using garlic for your health?"

"Well, great claims are made that garlic can stave off heart disease, colds and fevers, and even impotence in men, but the evidence is pretty inconclusive."

"Yeah, I've heard the spiel on all it can cure or keep you from getting. What I'm driving at is the form it comes in. Isn't there some kind of garlic pill that you can take?"

"Capsules? Yes. There are these large garlic capsules that you can buy at any health food store. They're supposed to be denatured so that they don't ruin your social life, and. . . ."

"Thanks, sis. You always come through for me. I just found out what I needed to know, and you've just made a whole bunch of people very happy."

"Any time. We're always open," said Janice, hanging up.

The next afternoon, when the old man strolled into the reference room with a jaunty, "Hello, sonny!" to him, Randy went over to him with a photocopied article he had found in a popular magazine.

"Excuse me, but I thought you'd be interested in reading this article which I took the liberty of making a copy of for you," he said, smiling, and trying not to inhale the waves of garlic which were reeking from the old man's mouth, and, seemingly even his pores.

The smile left the old man's face. "I thought we took care of this yesterday," he said.

"Yes, but this article has information on garlic capsules that are odorless when swallowed and contain full-potency equivalents of two cloves apiece. You just take one each day. . . ."

"Listen, son," said the man slowly. "I figure you mean well, so I'm not taking offense at what you're trying to do. But I really don't want to have you telling me how to run my private life. Tell you what. I'll make you a deal. You don't tell me what kind of medicines to take and I'll keep clear of your selection of books for this library, fair enough?"

Turning, the man walked away, trailing garlic in his wake, seemingly not angry, but having told Randy to butt out in a most forceful manner. Randy sighed and went back to the reference desk, wondering if there was anything else that he could do about this problem, and, if so, what.

Questions for Discussion

1. Is a garlic-eating patron really a problem for a library? At what point, if ever, does it call for some sort of action on the part of staff members?
2. If you were Randy, would you have discussed this matter with the man at all?
3. Now that the genleman has forcefully told Randy to leave him alone about his habit, how should Randy proceed?
4. Should a public library's staff procedure manual cover such problems as offensive personal odors in its guidelines for dealing with objectionable patrons?

Resources

1. DeRosa, Frank J. "The Disruptive Patron." *Library and Archival Security* 3 (Fall/Winter 1980): 29–37.
   Includes a section on a group of problem patron types "who rarely represent a threat to life or limb, but whose presence does cause an assault on other patrons' and staff members' senses (usually sight and smell) and exclude from use not only their seat but all seats within a 20 foot radius." DeRosa makes recommendations as to how to deal with such patrons.
2. Groark, James J. "Assertion: A Technique for Handling Troublesome Patrons." *Catholic Library World* 51 (November 1979): 172–73.

Explains that human rights do not extend to all forms of behavior in libraries and indicates ways in which library staff members may impose rules on recalcitrant or indignant patrons. See also Janette Caputo's *The Assertive Librarian* (Phoenix, AZ: Oryx Press, 1984) for an excellent discussion of library rights and responsibilities.

3. Schenectady County Public Library's *Problem Patron Manual* (page 39, see Case 1 for citation) has a section on ''Smelly Patrons,'' and how to handle them.

Case 36
Computers Are the Devil's Spawn

Pat Broughton, the director of the River Bend Public Library, was in an "up" frame of mind. A concentration of lucky circumstances had led to the purchase of four shiny new microcomputers, available at an extremely favorable price through the largesse of a computer company. The micros, complete with disk drives and assorted software with business, education, and leisuretime capabilities, had just been delivered and were now installed in the small room that housed the microform readers adjacent to the reference department.

Better yet, Pat had scored a media coup in her ability to get a reporter for the city's newspaper to write a feature article describing the computers and indicating to readers the uses to which they could be put. Unfortunately, as Pat saw things, the reporter had overemphasized the "Pac-Man" aspects of the micros and their software, and the library staff had been told to brace themselves for a spate of game-players, who probably wouldn't have educational enrichment on their minds. Still, she thought to herself, the games and graphics would give them familiarity with the use of computers, so that at some later time perhaps a bit of knowledge might be incorporated into their experience.

The article had, indeed, brought numerous students and adults to the library to check out the possibilities of microcomputers, even if they couldn't check out the computers themselves. Pat was aware that a different type of micro could be purchased by the library for just under $50 each and that some libraries were circulating them to be taken home and run in tandem with a home television set.

For now, however, Pat was grateful for the attention her library was receiving and was carefully trying to build a strong library of floppy disks containing a variety of programs for use by library patrons. She believed that these new acquisitions would demonstrate to the community that the library was very relevant, very "state-of-the-art," and very much in tune with community interests. For the most part, she was right. Not everyone agreed, however.

It just so happened that, coincident with the installation of the micros and their attendant publicity, River Bend had been hosting a convention of fundamentalist ministers and lay practitioners who had come from all over the midwest to coordinate political strategy for the upcoming elections in November. The morning edition of the *River Bend Herald* which contained the feature article on Pat's new machines happened to have been read by the Reverend Tom Jenkins and the Reverend Henry Farnham, two ministers with large followings in their respective religious communities. Both were fire-and-brimstone preachers of remarkable charismatic power and political conservative beliefs, who publicly and regularly denounced license and sin in America.

Whether through religious fervor or political opportunism, Reverends Jenkins and Farnham seized on the library's new microcomputers as tokens of the deterioration of society in River Bend and began a campaign of attack against them and the library, for making them available. From their pulpits, and on Farnham's Sunday morning television program shown locally, they inveighed against computers as implements of a technocratic society in league with Satan himself. To the approval of some (and to the amusement of most of the others), the computer industry, and those who bought and used them, were variously linked with the devil, the Russians, all Communists everywhere, drug abuse, sexual license, and "secular humanism," which was singled out for attack without benefit of definition. Jenkins delivered himself of several passionate and blistering tirades against modern technology as guest speaker at several local churches on successive days, and the newspaper sent reporters around to interview him concerning Pat's much-heralded machines. Aside from rhetoric, the principal thrust of the ministers' anger was that young people would spend countless hours playing games in which electronic creatures ate or were eaten by other electronic creatures, which was senseless, violent, and a waste of time. Such games also fostered competitiveness and pride, the ministers proclaimed, and were not deemed wholesome and constructive employment of leisure time by parents or teachers.

Pat became aware of this withering barrage of criticism when several people called or stopped in to register complaints about the availability of the computers. Attack even came from another quarter, when the proprietor of a nearby arcade objected to the library's giving people free games, while he was in business to sell them at a quarter a play. Despite the fact that she had read the angry words of the ministers, she was somehow taken aback by the outpouring of strong sentiment on the parts of parents and even some children against the continued availability of games for those who came into the library.

Nothing much happened, however, concerning the computers until a particularly hot and humid Thursday morning, when Pat was greeted by a line of well-dressed and well-behaved pickets, walking up and down in front of the library's front door, carrying signs and placards, variously marked with large, black lettering. Among these, Pat read:

"Computers are the Devil's Spawn!"

"Automation is the downfall of our nation!"

"What this library needs is more and better BOOKS!"

The picket line parted to let Pat through as she arrived at the door, and one member asked her if three of their number could come to her office to discuss their complaint in private. Pat saw no choice but to agree, and so three well-dressed people followed her into the building and entered her office after her.

Inside, one of them, identifying himself as the Reverend Farnham, presented Pat with a petition demanding that the computers be either removed or locked away from young people. Pat didn't have time to examine the signatures on the petition, but she was sure that there were at least 300 names. As she confronted the picketers' representatives, Reverend Farnham asked her mildly if she truly believed that the money spent on the computers and the programs she had bought might not be better spent on good books and approved materials for children.

Not wishing to blurt out any unconsidered answer, Pat graciously excused herself for a moment and backed into the small washroom adjacent to her office. Safe for a moment behind the locked door, she ran cool water over her hands and studied herself in the mirror as she tried to think about what she was going to say when she came out.

Questions for Discussion

1. As Pat Broughton, how would you deal with a group of well-behaved yet determined picketers who have come to your library with a petition aimed at getting you to remove, restrict, or suppress something in the library?
2. What arguments can you marshall to counter the allegations of those who charge that the computer is everything from an ungodly devil's tool to a complete waste of time?

3. In any event, what can you think of that would permit the library to keep its machines and still retain the good will of the community?
4. How can a library best use free publicity in the news media to its own advantage so that the promotion accomplishes something positive for the library?

Resources

1. Robotham, John, and Shields, Gerald. *Freedom of Access to Library Materials*. New York: Neal-Schuman Publishers, Inc., 1982.
   Describes cases in which libraries were challenged by religiously motivated persons demanding censorship.
2. Sanford, Bruce W. "The Information-less Age." *Special Libraries* (October 1983): 317–21.
   Details the attempts of right-wing groups to get libraries to remove or restrict material they find offensive or threatening.

Once again, the reader is invited to browse through the pages of the American Library Association's *Intellectual Freedom Manual* (2d edition) Chicago, American Library Association, 1983. In it, numerous policies and lines of defense are presented so that a library may be prepared for assaults on its provision of material or equipment from political or religious groups. It is also instructive to read the ALA's *Newsletter on Intellectual Freedom*, which comes out every two months, and has a bibliography of current writing about censorship attempts on its last page. See Case 22 for ordering information.

Case 37
Barbecue for One

The first thing Emilia Parsons noticed about Sam Perkins was the tangy, spicy, powerful aroma of the food he was eating. She noticed, just before dinnertime on a Thursday in early spring, the smell of food, delicious and mouth-watering, coming from somewhere out in the library's stacks. It made her both curious and aware that it had been a long time since lunch.

Rounding a stack aisle, she followed her nose to one of the small, square worktables back in the stacks, and there sat a man, hulking and enormous in bib overalls and a faded T-shirt, eating what seemed to be a whole slab of spareribs and assorted side dishes out of cardboard containers.

Hastily rising when he saw the librarian, the huge man brushed ineffectually at crumbs and stains on his clothing and smiled weakly down at her. "Evenin', ma'am," he managed to say when he had swallowed whatever was in his mouth.

"What do you think you're doing back here?" Emilia asked, trying not to raise her voice. "Who gave you permission to . . . to . . . use the stack area as a dining hall? No eating is permitted in the library. You can't just come in here and make yourself at home, you know!" Emilia had run out of things to say and just gaped at the man who, still smiling, was trying to extricate something from between two of his teeth.

"Aahhh. See, it's rainin' out, and I thought . . . uhh . . . where are my manners? My name's Samuel Perkins but you can call me Sam. Everyone does. Just got to town today. Hitchhiked. Got laid off over in Youngstown when they closed down the auto plant, and I come here to River Bend hopin' there's work for a strong man to do here. But the woman down at the employment office told me I'd have to come back tomorrow, so. . . ."

"Look, Mr. Perkins. . . ."

"Call me Sam." The large man picked nervously at a spot of barbecue sauce that had remained on the wooden table.

"Very well. Sam. I sympathize with your situation, but the library has rules, and. . . ."

"Awww, ma'am. I don't want to hurt nobody or break no rules. But I need a job and I was told that I can't apply for one until tomorrow. Meantime, it's rainin' enough to drown a duck out there, and I needed someplace to eat and maybe wait until the rain stops. So I went to the place called "The Rib Joynt" down on 4th Street . . . 4th Avenue . . . whatever . . . and they don't have no tables to eat at, so I tucked this food under my arm and lit out for the library. Figured it'd be warm and dry and I could find a bulletin board with odd jobs advertised and get a book to read until you close tonight. Then, tomorrow, I gotta find work. Need money, but I ain't afraid of hard work. Look at these arms!"

Sam Perkins flexed one of his biceps for Emilia's benefit, and she couldn't help smiling at his engaging and friendly manner. She paused to consider what she was going to say next. "Look, Sam, the thing of it is that we can't just let you hang out in here and bring your meals out into the stacks. Why don't you just pack up everything you came in with," she said, noticing the cheap cardboard suitcase beside him, "and find someplace else to wait?"

"Lady, I'd like to do just that, but fact is I got no place else to go. Now tomorrow, I'm bound to find work in construction or some such trade, but today I got no place. Figured I'd just sit and read . . . not bother nobody . . . until the library closes. Then I'd ask somebody where a shelter is for homeless men like me, and tomorrow, I'd be workin' and able to pay for my bed."

"Well, I can help you with the address of the shelter. It's not too far to walk. And I suppose you could stay here in the library until 9:00 when we close tonight, if you promise not to eat or sleep here. If it weren't raining," she gestured vaguely toward the outside which couldn't be seen from the windowless stack aisle in which they were talking, "I'd ask you to leave now, but under the circumstances. . . ."

"I thank you, Miz. . . ."

"Parsons."

"Miz Parsons. You're a good sport. And you won't have no trouble out of me, I promise."

"All right then, Sam. Mind the rules, now."

"I'll do it, ma'am."

The following day brought even more miserable weather, and a pelting storm reminded Emilia Parsons of her encounter with Sam Perkins. She fervently hoped that the big man was working today, and that it was inside out of the rain. Just before lunch, she was going out to the stacks for a back issue of a journal requested by a patron when she smelled pizza.

She knew even before she rounded the corner that she would find Sam Perkins seated at his "dining table," and she was not surprised to find him in the same position as the previous day, stuffing large triangles of pizza into his mouth.

"Wait a minute, Miz Parsons," Sam held up a massive hand. "Before you say anything about this, hear me out."

"This better be good, Sam. Give me one good reason why I shouldn't call security to have you thrown out of here."

"Yeah. Well, the good news is that I found work. Over at the brickyard on Central Avenue. The bad news is that I start tomorrow. So today, I needed someplace to go, and it takes a lot of food to keep a guy like me going, and. . . ."

"And you thought you'd prevail on my kindness again," said Emilia accusingly.

"Well, I suppose so. But after today, I'm out of your hair. I promise. And today's weather's even worse than yesterday's. Can't argue with that, can you?"

"I suppose not," said Emilia tonelessly.

"Then . . . what do you say? One more time?"

"Yes, all right! But this is the last time you'll bring your meals here to eat them. You promise me that, Sam?"

"Sure do. I promise."

"That's the trouble. You said the same thing yesterday." Declining the offer of a slice with sausage and mushrooms, Emilia Parsons walked briskly out of the stack area in the History and Travel department feeling that she'd lost something but had also gained something.

Questions for Discussion

1. When may library regulations be waived or ignored to fit extenuating circumstances or personal judgement?
2. As Emilia, what would you have done about Sam Perkins' choice of mealtime tables, given all the circumstances of the case?
3. In general, how would you attempt to ensure that privileges granted to patrons do not come to be looked upon as rights?

Resources

1. Caputo, Janette. *The Assertive Librarian*. Phoenix, AZ: Oryx Press, 1984.
   Caputo provides plenty of tips and techniques for acting assertively; see Chapter 5, "Verbal Assertion."
2. Griffith, Jack W. "Of Vagrants and Vandals and Library Things." *Wilson Library Bulletin* (June 1978): 759+.
3. Schenectady Public Library's *Problem Patron Manual* (page 31, see Case 1 for citation) has a section dealing with loiterers.

Case 38
Unstifled Creativity

The sound of very young children giggling uncontrollably was music to Bonnie McKibben's ears. Bonnie, a children's librarian at the River Bend Public Library, reflected as she listened to the sound of several kids breaking up with laughter that, if there were one thing that made her feel warm and happy, it was the laughter of the young and innocent.

Smiling to herself, she arose to search out the source of so many happy young voices. She strolled across the floor of the children's room until she identified the giggling as wafting out of the girls' room which stood adjacent to the door of the department. Maybe the sound of innocent merriment wasn't so innocent, after all, she thought to herself as she pushed open the washroom door and walked in.

There, frozen in attitudes of being caught in the act, were four young girls, variously situated around the small, tiled room. They had all stopped giggling now, and Bonnie could see what they had accomplished with their enthusiasm for play. The floor was awash with water, which streamed from all three of the toilets, obviously jammed up with thick soggy wads of bathroom tissue. More tissue festooned the stall doors as garlands, both wet and dry, had been tossed over the partitions from small hand to hand. Finally, as a centerpiece, a free-form sculpture of damp paper wads had been assembled in the middle of the tiled floor.

After their initial surprise had dissipated, the four girls, ranging in age from perhaps eight to ten, ran from the room, shrieking in mingled delight and alarm. Bonnie stood there for a few beats, transfixed with shock, watching water from one of the toilets begin to reach her shoes on its course to the drain. Then without considering a course of action, she ran to the door, pulled it open, and bellowed loudly into the children's area, "You four girls, get in here! NOW!"

She couldn't see any of them, as a matter of fact, but every head in the place swung toward her as she advanced into the department. Her eyes searched angrily for the culprits, with no success until the nervous giggling of one child, followed by a chorus of "Shhhhh!!!" sounds from several others, came to her ears from a range of counter-high shelving in the corner farthest from the door. Marching over to the shelves, she demanded, sternly, "All right, girls. Get out here this instant!" in a voice so compelling that it even surprised herself.

Hesitantly, and somewhat sullenly, the girls filed out from where they had been crouching behind a range of book-filled shelving, eyes downcast like whipped puppies. Bonnie recognized two of the four as regulars in the department, and called them by name. "Chrissie! Ginny! I'm shocked and terribly disappointed in you both. And the rest of you, what do you think you're doing, making such a mess of the bathroom like that?"

Silence greeted this question, as the four girls studied their sneakers or fixed their eyes on faraway points. "Well? I'm waiting! Why did you do that with the toilet paper?"

No one spoke. Finally, Bonnie lost her temper. "Nothing to say, eh? Well, I'll tell you what you little monsters are going to do right now. You're all going back in there and clean up that bathroom until it looks like it did before you got in there. Then you're all going to give me your names and phone numbers, and I'm going to call your parents and tell them about your disgraceful behavior. Then we'll see if you ever get to come here to the library again!"

This speech was designed to inspire fear and anxiety in the young girls, and it seemed to have done so. One of the girls began sobbing audibly, while the other three looked just plain terrified. "All right, march!" shouted Bonnie, pointing to the bathroom door with an abrupt motion of her arm.

For a moment, none of them moved. Then Ginny, one of the girls that Bonnie had seen before, quietly said, "But we have to go home."

"When?"

"Now."

"Is one of your mothers picking you up?"

Two of the girls nodded yes, and the other two signalled no.

"Oh, go on, get out of here!" hissed Bonnie, her voice and face filled with disgust. The girls needed no further invitation and broke formation, gathering their coats and running out of the department and up the stairs without a word or a backward glance. She reported the incident to custodial services but somehow Bonnie's day was spoiled after that. She just couldn't seem to shake her anger over the incident, but eventually she forgot and when she got home she sank gratefully into a restful sleep.

The next morning when Bonnie got to work she walked into the girls' restroom and saw that somehow, during the night, all evidence of the desecration of the facility had been removed. "Good old Peter!" she said softly to herself, thinking of the library's faithful and hardworking janitor. Except for the loss of an undisclosed number of rolls of toilet paper, everything was as it had been, and Bonnie supposed that she might have overreacted to girls just being girls on the previous afternoon.

Later in the day, she got a call from Pat Broughton, the library's director, who asked her to come upstairs immediately for a few moments. Wondering what it was all about, Bonnie dutifully reported to the administrative office, feeling a sense of foreboding. When she got there, she knocked and walked into Pat's office where two well-dressed women were seated smoking and ominously glaring at her.

"Oh, Bonnie," said Pat, cheerfully. "Come in and sit down. First close the door, would you? Thank you. I don't think you know Estelle Haddix and Joan Gold, do you? They're the mothers of two of the little girls you had an encounter with yesterday."

"I see," said Bonnie, nervously plumping into a chair. "Pleased to meet you both."

Both women nodded, but neither smiled.

Pat cleared her throat. "Bonnie, these women are here because their daughters came home yesterday with a disturbing story. They were told that you shouted and verbally abused their daughters in the middle of the children's department. Do you have any comment on these allegations?"

Bonnie liked Pat Broughton and knew her well; her uncharacteristic and formal language almost made Bonnie laugh out loud, but it was clear that this was no laughing matter. If she were not mistaken, this had all the earmarks of a hanging party. She swallowed nervously and asked, "Just what did your daughters tell you happened yesterday?"

"Our daughters told us that you threw a fit in the children's department, accusing them of vandalism or some such thing in the bathroom," said the woman who had been introduced as Estelle Haddix. "Worse than that, my Ginny couldn't get to sleep last night, and she was crying so hard when she told me what you had done that she threw up. Joan says that her little Chrissie had a similar reaction to your blow-up, isn't that right, Joanie?"

Joan Gold nodded glumly, obviously content to let her companion do the talking for her.

"So what we've come here to find out," continued Estelle, "is your version of the incident. We all know that little girls can exaggerate, so we're willing to hear that you didn't yell at them and didn't threaten them and didn't accuse them of trying to destroy the girls' room. Just tell us you never did those things, and we'll be on our way. But if you *did* do those things," she added, menacingly, "please be prepared to explain your unconscionable behavior with reference to small children in front of everybody within earshot!"

Bonnie, flinching at the unexpected anger in the woman's voice, decided that it might be better if she didn't react just yet, and she looked hopefully over at Pat Broughton, her employer and friend, to say something diplomatic and soothing to the women in her behalf. Pat, however, said nothing, leaning forward to listen to whatever Bonnie would say. Finally, Pat smiled an uncertain smile and offered, "Suppose you just tell us in your own words what happened yesterday, Bonnie. Take your time, but tell us who was there, what was said, and how you left it, will you?"

Slowly, after a couple of deep breaths, Bonnie recounted faithfully the sequence of events that had led to the conversation they were all having now. Trying to be thorough, she scrupulously attempted to represent the facts as they were known to her. She ended with an apology for any traumatizing effects that might have lingered in the girls' minds, but she reemphasized her conviction that she had been justified in coming down hard on the small vandals and hoped that they had learned something about proper behavior in the library from it.

"I don't care for your attitude or your tone," said Estelle Haddix. "My daughter is in the gifted and talented classes at school, and she's tested out at having a potentially genius-level IQ. Sure, she's a little high strung, maybe, but she's a good kid, and if you're going to overract to a little unstifled creativity, maybe you don't belong in charge of children, did you ever think of that?"

"Overreact? How can you say that?" burst out from Bonnie's mouth. "If you taught your brats better manners, there'd be no. . . ."

"Bonnie? Thank you. That's quite enough. Now, why don't you just get back to your desk and we'll talk later. Again, thank you for coming in!" Pat was making frantic signals with her eyebrows and hands for Bonnie to leave quietly and quickly, before further conflict erupted.

Flushed and trembling, Bonnie McKibben drew herself out of her chair, afraid to look at the women for fear of what she might say to them. "Excuse me," she mumbled, and strode angrily to the door, opening and closing it softly, so as not to give the appearance of having slammed it.

The last thing she heard as she brought the door of Pat's office gently closed was the voice of the angry Estelle Haddix saying, "Clearly someone emotionally unsuited to her job, wouldn't you say?"

This was too much. Bonnie flung the door wide, prepared to shout her outrage and anger into the faces of the complaining women and Pat Broughton's face, too, but something in Pat's expression saved her at the last moment from committing the unpardonable sin of screaming profanity at members of the public in the library. Wordlessly, her whole body trembling, she crept softly from the room, leaving the door open this time, and made it to the top of the stairwell and a measure of privacy before the tears came welling out of her eyes and began running down her face.

Questions for Discussion

1. To what extent do you think library staff members have the right to compel misbehaving children (or anyone) to do something or to cease doing it in the library?
2. Is a library director's first obligation that of backing up staff members in conflict situations with members of the public, or is it safer to conclude that "the customer is always right"?
3. As Bonnie, what would you do or say now?
4. As Pat, what would you do or say now?

Resources

1. DeRosa, Frank J. "The Disruptive Patron." *Library and Archival Security* 3 (Fall/Winter 1980): 29–37.
2. Driscoll, Alice. "A Dilemma for Today's Public Librarian: The Problem Patron." *Southeastern Librarian* 15 (Spring 1980): 15–21.
   Includes advice on dealing with small-scale vandalism in the library building.
3. Grotophorst, Clyde W. "The Problem Patron: Toward a Comprehensive Response." *Public Library Quarterly* 1 (Winter 1979): 345–53.
4. Lincoln, Alan Jay. *Crime in the Library*. New York: Bowker, 1984. 177p.
   Includes statistical surveys of public libraries. One table includes findings that vandalism inside buildings is reported by forty-five percent of the libraries with annual circulation over 98,000.
5. Schenectady County Library's *Problem Patron Manual* (page 19, see Case 1 for citation) has a section dealing with "children who become disruptive."

Case 39
You Need It WHEN???

Nancy Groves had just about had it. Doing reference work was normally easy and usually fun, but today she wondered whether she wouldn't have been wiser to accept her sister's offer to take her into the travel agency family business rather than going to library school four years ago. Nancy, a young reference librarian at the River Bend Public Library, was not in the habit of complaining about her work. True, she wasn't quite as idealistic and altruistic as she had been in her first days on the job, but she figured that to be the acquisition of wisdom as well as the end of innocence.

Today, the problem was heat. Intense, baking heat in the building, together with windows not intended to be opened, contributed to perhaps the longest and most difficult day Nancy had ever spent at the library. The building, built in the mid-1960s, when hermetically sealed structures were popular and energy was comparatively cheap, was normally cooled in summer by a large external refrigeration unit. Today, however, the air conditioner had failed. A repairman, summoned by the administration department to fix the system, had tinkered about for some time in the bowels of the machine, and then emerged, covered with perspiration and grease, to explain that he'd need at least one day to get the necessary parts (he mumbled something about bushings, but Nancy didn't know what they were or did) from a supplier in St. Louis. So it was stiflingly hot in the library, and the few fans the staff could find and deploy only managed to push hot air around.

One benefit of the discomfort inside the library on this unseasonably hot evening in late May, Nancy reflected to herself, was that there was an appreciably smaller number of people to be dealt with. All day, Nancy had watched the front doors as individuals, families, and groups had arrived, ready to beat the heat and read or study in air-conditioned comfort, only to leave within minutes, fanning themselves furiously with whatever books they happened to be carrying. It was, without exaggeration, a swamp inside the library this evening, and Nancy wondered why the city government had not found it appropriate and merciful to allow the library to close down until the cooling system was fixed. Telephone calls down to City Hall, however, were for naught, and the library had remained open all day. Thirty more minutes, thought Nancy appreciatively, and she could go home, undress, sip iced tea, watch a little television, and slip between crisp sheets in her deliciously chilly bedroom.

As she was smiling in anticipation of the way the day would end, Nancy became aware that two people stood before her at the reference desk. One of them was a small, plump woman with darting blue eyes, and the other one was a slack-jawed teenage boy, who was humming softly to himself and paying little attention to the cascade of words that issued from the woman's mouth.

"Hello," the woman began. "This is Sheldon," she said, indicating the boy, who was now rearranging things on the reference desk, "and he has to do a term paper on the, ah, metaphysical aspects of Shakespeare's tragedies."

Despite her fatigue and the heat, Nancy perked up. A question about Shakespeare's works she could always handle, due to her background as an English major and, briefly, a teacher. Turning to Sheldon, she inquired politely about the nature and dimensions of the assignment and was per-plexed and somewhat deflated when Sheldon only shrugged and looked at his mother.

If the son was at a loss for words, however, the mother never seemed to be. "Sheldon has to examine five of the tragedies of Shakespeare," she recited, "and draw together common threads indicating metaphysical thought and philosophy."

"Oh," sighed Nancy Groves, glancing unobtrusively at the big clock on the wall. "Well, we can help Sheldon get started, anyway, and then, if he'll come back tomorrow, when the air conditioner ought to be working, I can set him up with some more sources to consult. How does that sound to you, Sheldon?"

By way of an answer, the young man looked again into the face of his mother, who continued to speak for him as though he were either mute or did not speak English. Cursing her luck for drawing this pair in the last half-hour of such a day, Nancy listened inattentively while the woman quacked on about the things Sheldon had to do in writing the assignment. By now, she was quite certain that Sheldon would have little or nothing to do with the intellectual or creative aspects of the paper. He was blessed or cursed with one of those mothers who not only pushed their young into doing their schoolwork, but who actually did the work for them when all else failed.

Trying not to yawn, Nancy waited more-or-less patiently until the woman said something that caused her to sit bolt upright in her chair and say, "What was that you just said?"

"I said," the woman explained, "that the paper has to be in tomorrow. I nagged and reminded Sheldon to do this paper from the moment it was assigned back in March, but no, he wanted to play handball. He spent his time down at the place where they have videogames. He wanted to go out for baseball. He. . . ."

"Excuse me," Nancy burst into the soliloquy. "Did you say that the paper is due *tomorrow?*"

The small woman paused in mid-thought and glared at her. "Didn't I just say that?"

Nancy looked again at the clock on the wall. It read 8:42.

"Well, you see, we're closing in less than twenty minutes, which makes it difficult to get the materials together in that time, let alone organize them and try to extract from them anything meaningful about metaphysics in Shakespeare.

Sheldon, who had not spoken since the pair had entered the building, suddenly said, "C'mon, ma. Let's go."

"Go?" shrilled his startled mother. "If we go now, your chance of ever getting a college education goes with us! No, sir! We're going to stay right here and get everything we can on Shakespeare and take it home and whip it into a great paper!"

Nancy dabbed at her brow with a small handkerchief as she gently reminded the woman that the library would be closing soon, so they'd better hurry. As they dashed off into the stacks, she told the mother (and the trailing Sheldon) that there might not be too many books of Shakespearean criticism left, since other school assignments normally kept the shelves picked clean until late June of each year.

Nancy scrambled worriedly through the 822.33 section of the stacks, throwing anything and everything she could find about *Macbeth, Othello,* and the other great tragedies into the arms of the passive boy and the fretting mother until the lights flickered and the voice of Freddie Bondanella came over the public-address system, announcing that the library was now closing and that all materials must be checked out immediately.

Declaring that she had done what she could do with the time she had, Nancy ushered the two patrons to the charge desk, where she stood there watching them check out half a dozen volumes. As they brushed past her, she repeated her offer to meet them at nine the following morning, if they would like.

"That's too little and too late," grumbled the mother. "This paper is due at nine in the morning."

"If you'd just told me a few days ago," said the young librarian unhappily, "I could have helped you more."

"A few days ago, I was out of town. Then, yesterday, I couldn't bring him down here. So here we are tonight, and you're throwing us out."

"I'm terribly sorry," Nancy explained, "but you can't expect just to waltz in here at the last moment and get everything handed to you on a platter, you know!" She felt the last vestige of her self-control leaving her. It had been a gruesome and broiling day, and she now just wanted to get home to a pair of shorts and several frosty glasses of iced tea.

"What's your name?" The woman was looking at her furiously.

Flustered, Nancy responded, "Groves. Ms. Groves, and if there is any problem. . . ."

"A problem?" sneered the angry woman. "Do you see that sign over there?"

Nancy followed the woman's pointing finger and saw the yellow and black sign affixed to the front of the reference desk. It said: "We're here to help. Ask us."

"Uh, yes. I see it."

"Well, it shouldn't be up there unless you mean it."

"We mean it," said Nancy. "It's just that. . . ."

"Expect a call from your supervisor in the morning, MIZ Groves," the woman called over her shoulder as she stomped angrily through the front door, literally dragging the book-laden Sheldon in her wake.

As she watched them make their way around the building to the parking lot in back, Nancy saw Irwin Rossiter turn the key in the door's lock and reverse the sign that said "Open" to the side saying "Closed" in the glass door.

"Bet you're glad this one's over, huh, kid?" said Irwin, perspiring freely in his blue guard's uniform shirt and trousers.

"I would be, Irwin," she replied, "but this one is a long way from over."

Questions for Discussion

1. How can a library make good on its promise to its community to be helpful without having to defend itself against unreasonable complaints when it cannot comply with every request for help?

2. As Nancy, how would you have handled the distraught mother and her indolent tone when they dropped their request for an "instant term paper" into your lap with so little time remaining on such a beastly night?
3. Would you, as Nancy, now call Martha Forsch, your supervisor, to present your side of the story in anticipation of the woman's complaint about you in the morning?
4. As head of the department Martha Forsch, upon receiving such a complaint, how would you react to the charge that your young staff member has been unhelpful, in contrast to the policy stated on the sign at the reference desk?

Resources

1. Groark, James J. "Assertion: A Technique for Handling Troublesome Library Patrons." *Catholic Library World* 51 (November 1979): 172–73.
   Some helpful hints on ways to "stand up to" intimidating or threatening patrons in the library.
2. Schenectady County Public Library's *Problem Patron Manual* (page 12, see Case 1 for citation) has a section that deals with treatment of "Angry or Irate Patrons."
3. Shuman, Bruce A. "Closing Time." Case 3 in *The River Bend Case Book*. Phoenix, AZ: The Oryx Press, 1981. 13–14.
   See this case which deals with a situation in which the reference librarian elects to remain after closing time with a patron who has a "rush deadline" on something she must do.

Case 40
And the Same to You!

For a moment, Randy Gardner couldn't believe that he'd heard him right. The well-dressed, pleasant-looking man had walked up to Randy at the reference desk, smiled warmly, and uttered a long and disconnected stream of profanity, apropos of nothing. Shocked as he was, Randy was also aware that there was no anger in the man's voice, and no apparent reason for the profanity. Most people, Randy included, used such language to show emotion or to intensify communication; this guy, however, didn't even seem to be aware that he was using it.

As Randy listened in mixed amusement and alarm, the inoffensive looking young man continued to rattle off invective both scatological and sexual, but with no discernible malice, or, even more strangely, no particular point. He was using a tone more conversational than heated, and the foul language coming out of his mouth was blunted by a demeanor of innocence and good humor.

Taking a deep breath, Randy asked if he could help the man find something in the library. The rejoinder came out, as before, as a torrent of unacceptable language, but the man's eyes seemed to say, "What are you staring for? I'm not doing anything unusual!" Randy had a quick decision to make, so he decided that as long as the man was doing nothing threatening he should be left pretty much alone to do as he chose. Poor fellow, thought Randy. He really had something seriously the matter. Faulty wiring in his head somewhere. How he found his way down to the library Randy didn't know, but with so many weirdos coming in every day this one was just another fascinating case, and milder than most.

As he sadly watched the man bumble around muttering to himself, Randy was struck with another thought. The harmless little man might not be so inoffensive in the view of children, or, say of Mrs. Gladding, wife of a local minister, who had given Randy fits ever since he had begun working in River Bend. In fact, the man couldn't just be permitted to go walking around the building cursing. The image-conscious library might have to do something about him, after all.

Brusquely, Randy walked over to the man, who was explaining the use of the card catalog to a startled teenager, using four-letter words almost exclusively. Grabbing the man firmly by the sleeve of his jacket, Randy propelled him outside the building, where he told him quickly that foul language had no place in the public buildings and that the man was not to return until he could keep his speech civil.

Amazingly, the man burst into tears, and ran away as fast as he could, shouting only the single word "Sorry!" over his shoulder as he scurried down the walk and around the corner. Randy suddenly felt terribly guilty but trudged back into the library figuring that he had done what needed to be done. That afternoon, in his unassigned period, Randy did some reading in the library's reference collection in psychology. He was both surprised and pleased to find out that there was a name, Tourette's Syndrome, for the man's affliction and that it could be lessened through the use of psychotherapy and a drug called Chlorpromazine. According to one source, the syndrome was not all that uncommon, and the symptoms were treatable in most victims.

The next afternoon, Randy looked up from *Publishers' Weekly* to find an attractive young woman standing before him.

"Mr. Gardner? Hi," she said. "I'm Susan Browning. My brother is Melvin Browning, and you threw him out of the library yesterday, remember?"

Randy swallowed twice and say, "Your brother is the guy who says something gross every other word that comes out of his mouth?"

Susan Browning looked sad. "Yes, that's my brother. Mel has been like this since he got out of the Army. It's called Tourette's Syndrome. . ."

"I know. I looked it up yesterday. Miss Browning, I'm really sorry that I had to escort your brother out of the building, but you must understand that we can't just turn our backs and let him roam the halls talking like that to kids and everybody else."

"Oh, I know that, Mr. Gardner," she replied. "Mel doesn't mean any harm. He thinks he's talking normally but somehow his words get scrambled up in his brain and they come out wrong. The reason I'm here is to ask you a big favor. You see, my brother can't work the way he is, so he's getting therapy three times a week to get him out of this problem he's got. He also gets pills to help him. But he seems to take some pleasure in coming to the library. Mel has always loved to read, and the doctors think that he should be encouraged to get out into the world more and not just hole up in his room with television and books. So I was wondering if you'd reconsider. I assure you that he's harmless. I wish I could promise you that he wouldn't use that dreadful language any more, but these things take time . . . maybe years."

"Well," said Randy, whose guilt at the way he had handled the man was now intensified, "could we maybe get him to stay far away from the children's area? Could he promise us that, at least?"

"I think so. Mel understands everything you say to him. He just has trouble expressing himself without profanity. But he's getting better. You should have heard him last year!"

"I can imagine. Well, why don't you bring him around and the three of us will have a little talk about the do's and don't's of hanging around in the library?"

Susan Browning smiled charmingly. "I'm way ahead of you. He's right outside. Just one moment." She darted out of the room and returned inside two minutes with an abashed and silent brother. Randy patiently told Melvin Browning that he was again welcome to use the library but that he would have to speak correctly to people or in their vicinity. Otherwise, he was to say nothing at all. To these terms and conditions, Melvin readily assented. A handshake sealed the deal, and a smiling and grateful brother and sister left the building together, leaving Randy to congratulate himself on a crisis averted. He was a sucker for happy endings, and this semed to be one of them, providing that Browning could keep his end of the bargain.

The following afternoon, Randy looked up and saw the man standing in front of his desk with a big smile on his face. Making the sign of locking his mouth and throwing away the key, Melvin walked off into the reference stacks. Randy returned to his work, thinking no more about the man until, about a hour later, he heard a commotion coming from over by the map tables in the corner. Two women and a man were loudly commanding Melvin Browning to get away from them, the woman emphasizing her points with jabs of her pink umbrella.

Silently, Melvin ran from the reference room, tears streaming from his eyes. Randy went over to the outraged trio of patrons, apologized for the shock and embarrassment of their experience, and told them that the man wouldn't be bothering them again. Gradually, they recovered their poise, and the reference area returned to normal.

Randy, however, returned to his desk, and after thinking about it, prepared notes for a list of options for Pat Broughton, his boss, to consider in dealing with the problem of Mr. Browning:

1. Ban the man from the building permanently.

2. Obtain the name of the man's physician or psychiatrist, and try to get the doctor to explain to the man why he was not welcome in the library under the present circumstances.

3. Call Susan Browning and explain to her that she must accompany her brother on his visits to the library and be ready to get him out of there if he exhibited any unacceptable behavior.

4. Try once again to talk to Melvin Browning concerning the seriousness of his conduct and the offense it might give to others.

Satisfied with his list, he went to Pat Broughton's office to explain the situation to her and to seek her guidance.

Questions for Discussion

1. As Randy, what would you have done upon first observing the man walking around the library mouthing obscenities?
2. What do you think of each of the four options that Randy has listed?
3. Does such behavior on the part of a patron, who seems otherwise harmless, warrant requiring that he leave the building and not return? As a taxpaying citizen, does he not have the right to use the library?
4. As Pat, having seen Randy's list of options, what would you tell Randy to do about Mr. Browning in the future?

Resources

Two articles cited previously deal with the definition of "the legitimate patron" and are designed to help librarians focus on behavior as a determinant of the appropriate action steps for the staff to take:

1. Vocino, Michael, Jr. "The Library and the Problem Patron." *Wilson Library Bulletin* 50 (January 1976): 372–73.
   Boldly states that libraries need not tolerate any problem behavior on the part of members of the public, and that offenders may legally be shown the door or called to the attention of the police.
2. Vogel, Betty. "The Illegitimate Patron." *Wilson Library Bulletin* 51 (September 1977): 65–66.
   Responds to Vocino's article by asking librarians to use compassion and tolerance when dealing with patrons who are more pathetic then dangerous.

See also Pary, Robert J. "The Psychotic Curse." *American Journal of Psychiatry* (May 1979): 715–16. Discusses symptoms and treatment of Gilles de la Tourette's Disorder, a very real disease of the mind, whose victims may or may not wander into your library someday.

Subject Index

Juvenile crime. *See* Children, Crime by; Youth gangs.

Kleptomania, 16

Language, unacceptable. *See* Obscene patron.
Lawsuit, 2, 9
Loiterer, 15, 30, 37
Lonely patron, 32

Mentally ill patron, 11, 13
Mugger. *See* Robbery.
Mutilation of materials. *See* Property damage.

Noise, excessive, 9, 13, 24

Obscene patron, 17, 19, 40
Odors, offensive, 15, 21, 35
Overdue materials, problems caused by. *See* delinquent borrower.

Paranoid patron. *See* Mentally ill patron.
Peeping Tom. *See* Voyeur.
Practical joker, 8
Profanity. *See* Obscene patron.
Property damage (or loss), 4, 10, 11, 12, 14, 16, 27, 38
Proselytizers, 33
Psychological problems. *See* Mentally ill patron.

Public official, complaint by, 25

Race relations, 10
Religious complainant, 22, 33, 36
Retarded patron, 14
Robbery, 5, 16
Rowdiness, juvenile, 5, 9, 24

Sexual offenses, 1, 6, 17, 19, 30
Sleeping patron, 15
Smells. *See* Odors, offensive.
Smoking patron, 21
Solicitation, 33, 34
Staring patron, 6

Teenage vandalism. *See* Property damage, Youth gangs.
Telephone threat, 3, 19
Theft. *See* Robbery.
Time-wasting patron, 32
Transient patron, 37

Unruly behavior, 7, 8, 9, 13, 15, 21, 24, 26, 30, 34, 37, 38

Vagrant, 15, 37
Vandalism. *See* Property damage.
Violence. *See* Fighting patrons.
Voyeur, 30

Witchcraft, 23

Youth gangs, 5, 9, 24